To Kathleen, Ralph and Oliver Roe, who are
'All which love is and does and can'

PENGUIN CLASSICS

her poems, ... worthy of publication. She became engaged in 1848 to James Collinson, an early member of the Pre-Raphaelite Brotherhood, of which her brothers Dante Gabriel and William Michael were among the founders. The engagement ended in 1850 on Collinson's conversion to Roman Catholicism, which clashed with Christina's High Anglicanism. Her father retired in 1853 and Christina planned to open a day school to earn money. This plan was eventually abandoned because of ill-health, which required her to live quietly.

In 1850 several of her poems had been published under a pseudonym in the Pre-Raphaelite magazine *The Germ*. More of her poems appeared in *Macmillan's Magazine* in 1861, of which 'Uphill' and 'A Birthday' received considerable critical praise. Christina went on to publish several collections of poetry, including *Goblin Market and Other Poems* (1862). She also published verse for children, including *Sing-Song: A Nursery Rhyme Book* (1872, illustrated by Arthur Hughes), short stories, prose-works, including a commentary on the Apocalypse, and a number of devotional works. A devout Anglican, she was drawn to the Tractarian or Oxford Movement, and much of her writing was religious in theme, with a strong sense of spiritual yearning and melancholy. She also wrote about the frustrations and renunciation of love and in 1866 rejected a proposal of marriage from Charles Cayley, on the grounds that he was not a Christian. From then on she lived somewhat reclusively, although continuing to write and to meet her brothers' friends, whose circle included Whistler, Swinburne and Charles Dodgson (Lewis Carroll). She died in 1894.

DINAH ROE is a lecturer at the University of Hertfordshire and a freelance writer whose interests include the nineteenth-century novel, Victorian poetry, and women's writing. Born and raised in the United States, she holds degrees from Vassar College (USA) and University College London. She has written *Christina Rossetti's Faithful Imagination* (2006), and is currently working on a book about the Rossetti family and their circle. She lives in London.

CHRISTINA ROSSETTI

Selected Poems

Text by R. W. CRUMP
Edited with an Introduction and Notes by DINAH ROE

PENGUIN BOOKS

PENGUIN CLASSICS

Published by the Penguin Group
Penguin Books Ltd, 80 Strand, London WC2R ORL, England
Penguin Group (USA) Inc., 375 Hudson Street, New York, New York 10014, USA
Penguin Group (Canada), 90 Eglinton Avenue East, Suite 700, Toronto, Ontario, Canada M4P 2Y3
(a division of Pearson Penguin Canada Inc.)
Penguin Ireland, 25 St Stephen's Green, Dublin 2, Ireland
(a division of Penguin Books Ltd)
Penguin Group (Australia), 250 Camberwell Road, Camberwell, Victoria 3124, Australia
(a division of Pearson Australia Group Pty Ltd)
Penguin Books India Pvt Ltd, 11 Community Centre, Panchsheel Park, New Delhi – 110 017, India
Penguin Group (NZ), 67 Apollo Drive, Rosedale, North Shore 0632, New Zealand
(a division of Pearson New Zealand Ltd)
Penguin Books (South Africa) (Pty) Ltd, 24 Sturdee Avenue, Rosebank, Johannesburg 2196, South Africa

Penguin Books Ltd, Registered Offices: 80 Strand, London WC2R ORL, England

www.penguin.com

This selection first published in Penguin Classics 2008
006

Texts copyright © Louisiana State University Press, 1979, 1986, 1990
Selection and editorial matter copyright © Dinah Roe, 2008
All rights reserved

The moral right of the editor has been asserted

Set in 10.25/12.25 pt PostScript Adobe Sabon
Typeset by Rowland Phototypesetting Ltd, Bury St Edmunds, Suffolk
Printed in England by Clays Ltd, St Ives plc

ISBN: 978-0-140-42469-0

www.greenpenguin.co.uk

ALWAYS LEARNING   **PEARSON**

Contents

Chronology   xii
Introduction   xvii
Further Reading   xxxvii
A Note on the Texts   xli

SELECTED POEMS

On Albina   3
Forget Me Not   3
Charade   3
Hope in Grief   4
On the Death of a Cat   5
Sappho   6
Heart's Chill Between   6
Death's Chill Between   8
Lines / given with a Penwiper   9
A Pause of Thought   10
Song ['She sat and sang alway']   10
Song ['When I am dead, my dearest']   11
Some ladies dress in muslin full and
    white   12
On Keats   12
Song ['Oh roses for the flush of
    youth']   13
Have you forgotten?   13
Sweet Death   14
An End   14

Dream-Land   15
Remember   16
Three Nuns   17
Portraits   24
'Consider the Lilies of the Field' ['Flowers
    preach to us if we will hear']   24
The P.R.B.   25
The Bourne   26
The World   26
From the Antique   27
Three Stages   27
Echo   30
My Dream   31
May   33
Shut Out   33
Amen   34
The Hour and the Ghost   35
The Lowest Room   37
A Triad   47
Love from the North   48
In an Artist's Studio   49
A Better Resurrection   49
'Whatsoever is right, that shall ye
    receive'   50
'The heart knoweth its own bitterness'
    ['When all the over-work of life']   51
A Birthday   52
An Apple-Gathering   53
Winter: My Secret   54
Maude Clare   55
At Home   57
Up-Hill   58
The Convent Threshold   59
'What good shall my life do me?'
    ['Have dead men long to wait?']   63
Winter Rain   64
L.E.L.   65
Goblin Market   67

'No, Thank You, John'   83
'Out of the Deep'   84
The Queen of Hearts   85
Consider   86
The Lowest Place   87
Beauty is Vain   87
What Would I Give?   88
Who Shall Deliver Me?   88
Twice   89
Jessie Cameron   91
The Prince's Progress   94
Memory   112
Amor Mundi   114
'The Iniquity of the Fathers Upon the
    Children'   115
A Daughter of Eve   131
A Smile and a Sigh   131
Autumn Violets   132
'They Desire a Better Country'   132
A Christmas Carol   134
Love me, – I love you   135
A city plum is not a plum   135
A baby's cradle with no baby in it   135
Hope is like a harebell trembling from
    its birth   136
A linnet in a gilded cage   136
If all were rain and never sun   136
If I were a Queen   136
What are heavy? sea-sand and sorrow   137
Brown and furry   137
A toadstool comes up in a night   137
If a pig wore a wig   137
How many seconds in a minute?   138
What is pink? a rose is pink   138
A pin has a head, but has no hair   139
When fishes set umbrellas up   139
The peacock has a score of eyes   139
The wind has such a rainy sound   140

Who has seen the wind?   140
When a mounting skylark sings   140
An emerald is as green as grass   141
What does the bee do?   141
I caught a little ladybird   141
Baby lies so fast asleep   142
Confluents   142
'Yet a little while'   143
Monna Innominata   143
Sonnets are full of love, and this my
     tome   152
The Key-Note   152
He and She   153
De Profundis   153
'Hollow-Sounding and Mysterious'   154
At Last   155
Mariana   155
Passing and Glassing   156
The Thread of Life   157
Touching 'Never'   158
An Old-World Thicket   159
Later Life: A Double Sonnet of
     Sonnets   165
'Judge nothing before the time'   177
Joy is but sorrow   178
'Redeeming the Time'   178
'Doeth well . . . doeth better'   178
A Castle-Builder's World   179
Piteous my rhyme is   179
If love is not worth loving, then life is
     not worth living   180
Roses on a brier   180
'Called to be Saints'   181
Of each sad word which is more
     sorrowful   181
Our heaven must be within ourselves   182
'A Helpmeet for Him'   182
O ye who love today   183

Lord, I am feeble and of mean
   account   183
What is the beginning? Love. What the
   course? Love still   183
As froth on the face of the deep   184
Patience must dwell with Love, for
   Love and Sorrow   184
Hope is the counterpoise of fear   184
'Subject to like Passions as we are'   185
Experience bows a sweet contented
   face   185
'Charity never Faileth'   186
Safe where I cannot lie yet   186
How great is little man!   186
'The Greatest of these is Charity'   187
'O Lucifer, Son of the Morning!'   188
Time seems not short   188
'Judge not according to the
   appearance'   189
St Peter   189
'Sit down in the lowest room'   190
'Consider the Lilies of the Field'.
   ['Solomon most glorious in
   array']   190
Our Mothers, lovely women pitiful   190
Babylon the Great   191
'Do this, and he doeth it'   191
'Standing afar off for the fear of her
   torment'   192
Vigil of St Bartholomew   192
'Who hath despised the day of small
   things?'   193
Tune me, O Lord, into one harmony   193

Notes   195
Index of Titles   253
Index of First Lines   258

Chronology

1824 Gabriele Rossetti arrives in London.

Death of Lord Byron.

1826 Marriage of Frances Mary Lavinia Polidori and Gabriele Rossetti.

1827 Publication of Tractarian poet John Keble's *The Christian Year* (Christina's copy contains her own illustrations in the margins).

1830 (*5 December*) Christina Rossetti born in London, the youngest of four siblings: Maria Francesca (b. 1827), Dante Gabriel (b. 1828) and William Michael (b. 1829).

Publication of Alfred Tennyson's *Poems, Chiefly Lyrical.*

1833 Oxford Movement begins with the start of the series of publications *Tracts for the Times.*

1837 Queen Victoria's reign begins.

1839 Christina first reads John Keats in *Hone's Everyday Book.*

1842 First surviving written poem, 'To My Mother on Her Birthday'.

1843 Begins attending services at Christ Church, Albany Street, along with mother Frances and sister Maria.

William Wordsworth becomes Poet Laureate.

1845 Christina suffers poor health and a nervous breakdown.

William Michael gets a job at the Inland Revenue.

Henry Newman's conversion to Roman Catholicism causes turmoil for Anglo-Catholics.

1847 *Verses: Dedicated to Her Mother* privately printed by Christina's grandfather Gaetano Polidori.

1848 Pre-Raphaelite Brotherhood (PRB) founded.

Publication of Monckton Milnes's *The Life Letters and Literary Remains of Keats*.

(*October*) First poems published in *The Athenaeum*.

Engagement to PRB painter James Collinson.

1850 (*January*) Poems appear in the first issue of the Pre-Raphaelite magazine *The Germ*.

Ends engagement with Collinson when he converts to Roman Catholicism.

Death of Wordsworth. Tennyson becomes Poet Laureate.

Publication of Elizabeth Barrett Browning's *Sonnets from the Portuguese*.

1853 Death of the Polidori grandparents.

Crimean War begins.

1854 (*March*) British involvement in Crimean War.

(*April*) Death of father.

1856 Crimean War ends.

1859 Christina volunteers at St Mary Magdalene Home for Fallen Women in Highgate.

1860 Friendship with Charles Bagot Cayley begins.

Dante Gabriel marries his muse, Elizabeth Siddal, and publishes *The Early Italian Poets*.

1861 First trip abroad, to France.

1862 (*February*) Death, from laudanum overdose, of Elizabeth Siddal.

(*April*) Publication of *Goblin Market and Other Poems*.

1864 Most probable date (according to Jan Marsh) that Christina stops volunteer work at St Mary Magdalene Home for Fallen Women.

1865 Last trip abroad, to Italy.

Publication of Lewis Carroll's *Alice's Adentures in Wonderland*.

1866 Publication of *The Prince's Progress and Other Poems*.

(*August*) Refuses Cayley's proposal of marriage.

1867 Mother, William Michael, Maria, Christina and aunts Eliza and Charlotte Polidori move to 56 Euston Square, Bloomsbury.

1870 Publication of *Commonplace and Other Short Stories*.

1871 Falls ill with Graves' disease.

1872 Publication of *Sing-Song: A Nursery Rhyme Book*.

1873 Maria enters the Anglican Sisterhood of All Saints.

1874 Publication of *Speaking Likenesses* and *Annus Domini: A Prayer for Each Day of the Year, Founded on a Text of Holy Scripture*.

1875 Publication of *Goblin Market, The Prince's Progress, and Other Poems*.

1876 Death of Maria.

1878 University of London admits women for the first time.

1879 Publication of *Seek and Find: A Double Series of Short Studies of the Benedicite*.

1881 Publication of *A Pageant and Other Poems* and *Called to be Saints: The Minor Festivals Devotionally Studied*.

1882 Death of Dante Gabriel.

Married Women's Property Act allows women to own property and earn money.

1883 Death of Cayley.

Publication of *Letter and Spirit*.

1885 Publication of *Time Flies: A Reading Diary*.

1886 Death of mother.

1888 Signs Mary Ward's anti-suffrage petition.

1892 Publication of *The Face of the Deep: A Devotional Commentary on the Apocalypse*.

Death of Tennyson. No immediate successor appointed as Poet Laureate.

1893 Publication of *Verses* (reprinted from *Called to be Saints, Time Flies* and *The Face of the Deep*).

1894 (*29 December*) Death of Christina.

1895 Publication of Ellen A. Proctor's *A Brief Memoir of Christina G. Rossetti. With a preface by W. M. Rossetti*.

1896 Publication of *New Poems, Hitherto Unpublished or Uncollected*.

Alfred Austin becomes Poet Laureate.

1897 Publication of Christina's *Maude: A Story for Girls* by William Michael.

1901 Death of Queen Victoria.

1904 Publication of *The Poetical Works of Christina Georgina Rossetti, with Memoir and Notes by William Michael Rossetti.*

Introduction

> Cecilia never went to school
> Without her gladiator.

The earliest lines that Christina Rossetti ever composed seem at first glance an inauspicious beginning for a girl who would grow up to become one of the greatest poets of the nineteenth century. But look again. This tiny 'poem', dictated by the five-year-old Rossetti when she was too young to write it down herself, contains in embryo the structure, ideas and themes characteristic of the poet's adult work. We have a young girl, the spectre of a school, and then, surprisingly, a gladiator appears. This meeting of the mundane and the extraordinary, the material and the magical, is described in the simple yet tightly controlled style which would shape Rossetti's best-known adult poetry, such as 'A Birthday' or 'Goblin Market', her most famous and widely studied poem. That Cecilia and her gladiator are united in metre as well as in purpose shows us that Rossetti's technical ability was keeping pace with her developing imagination.

Of Rossetti's first effort, her brother William Michael wrote, 'There was no reason for coupling "gladiator" with "Cecilia"', beyond the fact that a '"gladiator" would be a man capable of showing some fight for "Cecilia" upon emergency.'[1] But here, as with the rest of Rossetti's poetry, 'showing some fight' is reason enough. Her poems, both secular and devotional, create imaginative arenas where gods meet mankind, muses face poets, and hope does battle with despair. That these arenas are often domestic, that their conflicts are drawn on a small scale, and that their combatants are often female, does not make their struggles any less heroic.

In Rossetti's poetry, ordinary household errands like grocery shopping can become extraordinary events rife with magical and transformative potential. In 'Goblin Market', for example, when young Laura exchanges a lock of her hair for the goblin merchants' enchanted fruit, she doesn't realize that her very self is part of the bargain. She begins to crave the fruit to the exclusion of all other wants, but the goblin men will only do business with her sister Lizzie. When Lizzie refuses to sample their fruit for herself, they turn violent and attempt to force-feed her their enchanted wares. Without tasting the fruit, she runs home and instructs Laura to suck its curative juices directly from her skin:

> "Hug me, kiss me, suck my juices
> Squeezed from goblin fruits for you,
> Goblin pulp and goblin dew.
> Eat me, drink me, love me;
> Laura, make much of me:
> For your sake I have braved the glen
> And had to do with goblin merchant men."
>
> (ll. 468–74)

The poem's fairy-tale world fascinated Victorian readers, most notably Lewis Carroll, who used it as an inspiration for *Alice's Adventures in Wonderland* (1865). According to William Michael, Christina Rossetti herself claimed that 'she did not mean anything profound by this fairy tale',[2] but this is part of its attraction. 'Goblin Market' has been able to retain its grip on both Victorian and modern imaginations precisely because Rossetti is not prescriptive about its meaning.

When Rossetti fell out of fashion in the twentieth century, it was 'Goblin Market' that resurrected her reputation. The scenes of goblin assault on Laura and Lizzie's virtue, as well as Lizzie's very carnal cure of her ailing sister, recaptured the imagination of the reading public in the 1970s and 1980s. Feminist classics like *The Madwoman in the Attic* (1979) discussed the poem in terms of female resistance and empowerment through sister-hood, while *Playboy* took a rather different view. The magazine reproduced the poem in 1973 for its 'Ribald Classics' series, accompanied by a Kinuko Craft illustration, which, unlike the poem itself, left little to the imagination. Although the devoutly religious Rossetti might not regard it as a compliment, that hers is the kind of poetry which engages both feminists and pornographers testifies to its universal and lasting appeal.

The feminist and not-so-feminist rehabilitation of Rossetti in the 1970s and 1980s opened the door for a re-evaluation of her life and work. The late 1980s and 1990s saw an unprecedented number of biographical and critical publications on Rossetti, a trend which continues into the new millennium, with books coming out at the rate of at least one per year. Christina Rossetti is now taking her rightful place alongside Alfred Lord Tennyson and Robert Browning as one of the nineteenth century's most important poets, and one of Victorian scholarship's most popular subjects. Her themes of love rejected, hope in grief, reserved anguish and resignation to the will of God, while not always fashionable, have proved durable.

Equally persistent has been Virginia Woolf's notion that Rossetti's unmarried status, religious faith and relative social isolation meant she was 'an instinctive poet' who 'saw the world from the same angle always' and never 'developed very much'.[3] From first to last, Rossetti's poems are of exceptional quality, but this high standard does not reflect a lack of develop-ment. This selection hopes to emphasize the evolution of the poet's style by presenting her poems in the order that they were written (where possible), rather than by the date of their publication. Viewed from this angle, it becomes evident that Rossetti's craftsmanship is deliberate, her poetry honed and refined over years of reading, writing and thinking. It is a tribute to her skill that this progression seems 'instinctive'.

Rossetti's wide-ranging imagination, which sustained her over a poetic career spanning fifty years, was hot-housed in the unconventional environment of her childhood home. The youngest of four children, she was born in London on 5 December 1830 to Frances (*née* Polidori) and Gabriele

Rossetti. Her father, an academic who became Professor of Italian at Kings College, was a Neapolitan exile whose Republican views had forced him to flee Italy for England in 1824. The Rossetti home on Charlotte Street near Portland Place enjoyed frequent visits from Gabriele's fellow-exiles, which meant that Christina and her three siblings, William Michael, Dante Gabriel and Maria, grew up in a highly politicized atmosphere.

Eschewing the middle-class custom of the day, Frances brought her children up without the aid of a nanny, while the family sitting-room served as their nursery. Their Anglo-Italian background meant that the children spoke English with their mother and Italian with their father, and they were as accustomed to pasta as they were to traditional English fare. They enjoyed frequent visits to the zoo at Regent's Park, where, biographers have suggested, Christina's lifelong love of animals began. The urban Rossetti children especially looked forward to visiting their maternal grandfather Gaetano Polidori's country house in Buckinghamshire. Gaetano doted on Christina, who was said to resemble her Polidori grandmother, the English beauty Anna Maria Pierce. A former secretary to the Italian poet Vittorio Alfieri and a translator of John Milton, Polidori encouraged his grand-daughter's literary talent, and published her first collection of poetry, *Verses: Dedicated to Her Mother*, in 1847 when the poet was only seventeen.

Christina and her elder sister Maria were home-schooled by their mother, a well-read, ambitious woman who fervently wished that her children 'should be distinguished through intellect'.[4] While the brothers remained agnostic, Christina and Maria followed their mother's religious example, becoming devout Anglo-Catholics. In 1843, when Christina was thirteen, the Rossetti women began attending services at Christ Church, Albany Street, where the dynamic Reverend Dodsworth influenced a generation of worshippers. He was a descendant of the Oxford Movement (1833–41), begun by John Keble and Henry Newman, among others, who had written a series of pamphlets called *Tracts for the Times*, promoting the restoration of religious rituals long abandoned by the Church of England. Their views, which came to be known as 'Tractarian', ignited fierce debates about reinstating practices such as confession, the use of religious icons and the establishment of 'Sisterhoods' of Anglican nuns. Maria Rossetti joined the Sisterhood of All Saints, Margaret Street, in 1873, but Christina was more at home following the Tractarian literary legacy, for part of their belief was that poetry itself could be a vehicle for the expression of divine truth.

Literature and poetry were as essential to the Rossetti household as religion and politics. Frances maintained a commonplace book containing selected passages from favourite poets and writers, to which her children also contributed. She taught them to take pride in their uncle John Polidori, who was Byron's travelling physician and the author of *The Vampyre* (1819). According to Christina's biographer Georgina Battiscombe, all of the children developed a special love of horror stories.[5] Along with many of her contemporaries, Christina was an admirer of Anne Radcliffe's gothic horror tales, such as *The Mysteries of Udolpho* (1794). Other early favourite writers were John Keats, Charles Maturin, Pietro Metastasio, Alexander Pope, Walter Scott and, of course, Dante Alighieri, of whom their father was so fond that he named Charles Dante Gabriel, their second child, after the poet. The family also played a game called *bouts rimés* (literally, 'rhymed ends'), which involved improvising sonnets within a given time-frame. William Michael observes that his sister was especially adept at these family competitions, noting that many of her sonnets were composed in under nine minutes. This untitled effort, later reprinted in her novella *Maude*, illustrates the skill of the eighteen-year-old Rossetti:

> Some ladies dress in muslin full and white,
> Some gentlemen in cloth succinct and black;
> Some patronise a dog-cart, some a hack,
> Some think a painted clarence only right.
> Youth is not always such a pleasing sight,
> Witness a man with tassels on his back;
> Or woman in a great-coat like a sack
> Towering above her sex with horrid height.
> If all the world were water fit to drown

> There are some whom you would not teach to swim,
> Rather enjoying if you saw them sink;
> Certain old ladies dressed in girlish pink,
> With roses and geraniums on their gown:—
> Go to the Bason, poke them o'er the rim.—

It is not difficult to believe this poem was composed by a poet whose Italian nickname in childhood was Vivace ('Lively'), but there was another, darker side to Rossetti's personality. As children, Christina and Dante Gabriel were known as 'the storms', by contrast with Maria and William Michael's 'the calms'. Rossetti could be tempestuous if she did not get her way. A frequently cited anecdote tells us how on being 'rebuked' by her mother on one occasion, she retaliated by cutting her own arm with a pair of scissors. In adolescence she developed a depressive strain, a condition which also affected her brother Dante Gabriel at different times during his life. Whether this is a question of artistic temperament or biological inheritance (their uncle John Polidori was a famous suicide) remains a mystery.

Her father also shared the passionate, sometimes depressive temperament of his two youngest children. In 1842, he fell seriously ill after his badly received, infamous publications on Dante, which insisted that the great poet's works had been written in a secret anti-papal code. Thoroughly incapacitated, he gave up work, forcing Frances and Maria into governessing, while his daily care fell to Christina. There was a failed attempt by the Rossetti women at running a girls' day school, but in 1845 the responsible William Michael became head of the family, stoically accepting a dull job at the Inland Revenue in order to support them, and to keep Dante Gabriel at art school.

Christina Rossetti herself experienced some kind of breakdown in 1845 when she was fifteen. She began to suffer from the various physical maladies that would plague her for the rest of her life. Still, she must have been made of pretty stern stuff, because, as William Michael notes, 'she survived every single member of the Rossetti and Polidori families, myself and my children alone excepted'.[6] Biographer Jan Marsh tells us that the diagnosis at the time, of angina pectoris, was unlikely, and points to a second-hand report of her medical notes in which her doctor mentioned that 'she was more or less out of her mind (suffering, in fact, from a form of insanity, I believe a kind of religious mania)'.[7] Whether the cause was physical or mental or a combination of the two, it seems that Rossetti recovered, though she endured the effects of ill-health all her life. It is tempting to suppose that it was after this breakdown that the poet's 'lively' spirit was suppressed, and the 'gloomy' poetry for which she would become famous began. But there is another way to view this sequence of events: after Rossetti's poetic career takes off, we hear no more of antics with scissors or episodes of being 'out of her mind'.

Rossetti's more severe symptoms appear to have lessened around the time that she began to publish her poetry. In 1848, 'Heart's Chill Between' and 'Death's Chill Between' appeared in *The Athenaeum* literary magazine, while in 1850 her poems were published in the magazine set up by Dante Gabriel and the rest of the Pre-Raphaelite Brotherhood, *The Germ: Thoughts Towards Nature in Poetry, Literature and Art*. Though the members of the Brotherhood were more famous, it was Christina who garnered the most critical praise. Publishing under the pseudo-medieval name of Ellyn Alleyn was her only real concession to the Pre-Raphaelite movement, which, guided by the spirit of Thomas Carlyle and the Arthurian poetry of Tennyson, pined for a lost, idealized medieval England. The Pre-Raphaelite Brothers' contributions to the first issue of *The Germ* included poems with titles such as 'My Beautiful Lady', 'Of My Lady in Death' and 'The Love of Beauty'. Christina Rossetti submitted 'Repining', a lengthy metaphysical debate between a woman and a Christ-figure.

While Rossetti's involvement with the Pre-Raphaelite artistic project remained peripheral, she formed a personal attachment to one of its quieter members, the painter James Collinson. Collinson was, though not a genius, a solid painter, whose presence in the rambunctious Pre-Raphaelite group seems odd in view of his retiring personality and reported tendency to fall asleep during the group's revels. He was also a religious man, a member of Christ Church, Albany Street, and seemingly perfect for the devout Christina Rossetti. But after the pair were engaged, Collinson suffered a religious crisis and converted to Roman Catholicism, and Rossetti refused to marry him. Anglo-Catholicism was always having to defend itself against accusations of 'Romish' or 'Papist' inclinations, and although Rossetti was not strictly anti-Catholic (in fact, she wrote a sympathetic sonnet about Newman's conversion to Catholicism), she seems to have felt that an inter-faith marriage was not compatible with her religion. This was not a decision she took lightly; William Michael describes it as 'a blow from which she did not fully recover for years'.[8]

But while she was recovering, she was also writing. Her father's death in 1854 presaged a flurry of activity; perhaps working kept grief at bay. Being rejected as a prospective Florence Nightingale nurse in the Crimean War did not prevent her from trying elsewhere; she joined the volunteers at the St Mary Magdalene Home for Fallen Women at Highgate, along with working at her family's day schools. In the run-up to her most famous volume of poetry, *Goblin Market and Other Poems* (1862), Rossetti published the short story 'The Lost Titian' in *Crayon* and 'Nick' in *National Magazine*, as well as poems in *Once a Week* and *Macmillan's Magazine*.

Goblin Market and Other Poems was a critical and commercial success, despite John Ruskin's bemusing warning to Dante Gabriel that 'your sister should exercise herself in the severest commonplace of metre until she can write as the public like'. He added that 'she must have the Form first'.[9] In fact, form almost always came first for Rossetti, and is a particular feature of 'Goblin Market', the subject of Ruskin's unfair critique. Echoing the sales-pitch of the goblin merchants, Rossetti's subliminal rhymes and rhythms transform what is essentially a shopping list into a catalogue of temptation:

> Apples and quinces,
> Lemons and oranges,
> Plump unpecked cherries,
> Melons and raspberries,

> Bloom-down-cheeked peaches,
> Swart-headed mulberries,
> Wild free-born cranberries,
> Crab-apples, dewberries,
> Pine-apples, blackberries,
> Apricots, strawberries;—
>
> (ll. 5–14)

The sheer profusion of fruit (more is listed further on in the poem) is the key to its appeal, as is the sing-song rhythm of alternating dactylic and trochaic feet, which mimics the sound of a vendor hawking his wares. There is also a rhythmic fore-warning of the loss of control which the fruit will provoke. Lines 5, 7 and 9 share the same dimeter, a dactyl followed by a trochee, while lines 6, 8 and 10 are comprised of two dactylic feet. But lines 11–14 unexpectedly unravel into exclusively dactylic dimeter, reflecting in metre how easy it is to get carried away by this magical fruit. The rhyme loses restraint along with the rhythm: where we might expect lines 5 and 6 eventually to find a corresponding rhyme, in fact after line 9 it becomes obvious that no such rhyme is forthcoming. Instead, we are given the same incantatory rhyming word, 'berries', whose sibilants rattle and hiss through every line like a tempting serpent.

Goblin Market and Other Poems proved Ruskin utterly wrong about Rossetti's grasp of 'form'. In fact, Rossetti is often at her best, and most sophisticated, when exploring a complex idea within the formal confines of, for example, the sonnet. 'Remember', one of her best-loved poems, is still frequently chosen for funerals and memorial services. Its deceptively simple form and 'day by day' language evoke the speaker's struggle to come to terms with the complex realities of mortality:

> Remember me when I am gone away,
>   Gone far away into the silent land;
>   When you can no more hold me by the hand,
> Nor I half turn to go yet turning stay.

Remember me when no more day by day
  You tell me of our future that you planned:
  Only remember me; you understand
It will be late to counsel then or pray.
Yet if you should forget me for a while
  And afterwards remember, do not grieve:
  For if the darkness and corruption leave
  A vestige of the thoughts that I once had,
Better by far you should forget and smile
Than that you should remember and be sad.

Encouraged by the success of *Goblin Market*, Rossetti prepared another volume of poetry, *The Prince's Progress and Other Poems*, which was published by Macmillan in 1866. It was greeted with less critical fanfare, but nonetheless contains some first-rate work, such as 'Twice', 'The Queen of Hearts', 'What Would I Give', 'Memory' and 'L.E.L.', as well as her rare political poems 'The Iniquity of the Fathers Upon the Children' and 'A Royal Princess'. That year also saw a second marriage proposal, this time from Charles Cayley, a scholar and translator who had been given Italian lessons by Gabriele. He was by all accounts the stereotypical absent-minded professor, abstracted and absorbed wholly by his work. Rossetti, who idealized the qualities of reserve and dutiful application, became great friends with Cayley. William Michael tells us that she turned down his proposal, however, because she had 'probed his faith, and found it either strictly wrong or woefully defective'.[10] Although biographers have wondered whether this was the true reason, speculating either that she was not in love, was afraid of sex, was possibly a lesbian, and so on, it is equally intriguing to take Rossetti at her word. Rossetti's primary relationship outside her family was with God. Age and experience did not cause this bond to weaken; rather the relationship only intensified. Always a deeply religious person, both in her life and in her art, Rossetti gave God the kind of attention other poets might lavish on a human muse.

In 1870, she published *Commonplace and Other Short Stories*, a prose-work which was not as well reviewed as her poetry, causing a temporary retreat from short fiction. In 1872, she returned to form with *Sing-Song*, a book of children's verse with illustrations by Arthur Hughes. Because they do not shy away from the darker aspects of childhood experience, these poems are as sophisticated and original as any of Rossetti's adult work, and deserve much more critical and popular attention than they have thus far received. Her succinct style, her eye for a startling image and her love of rhyme and rhythm serve her children's poetry well, as is evident in this untitled piece:

> An emerald is as green as grass;
> A ruby red as blood;
> A sapphire shines as blue as heaven;
> A flint lies in the mud.
>
> A diamond is a brilliant stone,
> To catch the world's desire;
> An opal holds a fiery spark;
> But a flint holds fire.

A substantial amount of Rossetti's poems for children have been included in this edition in the hope that they will be rediscovered by a new generation of readers.

Between the publication of *Commonplace* and *Sing-Song*, Rossetti fell victim to Graves' disease, a malfunction of the thyroid gland, some symptoms of which are weight gain, goitre, protruding eyes and mood changes. William Michael informs us that his sister lost her good looks to this incurable illness. Her joking references to herself as 'the fat poetess' in her letters cannot quite conceal the very real pain this transformation caused her. Difficult times followed, including Dante Gabriel's mental breakdown and Maria Rossetti's moving out of the family home to become an Anglican nun.

In this time of upheaval, Christina turned once again to writing, producing a collection of prayers, the somewhat clumsily subtitled *Annus Domini: A Prayer for Each Day of the Year, Founded on a Text of Holy Scripture* (1874). In the same year, she published *Speaking Likenesses*, a collection of short stories for children which was received with lukewarm reviews but sold well. Such was her popularity that in 1875 Macmillan published a collected edition of her poems, *Goblin Market, The Prince's Progress, and Other Poems*, but the following year brought more heartbreak with the death of Maria from cancer at the age of forty-nine. A passage from Rossetti's devotional prose-work of 1885, *Time Flies: A Reading Diary*, gives us a portrait in miniature of their close relationship. Maria is terminally ill, and the sisters are planning her memorial service. When the notoriously unfashionable Christina reveals her plan to wear an outmoded outfit to the funeral, her sister remarks tartly, 'Why make everything as hopeless looking as possible?'[11]

Like *Time Flies*, the rest of Rossetti's devotional prose-works were very popular, and generated more income than her poetry. Often a mix of poetry and prose, these volumes were intended to supplement other Christian readings, and to provide food for thought. Devotional writing was a way for women of a theological bent to participate in discussions usually reserved for official, male members of the clergy. Rossetti, whose relationship with her religion was as intellectual as it was spiritual, struggled powerfully with issues of faith, and took both her subject matter and her audience very seriously.

Although she is accused by William Michael of being 'over-scrupulous' as a Christian, she is determined not to be so as a writer. Early on in *Time Flies* she displays a poet's respect for form: 'Scrupulous Christians need special self-sifting. They too often resemble translations of the letter in defiance of the spirit: their good poem has become unpoetical.' We expect a devout Christian like Rossetti to argue that 'unpoetical' poems are redeemed by their 'good' message, but instead she challenges this commonplace. Morality and artistic merit are linked, but not in the way we might anticipate. 'Scrupulous persons', in fact, endanger the Christian message: 'Their aim is to be accurate; a worthy aim: but do they achieve accuracy? Such handling as blunts the pointed and flattens the lofty cannot boast of accuracy.' The 'spirit' in which 'the letter' of Christianity is communicated is important to its meaning, as Rossetti makes clear: 'he (or she) cannot be an efficient Christian who exhibits the religion of love as unlovely.'[12]

Readers responded to her frank, thoughtful style, ensuring that her prose-works went into multiple editions. Although *Time Flies*, with its diary-style entries and poems, would be of most interest to the general reader, her other works – *Annus Domini, Seek and Find: A Double Series of Short Studies of the Benedicite* (1874), *Called to be Saints: The Minor Festivals Devotionally Studied* (1881), *Letter and Spirit* (1883) and *The Face of the Deep: A Devotional Commentary on the Apocalypse* (1892) – give fascinating insight both into High Church theology and women's place within it, as well as providing the original context for some of Rossetti's most beautiful poems. These works also reveal Rossetti's keen intellect, original thought, sense of humour, and sense of herself as a writer.

Along with the prose-works, Rossetti kept producing poetry, releasing *A Pageant and Other Poems* in 1881. This volume confirms Rossetti's status as a master sonneteer, with 'Monna Innominata', 'Later Life: A Double Sonnet of Sonnets' and 'The Thread of Life'. The most famous of these, 'Monna Innominata' ('Unnamed Lady'), is a bravura sequence of fourteen Petrarchan sonnets describing the love of a female poet for her male muse. Technically and emotionally complex, these sonnets draw on Dante's *Commedia* and Petrarch's *Canzoniere* to imagine what a troubadour's muse might say 'Had such a lady spoken for herself'. Probably, Rossetti tells us in the preface to this poem, 'the portrait left us might have appeared more tender, if less dignified, than any drawn even by a devoted friend'. 'Monna Innominata' picks up a theme originally explored in a sonnet of 1856 entitled 'In an Artist's Studio', about Dante Gabriel's obsessive paintings of his lover, Elizabeth Siddal. Although the painted woman is 'Fair as the moon and joyful as the light' (l. 11), the painter has depicted her 'Not as she is, but as she fills his dream' (l. 14).

Dante Gabriel's mental and physical health had been deteriorating for some time, and the depression that had claimed the life of his suicidal uncle John Polidori at last appeared to claim him. His mental state was not helped by the chloral and morphia he was prescribed, and, after suffering a minor stroke and kidney failure, he died at Birchington in Kent in 1882. He was followed by his mother Frances in 1886, whose death dealt quite a blow to Christina, who was closer to her mother than to any other person in her life. In the interim, her would-be fiancé and lifelong close friend Charles Cayley had also died (1883).

Rossetti's final and most financially successful volume of poetry, *Verses* (1893), culled poems from her devotional prose-works *Called to be Saints*, *Time Flies* and *The Face of the Deep*. Characteristic of Rossetti, it is a sober yet hopeful collection, its more mature voice inviting comparison with the gambolling goblins of Rossetti's youthful poetry. It is heaped with many forgotten and overlooked treasures which challenge the idea that her devotional work is 'overscrupulous', pious or unthinking. Take, for example, the following untitled poem whose first line, with its striking and inventive internal rhyme, is anything but 'piteous':

> Piteous my rhyme is
> What while I muse of love and pain,
> Of love misspent, of love in vain,
> Of love that is not loved again:
> And is this all then?
> As long as time is,
> Love loveth. Time is but a span,
> The dalliance space of dying man:
> And is this all immortals can?
> The gain were small then.
>
> Love loves for ever,
> And finds a sort of joy in pain,
> And gives with nought to take again,
> And loves too well to end in vain:
> Is the gain small then?
> Love laughs at "never,"

> Outlives our life, exceeds the span
> Appointed to mere mortal man:
> All which love is and does and can
>   Is all in all then.

One of the primary aims of this edition is to draw attention both to Rossetti's unjustly neglected devotional poems, and to the heavy influence of the Bible in Rossetti's works. The sheer number of biblical allusions is nearly overwhelming, yet their treatment within the poetry should not be regarded as uninformed or unsophisticated. Half of her approximately 1,200 poems are specifically designated as devotional, but the remainder refer to the Authorized Version of the Bible so often that the distinction between secular and devotional work borders on hair-splitting. Although some critics have suggested that knowledge of the Bible is not required for an understanding or appreciation of Rossetti's poetry, it would be extraordinary, not to mention counterproductive, to recommend that readers should continue in ignorance. Rossetti is as much a descendant of the Hebrew poet of the Song of Solomon as she is of Dante or Tennyson. Perhaps Rossetti's gender, or her lack of official religious rank, is responsible for this attitude: it is difficult to imagine anyone suggesting to readers of William Vaughan, George Herbert or Gerard Manley Hopkins that biblical literacy does not enhance the experience of reading their work. As Betty S. Flowers noted in her introduction to the *Complete Poems*, an understanding of Rossetti's religious poems' literary and spiritual relationship to the Bible means that they can no longer be dismissed as slavish reiterations of Christian dogma.[13]

'Babylon the Great', for example, is a devotional poem based on Revelation 17:1–6, which could hardly be described as unimaginative or dully pious:

> Foul is she and ill-favoured, set askew:
>   Gaze not upon her till thou dream her fair,
>   Lest she should mesh thee in her wanton hair,
> Adept at arts grown old yet ever new.
> Her heart lusts not for love, but thro' and thro'

> For blood, as spotted panther lusts in lair;
>   No wine is in her cup but filth is there
> Unutterable, with plagues hid out of view.
> Gaze not upon her, for her dancing whirl
>   Turns giddy the fixed gazer presently:
>   Gaze not upon her, lest thou be as she
>   When at the far end of her long desire,
> Her scarlet vest and gold and gem and pearl
>   And she amid her pomp are set on fire.

Elements of gothic horror and Pre-Raphaelite *femme fatale* imagery combine with the apocalyptic language of Revelation to create a memorable anti-sonnet; so corrupting is the Whore of Babylon that she has perverted even the sonnet itself. Instead of the fourteen lines of love we might traditionally expect, we get a monstrous dark parody, where corrupted love goes up in flames. But Rossetti's God soothes as often as he punishes:

> As froth on the face of the deep,
>   As foam on the crest of the sea,
> As dreams at the waking of sleep,
>   As gourd of a day and a night,
> As harvest that no man shall reap,
>   As vintage that never shall be,
> Is hope if it cling not aright,
>   O my God, unto Thee.

The surface simplicity of this untitled poem enacts the very 'froth' it describes: it is our understanding of these images' deeper biblical resonances which takes us beneath their surface meaning. For example, the first line's 'froth' becomes even more significant when we connect it to Genesis 1:2: 'And the earth was without form, and void; and darkness was upon the face of the deep. And the Spirit of God moved upon the face of the waters.' 'Froth' here is not simply froth in the secular sense, but also, more darkly, it evokes the absence of 'the Spirit of God'. Rossetti's poem puts metaphor itself to work in service of its point about disconnection from God. The word 'As' continually promises a comparison, but leads nowhere until it 'clings' to God in the final line.

The great critical and financial success of *Verses* might have suggested Rossetti to Queen Victoria as a successor for Poet Laureate, a post which had been empty since Tennyson's death in 1892, and in fact would not be filled until 1896, two years after Rossetti's death. Certainly, there were many who thought Christina Rossetti should be in the running, notably Lewis Carroll: 'If only the Queen would consult *me* as to whom to make Poet Laureate! I would say, "for once, Madam, take a *lady*!"' He further lamented, and quite rightly, 'But *they never consult the right people*.'[14]

The 'right people' to consult in Rossetti studies have so far been the male members of her family. Much has been written on Rossetti and the Pre-Raphaelite Brotherhood, and we also have her brother William Michael's painstaking notes on his sister's poems, some of which are reproduced in this edition. His opinion is of course valid, and his notes on his sister's activities and those of the Pre-Raphaelites are invaluable resources for the Victorian student. Yet Rossetti scholarship is currently finding more 'right people' to consult about Christina Rossetti, including her mother Frances and sister Maria, whose activities may have been less public than those of the Pre-Raphaelite Brotherhood, but were no less important to Christina's literary development. Mary Arseneau has recently written a book on their contributions, further suggesting the importance of the Polidori aunts, Charlotte and Eliza, for whom Christina cared until their deaths.[15]

The other 'right people' to consult in the study of Rossetti are the writers whose influence her work proudly displays. Because of her lack of formal education, religious or otherwise, it is tempting to regard Rossetti as a somewhat naïve autodidact rather than a deliberate, intelligent and skilled artist. Indeed, Virginia Woolf wrote that 'years of traffic with men and books did not affect you in the least'.[16] But no poet traffics with Wordsworth, Coleridge, Shelley and Keats, and remains unaffected. The Romantics, both first and second generation, leave their mark on Rossetti's work, particularly Keats. With uncon-

ventional educations and close family ties, Keats and Rossetti
both wrote from the margins of a more famous inner circle of
poets. Rossetti's poems respond strongly to Keats, especially
her early work, which laments being 'Shut Out', often 'hears
the nightingale / That sadly sings' in 'Dream-Land', and yearns
for 'Sweet Death'.

It has been observed that, in contrast to Keats, Rossetti has
not bequeathed us letters which reveal her personality or artistic
intentions. But this is another case of not consulting the right
people, or in this case, the right books. For a Keatsian level of
autobiographical confession from Rossetti, it is necessary to
consult her devotional prose-works, particularly *Letter and
Spirit*, *Time Flies* and *The Face of the Deep*. If these neglected
works were made widely available in affordable, accessible,
annotated editions, they would do much to challenge Rossetti's
reputation as too morbid, humourless, pious, or uninvolved in
the affairs of the world. The notes to this edition indicate poems
which appeared originally in Rossetti's devotional prose-works
and include, where particularly relevant, the prose passages
following or preceding the poems.

The notes also 'translate' the Victorian language of flowers
for the modern reader. An acquaintance with the coded signifi-
cance of flowers in nineteenth-century culture enriches our
understanding of Rossetti's poems. For example, in 'Three
Stages' the speaker concludes 'My happy happy dream is
finished with', and, as a consequence, she determines that her
'spirit shall keep house alone, / Accomplishing its age' (part 2,
ll. 1, 23–4). But this solitary retreat is not all it seems, as the
plants growing in its garden tell us:

> There other garden beds shall lie around
>   Full of sweet-briar and incense-bearing thyme;
> There I will sit, and listen for the sound
>   Of the last lingering chime.

> (ll. 25–8)

In the language of flowers, thyme is a symbol of activity, while
sweet-briar is an emblem of poetry. To 'keep house alone' is

one thing, but to cultivate poetry in place of companionship is quite another. Rossetti coaxes the 'garden' of these final four lines into life so that the stanza achieves what the speaker, who sits and listens 'for the sound', merely longs for. The *abab* rhyming scheme allows the concluding 'chime' to linger, as the 'sound' quite literally chimes with the proceeding rhyme-word, 'thyme'. The speaker of this poem may be resigned, but the poem itself remains vital and active.

Rossetti writes in *Letter and Spirit* that 'To do anything whatsoever, even to serve God, "with all the strength," brings us into continual collision with that modern civilized standard of good breeding and good taste which bids us avoid extremes.'[17] Despite Rossetti's reputation for personal reserve and faithful resignation, hers is a poetics which does not shy away from collision and confrontation. In an era which was suspicious of professional women writers, not to mention female religious thinkers, her battle took place in public, in the form of her published, paid work. The five-year-old Rossetti had provided 'Cecilia' with a gladiator to walk her to school. The adult Rossetti made poetry itself her champion. Whether it is Laura of 'Goblin Market' resisting the monstrous merchants, the muse of 'Monna Innominata' turning to face her troubadour, or the speaker of hundreds of devotional poems asking difficult questions of God, Rossetti's poetry always stands up to bullies. In the spirit of the demure but quietly confident sister of 'The Lowest Room', Rossetti compels us to wonder, 'Why should not you, why should not I / Attain heroic strength?'

NOTES

1. William Michael Rossetti, 'Memoir' from *The Poetical Works of Christina Georgina Rossetti, with Memoir and Notes by William Michael Rossetti* (Macmillan, 1904), p. xlix. (Referred to as 'Memoir' in subsequent notes.)

2. William Michael Rossetti, 'Notes' from *The Poetical Works*, p. 459.

3. Virginia Woolf, *The Common Reader: Second Series* (Hogarth Press, 1932), p. 242.

4. William Michael Rossetti, *Dante Gabriel Rossetti: His Family Letters. With a Memoir by William Michael Rossetti*, vol. 1 (Ellis and Every, 1895), p. 22.

5. Georgina Battiscombe, *Christina Rossetti: A Divided Life* (Constable, 1981).

6. 'Memoir' l.

7. Quoted in Jan Marsh, *Christina Rossetti: A Literary Biography* (Jonathan Cape, 1994), p. 52.

8. 'Memoir' lii.

9. John Ruskin to Dante Gabriel Rossetti, 24 January 1861, *Letters of Dante Gabriel Rossetti*, ed. Oswald Doughty and John Robert Wahl, vol. 2 (Clarendon Press, 1965), p. 391.

10. 'Memoir' liii.

11. *Time Flies: A Reading Diary* (Society for Promoting Christian Knowledge, 1885), p. 213.

12. Ibid, pp. 2–3.

13. Betty S. Flowers, *Christina Rossetti: The Complete Poems* (Penguin, 2001).

14. *The Letters of Lewis Carroll*, ed. M. C. Cohen with Roger Lancelyn Green, vol. 2 (Macmillan, 1979), p. 986.

15. Mary Arseneau, *Recovering Christina Rossetti* (Palgrave, 2004).

16. *The Common Reader*, p. 242.

17. *Letter and Spirit: Notes on the Commandments* (Society for Promoting Christian Knowledge, 1883), p. 19. Rossetti's quotation 'with all the strength' refers to the First Commandment's injunction to worship only one God, as described in Mark 12:28–34. The quotation is from verse 33: 'And to love him with all the heart, and with all the understanding, and with all the soul, and with all the strength, and to love his neighbour as himself, is more than all whole burnt offerings and sacrifices.'

Further Reading

COLLECTED POEMS

Rossetti's elder brother, William Michael, collected a large number of her poems for *The Poetical Works* (1904), organizing them, rather idiosyncratically, according to theme. The complete poems remained unavailable until Rebecca Crump's definitive three-volume variorum edition (*The Complete Poems of Christina Rossetti*, Louisiana State University Press, 1979–90). Crump arranged the poems according to the volumes in which they originally appeared, and included special sections for poems separately published, privately printed or unpublished during the poet's lifetime. This edition remains the gold standard for Rossetti scholars. Betty S. Flowers followed Crump's model for the 2001 single-volume paperback *Christina Rossetti: The Complete Poems* (Penguin, 2001). Her annotations include William Michael's notes from *The Poetical Works* and passages from Rossetti's devotional prose-works.

LETTERS

Christina Rossetti's letters have been collected and annotated by Antony H. Harrison in four volumes in *The Letters of Christina Rossetti* (University of Virginia Press, 1997–2004). Harrison's is the standard edition. See also Lona Mosk Packer's *The Rossetti–Macmillan Letters* (University of California Press, 1963) for their focus on Dante Gabriel and Christina Rossetti's relationship with their publisher.

PROSE

Originally published by the Society for the Promotion of Christian Knowledge (SPCK), and out of print since the early twentieth century, four of Rossetti's devotional prose-works were issued in facsimile reprint editions in 2003 by Thoemmes Press, introduced by Maria Keaton: *Called to be Saints: The Minor Festivals Devotionally Studied, Letter and Spirit: Notes on the Commandments Time Flies: A Reading Diary* and *The Face of the Deep: A Devotional Commentary on the Apocalypse*. Rossetti's other devotional prose-works, *Annus Domini: A Prayer for Each Day of the Year, Founded on a Text of Holy Scripture* (1874) and *Seek and Find: A Double Series of Short Stories of the Benedicite* (1879), are not included in the Thoemmes editions, and remain out of print. Selections from the devotional prose can also be found in David A. Kent and P. G. Stanwood's *Selected Prose of Christina Rossetti* (Palgrave, 1998).

A good single source of Rossetti's short stories is Jan Marsh's edition of *Christina Rossetti: Poems and Prose* (Dent, 1994), which contains 'Maude', 'Nick', 'Hero', 'The Lost Titian', 'Vanna's Twins', 'Commonplace' (all 1870) and 'Speaking Likenesses' (1874). Another wide selection can be found in Kent and Stanwood's *Selected Prose*, which contains 'Commonplace', 'The Lost Titian', 'Nick', 'Prose and Cons', 'Maude' and 'Speaking Likenesses'. 'Commonplace' has been reprinted separately (Hesperus Press, 2005), with an introduction by Andrew Motion.

Also of interest are Rossetti's articles on Dante – 'Dante, An English Classic' for the *Churchman's Shilling Magazine and Family Treasury* (1867) and 'Dante. The Poet Illustrated Out of the Poem' for *The Century Illustrated Monthly Magazine* (1884) – which can be found in Kent and Stanwood's *Selected Prose*.

CRITICAL AND SCHOLARLY
BOOKS ON ROSSETTI

The mid-1980s revival of interest in Rossetti resulted in land-mark publications such as: Dolores Rosenblum, *Christina Rossetti: The Poetry of Endurance* (Southern Illinois University Press, 1986); the essay collection *The Achievement of Christina Rossetti*, ed. David A. Kent (Cornell University Press, 1987); and Antony H. Harrison, *Christina Rossetti in Context* (University of North Carolina Press, 1988). The 1990s continued to place Rossetti 'in context', with Diane D'Amico's study of the poet's artistic relationship to Anglo-Catholicism in *Christina Rossetti: Faith, Gender, and Time* (Louisiana State University Press, 1999), while Mary Arseneau, Antony Harrison and Lorraine Janzen Kooistra edited the significant collection *The Culture of Christina Rossetti: Female Poetics and Victorian Contexts* (Ohio University Press, 1999).

More recent publications include Alison Chapman's *The Afterlife of Christina Rossetti* (Palgrave, 2000), Lorraine Janzen Kooistra's *Christina Rossetti and Illustration: A Publishing History* (Ohio University Press, 2002), Lynda Palazzo's *Christina Rossetti's Feminist Theology* (Palgrave, 2002), Mary Arseneau's *Recovering Christina Rossetti* (Palgrave, 2004), Constance Hassett's *Christina Rossetti: The Patience of Style* (University of Virginia Press, 2005) and Dinah Roe's *Christina Rossetti's Faithful Imagination: The Devotional Poetry and Prose* (Palgrave, 2007).

BIOGRAPHIES OF ROSSETTI

There are many biographies of Christina Rossetti, but curiously the most significant are both the most distant and the most recent. Ellen A. Proctor's *A Brief Memoir of Christina G. Rossetti. With a preface by W. M. Rossetti* (SPCK, 1895), written by Rossetti's late-life friend shortly after the poet's death, is notable for its personal, intimate tone and its small-scale rendering of a poet usually considered larger-than-life. Although authorized, and so to some extent censored by William Michael, Mackenzie Bell's *Christina Rossetti: A Biographical and Critical Study* (Hurst and Blackett, 1898) contains a wealth of biographical information and acute poetic analysis. Lona Mosk Packer's *Christina Rossetti* (University of California Press, 1963), though most famous for its speculation about an affair between Rossetti and the painter William Bell Scott, is an easy read, and a good place for readers new to Rossetti to begin. *Christina Rossetti: A Divided Life* by Georgina Battiscombe (Constable, 1981) holds a similar appeal. *Christina Rossetti: A Literary Biography* (Jonathan Cape, 1994), Jan Marsh's balanced, thoughtful and comprehensive study of the poet's literary and personal life, is easily the best of the twentieth-century selection, and is strongly recommended.

A Note on the Texts

I have used R. W. Crump's definitive texts of the poems, as well as the composition and publication dates she provides. For Rossetti's published poems, Crump follows the copy-text of the English first editions, because these incorporated revisions and changes that Rossetti herself suggested to her publisher (Macmillan). Crump's texts also incorporate some of Rossetti's revisions which appeared for the first time in the 1875 volume, *Goblin Market, The Prince's Progress, and Other Poems*. For poems which Rossetti did not include in her published collections, such as those published separately in anthologies, privately printed or never published at all, Crump consulted sources such as manuscripts, authorial rough drafts, letters and individual printings of poems in journals. Her emendations include restoring house spellings to manuscript spellings, correcting typesetting errors, and adopting manuscript paragraphing where the printed paragraphing deviated from the poet's customary practices.

The punctuation and headings are exactly as in Crump's texts, which, because they preserve the 'look' of the poems as well as their grammar, maintain their visual integrity. For example, like Emily Dickinson (whom she inspired), Rossetti often uses dashes as a musical device. These visually express a drawing out of emotion, a reaching out, or a 'something almost being said' (to quote 'The Trees', by unlikely Rossetti admirer Philip Larkin). After a colon brings the reader up short, a dash can open the line up again.

In this edition, the poems are presented according to their date of composition, where possible. Multi-part poems

composed over a period of years are listed by their final compo-
sition date rather than by the date of the first part to be written.
Where the composition date is unknown, the poems are
arranged by the date of first publication. Poems sharing a publi-
cation date, but whose composition date is unknown, such as
the children's poems, are presented in the same order as in the
anthology in which they originally appeared.

SELECTED POEMS

On Albina.

The roses lingered in her cheeks,
  When fair Albina fainted;
Oh! gentle Reader, could it be
  That fair Albina painted?

Forget Me Not.

1

"Forget me not! Forget me not!"
  The maiden once did say,
When to some far-off battle-field
  Her lover sped away.

2

"Forget me not! Forget me not!"   5
  Says now the chamber-maid
When the traveller on his journey
  No more will be delayed.

Charade.

My first may be the firstborn,
  The second child may be;
My second is a texture light
  And elegant to see:
My whole do those too often write   5
  Who are from talent free.

Hope in Grief.

Tell me not that death of grief
Is the only sure relief.
Tell me not that hope when dead
Leaves a void that nought can fill,
5   Gnawings that may not be fed.
Tell me not there is no skill
That can bind the breaking heart,
That can soothe the bitter smart,
When we find ourselves betrayed,
10   When we find ourselves forsaken,
By those for whom we would have laid
Our young lives down, nor wished to waken.
Say not that life is to all
But a gaily coloured pall,
15   Hiding with its deceitful glow
The hearts that break beneath it,
Engulphing as they anguished flow
The scalding tears that seethe it.
Say not, vain this world's turmoil,
20   Vain its trouble and its toil,
All its hopes and fears are vain,
Long, unmitigated pain.
What though we should be deceived
By the friend that we love best?
25   All in this world have been grieved,
Yet many have found rest.
Our present life is as the night,
Our future as the morning light:
Surely the night will pass away,
30   And surely will uprise the day.

ON THE DEATH OF A CAT,
A Friend of Mine, Aged Ten Years and a Half.

Who shall tell the lady's grief
When her Cat was past relief?
Who shall number the hot tears
Shed o'er her, beloved for years?
Who shall say the dark dismay   5
Which her dying caused that day?

Come, ye Muses, one and all,
Come obedient to my call.
Come and mourn, with tuneful breath,
Each one for a separate death;   10
And while you in numbers sigh,
I will sing her elegy.

Of a noble race she came,
And Grimalkin was her name.
Young and old full many a mouse   15
Felt the prowess of her house:
Weak and strong full many a rat
Cowered beneath her crushing pat:
And the birds around the place
Shrank from her too close embrace.   20
But one night, reft of her strength,
She laid down and died at length:
Lay a kitten by her side,
In whose life the mother died.
Spare her line and lineage,   25
Guard her kitten's tender age,
And that kitten's name as wide
Shall be known as her's that died.

And whoever passes by
30   The poor grave where Puss doth lie,
Softly, softly let him tread,
Nor disturb her narrow bed.

Sappho.

I sigh at day-dawn, and I sigh
When the dull day is passing by.
I sigh at evening, and again
I sigh when night brings sleep to men.
5   Oh! it were better far to die
Than thus for ever mourn and sigh,
And in death's dreamless sleep to be
Unconscious that none weep for me;
Eased from my weight of heaviness,
10   Forgetful of forgetfulness,
Resting from pain and care and sorrow
Thro' the long night that knows no morrow;
Living unloved, to die unknown,
Unwept, untended and alone.

HEART'S CHILL BETWEEN.

I did not chide him, tho' I knew
    That he was false to me:
Chide the exhaling of the dew,
    The ebbing of the sea,
5   The fading of a rosy hue,
    But not inconstancy.

Why strive for love when love is o'er?
    Why bind a restive heart?
He never knew the pain I bore

In saying: "We must part;   10
  Let us be friends, and nothing more":—
    Oh woman's shallow art!

But it is over, it is done;
    I hardly heed it now;
So many weary years have run   15
    Since then, I think not how
Things might have been; but greet each one
    With an unruffled brow.

What time I am where others be
    My heart seems very calm,   20
Stone calm; but if all go from me
    There comes a vague alarm,
A shrinking in the memory
    From some forgotten harm.

And often thro' the long long night   25
    Waking when none are near,
I feel my heart beat fast with fright,
    Yet know not what I fear.
Oh how I long to see the light
    And the sweet birds to hear!   30

To have the sun upon my face,
    To look up through the trees,
To walk forth in the open space,
    And listen to the breeze,
And not to dream the burial place   35
    Is clogging my weak knees.

Sometimes I can nor weep nor pray,
    But am half stupified;
And then all those who see me say
    Mine eyes are opened wide,   40
And that my wits seem gone away:—
    Ah would that I had died!

Would I could die and be at peace,
  Or living could forget;
My grief nor grows nor doth decrease,
  But ever is:—and yet
Methinks now that all this shall cease
  Before the sun shall set.

DEATH'S CHILL BETWEEN.

Chide not; let me breathe a little,
  For I shall not mourn him long.
Tho' the life-cord was so brittle
  The love-cord was very strong.
I would wake a little space
Till I find a sleeping-place.

You can go, I shall not weep;
  You can go unto your rest;
My heart-ache is all too deep,
  And too sore my throbbing breast.
Can sobs be, or angry tears,
Where are neither hopes nor fears?

Tho' with you I am alone,
  And must be so everywhere,
I will make no useless moan;
  None shall say: "She could not bear;"
While life lasts I will be strong,
But I shall not struggle long.

Listen, listen! everywhere
  A low voice is calling me,
And a step is on the stair,
  And one comes ye do not see.
Listen, listen! evermore
A dim hand knocks at the door.

Hear me: he is come again;   25
   My own dearest is come back.
Bring him in from the cold rain;
   Bring wine, and let nothing lack.
Thou and I will rest together,
Love, until the sunny weather.   30

I will shelter thee from harm,
   Hide thee from all heaviness;
Come to me, and keep thee warm
   By my side in quietness.
I will lull thee to thy sleep   35
With sweet songs; we will not weep.

Who hath talked of weeping? yet
   There is something at my heart
Gnawing, I would fain forget,
   And an aching and a smart—   40
Ah my Mother, 'tis in vain,
For he is not come again.

Lines
given with a Penwiper.

I have compassion on the carpeting,
   And on your back I have compassion too.
The splendid Brussels web is suffering
   In the dimmed lustre of each glowing hue;
And you the everlasting altering   5
   Of your position with strange aches must rue.
Behold, I come the carpet to preserve,
And save your spine from a continual curve.

A PAUSE OF THOUGHT.

I looked for that which is not, nor can be,
 And hope deferred made my heart sick in truth:
 But years must pass before a hope of youth
  Is resigned utterly.

5 I watched and waited with a steadfast will:
 And though the object seemed to flee away
 That I so longed for, ever day by day
  I watched and waited still.

Sometimes I said: This thing shall be no more;
10 My expectation wearies and shall cease;
 I will resign it now and be at peace:
  Yet never gave it o'er.

Sometimes I said: It is an empty name
 I long for; to a name why should I give
15 The peace of all the days I have to live?—
  Yet gave it all the same.

Alas, thou foolish one! alike unfit
 For healthy joy and salutary pain:
 Thou knowest the chase useless, and again
20 Turnest to follow it.

SONG.

She sat and sang alway
 By the green margin of a stream,
Watching the fishes leap and play
 Beneath the glad sunbeam.

I sat and wept away 5
   Beneath the moon's most shadowy beam,
Watching the blossoms of the May
   Weep leaves into the stream.

I wept for memory;
   She sang for hope that is so fair: 10
My tears were swallowed by the sea;
   Her songs died on the air.

SONG.

When I am dead, my dearest,
   Sing no sad songs for me;
Plant thou no roses at my head,
   Nor shady cypress tree:
Be the green grass above me 5
   With showers and dewdrops wet;
And if thou wilt, remember,
   And if thou wilt, forget.

I shall not see the shadows,
   I shall not feel the rain; 10
I shall not hear the nightingale
   Sing on, as if in pain:
And dreaming through the twilight
   That doth not rise nor set,
Haply I may remember, 15
   And haply may forget.

Some ladies dress in muslin full and white,
Some gentlemen in cloth succinct and black;
Some patronise a dog-cart, some a hack,
    Some think a painted clarence only right.
5   Youth is not always such a pleasing sight,
Witness a man with tassels on his back;
Or woman in a great-coat like a sack
    Towering above her sex with horrid height.
If all the world were water fit to drown
    There are some whom you would not teach to
10   swim,
  Rather enjoying if you saw them sink;
  Certain old ladies dressed in girlish pink,
With roses and geraniums on their gown:—
    Go to the Bason, poke them o'er the rim.—

On Keats.

A garden in a garden: a green spot
  Where all is green: most fitting slumber-place
  For the strong man grown weary of a race
Soon over. Unto him a goodly lot
5 Hath fallen in fertile ground; there thorns are not,
  But his own daisies: silence, full of grace,
  Surely hath shed a quiet on his face:
His earth is but sweet leaves that fall and rot.
What was his record of himself, ere he
10   Went from us? *Here lies one whose name was writ*
  In water: while the chilly shadows flit
    Of sweet Saint Agnes' Eve; while basil springs,
    His name, in every humble heart that sings,
Shall be a fountain of love, verily.

SONG.

Oh roses for the flush of youth,
　　And laurel for the perfect prime;
But pluck an ivy branch for me
　　Grown old before my time.

Oh violets for the grave of youth,　　　　　5
　　And bay for those dead in their prime;
Give me the withered leaves I chose
　　Before in the old time.

Have you forgotten?

Have you forgotten how one Summer night
　　We wandered forth together with the moon,
　　While warm winds hummed to us a sleepy tune?
Have you forgotten how you praised both light
And darkness; not embarrassed yet not quite　　5
　　At ease? and how you said the glare of noon
　　Less pleased you than the stars? but very soon
You blushed, and seemed to doubt if you were right.
We wandered far and took no note of time;
　　Till on the air there came the distant call　　10
Of church bells: we turned hastily, and yet
Ere we reached home sounded a second chime.
　　But what; have you indeed forgotten all?
Ah how then is it I cannot forget?

SWEET DEATH.

The sweetest blossoms die.
   And so it was that, going day by day
   Unto the Church to praise and pray,
And crossing the green churchyard thoughtfully,
5   I saw how on the graves the flowers
   Shed their fresh leaves in showers,
And how their perfume rose up to the sky
   Before it passed away.

The youngest blossoms die.
10   They die and fall and nourish the rich earth
   From which they lately had their birth;
Sweet life, but sweeter death that passeth by
   And is as though it had not been:—
   All colours turn to green;
15   The bright hues vanish and the odours fly,
   The grass hath lasting worth.

And youth and beauty die.
   So be it, O my God, Thou God of truth:
   Better than beauty and than youth
20   Are Saints and Angels, a glad company;
   And Thou, O Lord, our Rest and Ease,
   Art better far than these.
Why should we shrink from our full harvest? why
   Prefer to glean with Ruth?

AN END.

Love, strong as Death, is dead.
Come, let us make his bed
Among the dying flowers:
A green turf at his head;

And a stone at his feet,   5
Whereon we may sit
In the quiet evening hours.

He was born in the Spring,
And died before the harvesting:
On the last warm Summer day   10
He left us; he would not stay
For Autumn twilight cold and gray.
Sit we by his grave, and sing
He is gone away.

To few chords and sad and low   15
Sing we so:
Be our eyes fixed on the grass
Shadow-veiled as the years pass,
While we think of all that was
In the long ago.   20

DREAM-LAND.

Where sunless rivers weep
Their waves into the deep,
She sleeps a charmèd sleep:
   Awake her not.
Led by a single star,   5
She came from very far
To seek where shadows are
   Her pleasant lot.

She left the rosy morn,
She left the fields of corn,   10
For twilight cold and lorn
   And water springs.
Thro' sleep, as thro' a veil,
She sees the sky look pale,
And hears the nightingale   15
   That sadly sings.

Rest, rest, a perfect rest
Shed over brow and breast;
Her face is toward the west,
    The purple land.
She cannot see the grain
Ripening on hill and plain;
She cannot feel the rain
    Upon her hand.

Rest, rest, for evermore
Upon a mossy shore;
Rest, rest at the heart's core
    Till time shall cease:
Sleep that no pain shall wake;
Night that no morn shall break,
Till joy shall overtake
    Her perfect peace.

REMEMBER.

Remember me when I am gone away,
    Gone far away into the silent land;
    When you can no more hold me by the hand,
Nor I half turn to go yet turning stay.
Remember me when no more day by day
    You tell me of our future that you planned:
    Only remember me; you understand
It will be late to counsel then or pray.
Yet if you should forget me for a while
    And afterwards remember, do not grieve:
    For if the darkness and corruption leave
    A vestige of the thoughts that once I had,
Better by far you should forget and smile
    Than that you should remember and be sad.

Three Nuns.

I.

"Sospira questo core
E non so dir perchè."

Shadow, shadow on the wall
    Spread thy shelter over me;
Wrap me with a heavy pall,
    With the dark that none may see.
Fold thyself around me; come: 5
Shut out all the troublesome
Noise of life; I would be dumb.

Shadow thou hast reached my feet,
    Rise and cover up my head;
Be my stainless winding sheet,   10
    Buried before I am dead.
Lay thy cool upon my breast:
Once I thought that joy was best,
Now I only care for rest.

By the grating of my cell   15
    Sings a solitary bird;
Sweeter than the vesper bell,
    Sweetest song was ever heard.*
Sing upon thy living tree:
Happy echoes answer thee,   20
Happy songster, sing to me.

When my yellow hair was curled
    Though men saw and called me fair,
I was weary in the world
    Full of vanity and care.   25

*"Sweetest eyes were ever seen." E. B. Browning.

Gold was left behind, curls shorn
When I came here; that same morn
Made a bride no gems adorn.

Here wrapped in my spotless veil,
    Curtained from intruding eyes,
30 I whom prayers and fasts turn pale
    Wait the flush of Paradise.
But the vigil is so long
My heart sickens:—sing thy song,
35 Blithe bird that canst do no wrong.

Sing on, making me forget
    Present sorrow and past sin.
Sing a little longer yet:
    Soon the matins will begin;
40 And I must turn back again
To that aching worse than pain
I must bear and not complain.

Sing, that in thy song I may
    Dream myself once more a child
45 In the green woods far away
    Plucking clematis and wild
Hyacinths, till pleasure grew
Tired, yet so was pleasure too,
Resting with no work to do.

50 In the thickest of the wood,
    I remember, long ago
How a stately oak tree stood,
    With a sluggish pool below
Almost shadowed out of sight.
55 On the waters dark as night,
Water-lilies lay like light.

There, while yet a child, I thought
    I could live as in a dream,
Secret, neither found nor sought:
    Till the lilies on the stream,   60
Pure as virgin purity,
Would seem scarce too pure for me:—
Ah, but that can never be.

2.

    "Sospirerà d'amore,
      Ma non lo dice a me."

I loved him, yes, where was the sin?
    I loved him with my heart and soul.   65
    But I pressed forward to no goal,
There was no prize I strove to win.
Show me my sin that I may see:—
Throw the first stone, thou Pharisee.

I loved him, but I never sought   70
    That he should know that I was fair.
    I prayed for him; was my sin prayer?
I sacrificed, he never bought.
He nothing gave, he nothing took;
We never bartered look for look.   75

My voice rose in the sacred choir,
    The choir of Nuns; do you condemn
    Even if, when kneeling among them,
Faith, zeal and love kindled a fire
And I prayed for his happiness   80
Who knew not? was my error this?

I only prayed that in the end
    His trust and hope may not be vain.
    I prayed not we may meet again:
85 I would not let our names ascend,
No, not to Heaven, in the same breath;
Nor will I join the two in death.

Oh sweet is death; for I am weak
    And weary, and it giveth rest.
90   The Crucifix lies on my breast,
And all night long it seems to speak
Of rest; I hear it through my sleep,
And the great comfort makes me weep.

Oh sweet is death that bindeth up
95   The broken and the bleeding heart.
    The draught chilled, but a cordial part
Lurked at the bottom of the cup;
And for my patience will my Lord
Give an exceeding great reward.

100 Yea, the reward is almost won,
    A crown of glory and a palm.
    Soon I shall sing the unknown psalm;
Soon gaze on light, not on the sun;
And soon, with surer faith, shall pray
105 For him, and cease not night nor day.

My life is breaking like a cloud;
    God judgeth not as man doth judge.—
    Nay, bear with me; you need not grudge
This peace; the vows that I have vowed
110 Have all been kept: Eternal Strength
Holds me, though mine own fails at length.

Bury me in the Convent ground
   Among the flowers that are so sweet;
   And lay a green turf at my feet,
Where thick trees cast a gloom around.   115
At my head let a Cross be, white
Through the long blackness of the night.

Now kneel and pray beside my bed
   That I may sleep being free from pain:
   And pray that I may wake again   120
After His Likeness, Who hath said
(Faithful is He Who promiseth,)
We shall be satisfied Therewith.

3.

"Rispondimi, cor mio,
   Perchè sospiri tu?
Risponde: Voglio Iddio,
   Sospiro per Gesù."

My heart is as a freeborn bird
   Caged in my cruel breast,   125
That flutters, flutters evermore,
   Nor sings, nor is at rest.
But beats against the prison bars,
   As knowing its own nest
Far off beyond the clouded West.   130

My soul is as a hidden fount
   Shut in by clammy clay,
That struggles with an upward moan;
   Striving to force its way
Up through the turf, over the grass,   135
   Up, up into the day,
Where twilight no more turneth grey.

Oh for the grapes of the True Vine
    Growing in Paradise,
140   Whose tendrils join the Tree of Life
      To that which maketh wise.
Growing beside the Living Well
    Whose sweetest waters rise
Where tears are wiped from tearful eyes.

145   Oh for the waters of that Well
      Round which the Angels stand.
Oh for the Shadow of the Rock
    On my heart's weary land.
Oh for the Voice to guide me when
150   I turn to either hand,
Guiding me till I reach Heaven's strand.

Thou World from which I am come out,
    Keep all thy gems and gold;
Keep thy delights and precious things,
155   Thou that art waxing old.
My heart shall beat with a new life,
    When thine is dead and cold:
When thou dost fear I shall be bold.

When Earth shall pass away with all
160   Her pride and pomp of sin,
The City builded without hands
    Shall safely shut me in.
All the rest is but vanity
    Which others strive to win:
165   Where their hopes end my joys begin.

I will not look upon a rose
    Though it is fair to see:
The flowers planted in Paradise
    Are budding now for me.
170   Red roses like love visible
    Are blowing on their tree,
Or white like virgin purity.

I will not look unto the sun
    Which setteth night by night:
In the untrodden courts of Heaven   175
    My crown shall be more bright.
Lo, in the New Jerusalem
    Founded and built aright
My very feet shall tread on light.

With foolish riches of this World   180
    I have bought treasure, where
Nought perisheth: for this white veil
    I gave my golden hair;
I gave the beauty of my face
    For vigils, fasts and prayer;   185
I gave all for this Cross I bear.

My heart trembled when first I took
    The vows which must be kept;
At first it was a weariness
    To watch when once I slept.   190
The path was rough and sharp with thorns;
    My feet bled as I stepped;
The Cross was heavy and I wept.

While still the names rang in mine ears
    Of daughter, sister, wife;   195
The outside world still looked so fair
    To my weak eyes, and rife
With beauty; my heart almost failed;
    Then in the desperate strife
I prayed, as one who prays for life,   200

Until I grew to love what once
    Had been so burdensome.
So now when I am faint, because
    Hope deferred seems to numb
My heart, I yet can plead; and say   205
    Although my lips are dumb:
"The Spirit and the Bride say, Come."

Portraits.

An easy lazy length of limb,
   Dark eyes and features from the south,
A short-legged meditative pipe
   Set in a supercilious mouth;
5   Ink and a pen and papers laid
   Down on a table for the night,
Beside a semi-dozing man
   Who wakes to go to bed by light.

A pair of brothers brotherly,
10   Unlike and yet how much the same
In heart and high-toned intellect,
   In face and bearing, hope and aim:
Friends of the selfsame treasured friends
   And of one home the dear delight,
15 Beloved of many a loving heart
   And cherished both in mine, good night.

"CONSIDER THE LILIES OF THE FIELD."

Flowers preach to us if we will hear:—
The rose saith in the dewy morn:
I am most fair;
Yet all my loveliness is born
5 Upon a thorn.
The poppy saith amid the corn:
Let but my scarlet head appear
And I am held in scorn;
Yet juice of subtle virtue lies
10 Within my cup of curious dyes.
The lilies say: Behold how we
Preach without words of purity.

The violets whisper from the shade
Which their own leaves have made:
Men scent our fragrance on the air,   15
Yet take no heed
Of humble lessons we would read.

But not alone the fairest flowers:
The merest grass
Along the roadside where we pass,   20
Lichen and moss and sturdy weed,
Tell of His love who sends the dew,
The rain and sunshine too,
To nourish one small seed.

The P.R.B.

The P.R.B. is in its decadence:—
for Woolner in Australia cooks his chops;
And Hunt is yearning for the land of Cheops;
D. G. Rossetti shuns the vulgar optic;
While William M. Rossetti merely lops   5
His B.s in English disesteemed as Coptic;
Calm Stephens in the twilight smokes his pipe
But long the dawning of his public day;
And he at last, the champion, great Millais
Attaining academic opulence   10
Winds up his signature with A.R.A.:—
So rivers merge in the perpetual sea,
So luscious fruit must fall when over ripe,
And so the consummated P.R.B.

THE BOURNE.

Underneath the growing grass,
   Underneath the living flowers,
   Deeper than the sound of showers:
   There we shall not count the hours
5 By the shadows as they pass.

Youth and health will be but vain,
   Beauty reckoned of no worth:
   There a very little girth
   Can hold round what once the earth
10 Seemed too narrow to contain.

THE WORLD.

By day she wooes me, soft, exceeding fair:
   But all night as the moon so changeth she;
   Loathsome and foul with hideous leprosy
And subtle serpents gliding in her hair.
5 By day she wooes me to the outer air,
   Ripe fruits, sweet flowers, and full satiety:
   But thro' the night, a beast she grins at me,
A very monster void of love and prayer.
By day she stands a lie: by night she stands
10 In all the naked horror of the truth
With pushing horns and clawed and clutching
      hands.
Is this a friend indeed; that I should sell
   My soul to her, give her my life and youth,
Till my feet, cloven too, take hold on hell?

From the Antique.

It's a weary life, it is; she said:—
    Doubly blank in a woman's lot:
I wish and I wish I were a man;
    Or, better than any being, were not:

Were nothing at all in all the world,   5
    Not a body and not a soul;
Not so much as a grain of dust
    Or drop of water from pole to pole.

Still the world would wag on the same,
    Still the seasons go and come;   10
Blossoms bloom as in days of old,
    Cherries ripen and wild bees hum.

None would miss me in all the world,
    How much less would care or weep:
I should be nothing; while all the rest   15
    Would wake and weary and fall asleep.

Three Stages.

I.

I looked for that which is not, nor can be,
    And hope deferred made my heart sick in truth;
But years must pass before a hope of youth
    Is resigned utterly.

I watched and waited with a steadfast will: 5
    And though the object seemed to flee away
That I so longed for; ever, day by day,
    I watched and waited still.

Sometimes I said: This thing shall be no more:
   My expectation wearies and shall cease;
  I will resign it now and be at peace:—
     Yet never gave it o'er.

Sometimes I said: It is an empty name
   I long for; to a name why should I give
  The peace of all the days I have to live?—
     Yet gave it all the same.

Alas, thou foolish one! alike unfit
   For healthy joy and salutary pain;
  Thou knowest the chase useless, and again
     Turnest to follow it.

2.

My happy dream is finished with,
   My dream in which alone I lived so long.
My heart slept—woe is me, it wakeneth;
    Was weak—I thought it strong.

Oh weary wakening from a life-true dream:
   Oh pleasant dream from which I wake in pain:
I rested all my trust on things that seem,
    And all my trust is vain.

I must pull down my palace that I built,
   Dig up the pleasure-gardens of my soul;
Must change my laughter to sad tears for guilt,
    My freedom to control.

Now all the cherished secrets of my heart,
   Now all my hidden hopes are turned to sin:
Part of my life is dead, part sick, and part
    Is all on fire within.

The fruitless thought of what I might have been
    Haunting me ever will not let me rest:
A cold north wind has withered all my green,
    My sun is in the west.   20

But where my palace stood, with the same stone,
    I will uprear a shady hermitage;
And there my spirit shall keep house alone,
    Accomplishing its age:

There other garden beds shall lie around   25
    Full of sweet-briar and incense-bearing thyme;
There I will sit, and listen for the sound
    Of the last lingering chime.

3.

I thought to deal the death-stroke at a blow,
    To give all, once for all, but nevermore;—
Then sit to hear the low waves fret the shore,
    Or watch the silent snow.

"Oh rest," I thought, "in silence and the dark;   5
    Oh rest, if nothing else, from head to feet:
Though I may see no more the poppied wheat,
    Or sunny soaring lark.

"These chimes are slow, but surely strike at last;
    This sand is slow, but surely droppeth thro';   10
And much there is to suffer, much to do,
    Before the time be past.

"So will I labour, but will not rejoice:
    Will do and bear, but will not hope again;
Gone dead alike to pulses of quick pain,   15
    And pleasure's counterpoise:"

I said so in my heart, and so I thought
    My life would lapse, a tedious monotone:
    I thought to shut myself, and dwell alone
20   Unseeking and unsought.

But first I tired, and then my care grew slack;
    Till my heart slumbered, may-be wandered too:—
    I felt the sunshine glow again, and knew
        The swallow on its track;

25 All birds awoke to building in the leaves,
    All buds awoke to fulness and sweet scent,
    Ah, too, my heart woke unawares, intent
        Oh fruitful harvest sheaves.

Full pulse of life, that I had deemed was dead,
30   Full throb of youth, that I had deemed at rest,—
    Alas, I cannot build myself a nest,
        I cannot crown my head

With royal purple blossoms for the feast,
    Nor flush with laughter, nor exult in song;—
35 These joys may drift, as time now drifts along;
        And cease, as once they ceased.

I may pursue, and yet may not attain,
    Athirst and panting all the days I live:
    Or seem to hold, yet nerve myself to give
40   What once I gave, again.

ECHO.

Come to me in the silence of the night;
    Come in the speaking silence of a dream;
Come with soft rounded cheeks and eyes as bright
    As sunlight on a stream;
5   Come back in tears,
O memory, hope, love of finished years.

Oh dream how sweet, too sweet, too bitter sweet,
   Whose wakening should have been in Paradise,
Where souls brimfull of love abide and meet;
    Where thirsting longing eyes   10
      Watch the slow door
That opening, letting in, lets out no more.

Yet come to me in dreams, that I may live
   My very life again tho' cold in death:
Come back to me in dreams, that I may give   15
   Pulse for pulse, breath for breath:
     Speak low, lean low,
As long ago, my love, how long ago.

MY DREAM.

Hear now a curious dream I dreamed last night,
Each word whereof is weighed and sifted truth.

I stood beside Euphrates while it swelled
Like overflowing Jordan in its youth:
It waxed and coloured sensibly to sight,   5
Till out of myriad pregnant waves there welled
Young crocodiles, a gaunt blunt-featured crew,
Fresh-hatched perhaps and daubed with birthday dew.
The rest if I should tell, I fear my friend,
My closest friend would deem the facts untrue;   10
And therefore it were wisely left untold;
Yet if you will, why, hear it to the end.

Each crocodile was girt with massive gold
And polished stones that with their wearers grew:
But one there was who waxed beyond the rest,   15
Wore kinglier girdle and a kingly crown,
Whilst crowns and orbs and sceptres starred his breast.
All gleamed compact and green with scale on scale,
But special burnishment adorned his mail
And special terror weighed upon his frown;   20

His punier brethren quaked before his tail,
Broad as a rafter, potent as a flail.
So he grew lord and master of his kin:
But who shall tell the tale of all their woes?
25   An execrable appetite arose,
He battened on them, crunched, and sucked them in.
He knew no law, he feared no binding law,
But ground them with inexorable jaw:
The luscious fat distilled upon his chin,
30   Exuded from his nostrils and his eyes,
While still like hungry death he fed his maw;
Till every minor crocodile being dead
And buried too, himself gorged to the full,
He slept with breath oppressed and unstrung claw.
35   Oh marvel passing strange which next I saw:
In sleep he dwindled to the common size,
And all the empire faded from his coat.
Then from far off a wingèd vessel came,
Swift as a swallow, subtle as a flame:
40   I know not what it bore of freight or host,
But white it was as an avenging ghost.
It levelled strong Euphrates in its course;
Supreme yet weightless as an idle mote
It seemed to tame the waters without force
45   Till not a murmur swelled or billow beat:
Lo, as the purple shadow swept the sands,
The prudent crocodile rose on his feet
And shed appropriate tears and wrung his hands.

What can it mean? you ask. I answer not
50   For meaning, but myself must echo, What?
And tell it as I saw it on the spot.

MAY.

I cannot tell you how it was;
But this I know: it came to pass
Upon a bright and breezy day
When May was young; ah pleasant May!
As yet the poppies were not born   5
Between the blades of tender corn;
The last eggs had not hatched as yet,
Nor any bird foregone its mate.

I cannot tell you what it was;
But this I know: it did but pass.   10
It passed away with sunny May,
With all sweet things it passed away,
And left me old, and cold, and grey.

SHUT OUT.

The door was shut. I looked between
 Its iron bars; and saw it lie,
 My garden, mine, beneath the sky,
Pied with all flowers bedewed and green:

From bough to bough the song-birds crossed,   5
 From flower to flower the moths and bees;
 With all its nests and stately trees
It had been mine, and it was lost.

A shadowless spirit kept the gate,
 Blank and unchanging like the grave.   10
 I peering thro' said: "Let me have
Some buds to cheer my outcast state."

He answered not. "Or give me, then,
 But one small twig from shrub or tree;
 And bid my home remember me
Until I come to it again."

The spirit was silent; but he took
 Mortar and stone to build a wall;
 He left no loophole great or small
Thro' which my straining eyes might look:

So now I sit here quite alone
 Blinded with tears; nor grieve for that,
 For nought is left worth looking at
Since my delightful land is gone.

A violet bed is budding near,
 Wherein a lark has made her nest:
 And good they are, but not the best;
And dear they are, but not so dear.

AMEN.

It is over. What is over?
 Nay, how much is over truly:
Harvest days we toiled to sow for;
 Now the sheaves are gathered newly,
 Now the wheat is garnered duly.

It is finished. What is finished?
 Much is finished known or unknown:
Lives are finished; time diminished;
 Was the fallow field left unsown?
 Will these buds be always unblown?

It suffices. What suffices?
　　All suffices reckoned rightly:
Spring shall bloom where now the ice is,
　　Roses make the bramble sightly,
　　And the quickening sun shine brightly,   15
　　And the latter wind blow lightly,
And my garden teem with spices.

THE HOUR AND THE GHOST.

BRIDE.

O love, love, hold me fast,
He draws me away from thee;
I cannot stem the blast,
Nor the cold strong sea:
Far away a light shines   5
Beyond the hills and pines;
It is lit for me.

BRIDEGROOM.

I have thee close, my dear,
No terror can come near;
Only far off the northern light shines clear.   10

GHOST.

Come with me, fair and false,
To our home, come home.
It is my voice that calls:
Once thou wast not afraid
When I woo'd, and said,   15
"Come, our nest is newly made"—
Now cross the tossing foam.

BRIDE.

Hold me one moment longer,
He taunts me with the past,
His clutch is waxing stronger,
Hold me fast, hold me fast.
He draws me from thy heart,
And I cannot withhold:
He bids my spirit depart
With him into the cold:—
Oh bitter vows of old!

BRIDEGROOM.

Lean on me, hide thine eyes:
Only ourselves, earth and skies,
Are present here: be wise.

GHOST.

Lean on me, come away,
I will guide and steady:
Come, for I will not stay:
Come, for house and bed are ready.
Ah, sure bed and house,
For better and worse, for life and death:
Goal won with shortened breath:
Come, crown our vows.

BRIDE.

One moment, one more word,
While my heart beats still,
While my breath is stirred
By my fainting will.
O friend forsake me not,
Forget not as I forgot:
But keep thy heart for me,
Keep thy faith true and bright;
Thro' the lone cold winter night
Perhaps I may come to thee.

BRIDEGROOM.

Nay peace, my darling, peace:
Let these dreams and terrors cease:
Who spoke of death or change or aught
      but ease?   50

GHOST.

O fair frail sin,
O poor harvest gathered in!
Thou shalt visit him again
To watch his heart grow cold;
To know the gnawing pain   55
I knew of old;
To see one much more fair
Fill up the vacant chair,
Fill his heart, his children bear:—
While thou and I together   60
In the outcast weather
Toss and howl and spin.

THE LOWEST ROOM.

Like flowers sequestered from the sun
      And wind of summer, day by day
I dwindled paler, whilst my hair
      Showed the first tinge of grey.

"Oh what is life, that we should live?   5
      Or what is death, that we must die?
A bursting bubble is our life:
      I also, what am I?"

"What is your grief? now tell me, sweet,
      That I may grieve," my sister said;   10
And stayed a white embroidering hand
      And raised a golden head:

Her tresses showed a richer mass,
　　Her eyes looked softer than my own,
15　Her figure had a statelier height,
　　　　Her voice a tenderer tone.

"Some must be second and not first;
　　All cannot be the first of all:
Is not this, too, but vanity?
20　　　　I stumble like to fall.

"So yesterday I read the acts
　　Of Hector and each clangorous king
With wrathful great Aeacides:—
　　　　Old Homer leaves a sting."

25　The comely face looked up again,
　　The deft hand lingered on the thread:
"Sweet, tell me what is Homer's sting,
　　　　Old Homer's sting?" she said.

"He stirs my sluggish pulse like wine,
30　　He melts me like the wind of spice,
Strong as strong Ajax' red right hand,
　　　　And grand like Juno's eyes.

"I cannot melt the sons of men,
　　I cannot fire and tempest-toss:—
35　Besides, those days were golden days,
　　　　Whilst these are days of dross."

She laughed a feminine low laugh,
　　Yet did not stay her dexterous hand:
"Now tell me of those days," she said,
40　　　　"When time ran golden sand."

"Then men were men of might and right,
　　Sheer might, at least, and weighty swords;
Then men in open blood and fire
　　Bore witness to their words,

"Crest-rearing kings with whistling spears;　45
　　But if these shivered in the shock
They wrenched up hundred-rooted trees,
　　Or hurled the effacing rock.

"Then hand to hand, then foot to foot,
　　Stern to the death-grip grappling then,　50
Who ever thought of gunpowder
　　Amongst these men of men?

"They knew whose hand struck home the death,
　　They knew who broke but would not bend,
Could venerate an equal foe　55
　　And scorn a laggard friend.

"Calm in the utmost stress of doom,
　　Devout toward adverse powers above,
They hated with intenser hate
　　And loved with fuller love.　60

"Then heavenly beauty could allay
　　As heavenly beauty stirred the strife:
By them a slave was worshipped more
　　Than is by us a wife."

She laughed again, my sister laughed;　65
　　Made answer o'er the laboured cloth:
"I rather would be one of us
　　Than wife, or slave, or both."

"Oh better then be slave or wife
70   Than fritter now blank life away:
Then night had holiness of night,
        And day was sacred day.

"The princess laboured at her loom,
        Mistress and handmaiden alike;
75 Beneath their needles grew the field
        With warriors armed to strike.

"Or, look again, dim Dian's face
        Gleamed perfect thro' the attendant night;
Were such not better than those holes
80   Amid that waste of white?

"A shame it is, our aimless life:
        I rather from my heart would feed
From silver dish in gilded stall
        With wheat and wine the steed—

85 "The faithful steed that bore my lord
        In safety thro' the hostile land,
The faithful steed that arched his neck
        To fondle with my hand."

Her needle erred; a moment's pause,
90   A moment's patience, all was well.
Then she: "But just suppose the horse,
        Suppose the rider fell?

"Then captive in an alien house,
        Hungering on exile's bitter bread,—
95 They happy, they who won the lot
        Of sacrifice," she said.

Speaking she faltered, while her look
   Showed forth her passion like a glass:
With hand suspended, kindling eye,
    Flushed cheek, how fair she was!   100

"Ah well, be those the days of dross;
   This, if you will, the age of gold:
Yet had those days a spark of warmth,
    While these are somewhat cold—

"Are somewhat mean and cold and slow,   105
   Are stunted from heroic growth:
We gain but little when we prove
    The worthlessness of both."

"But life is in our hands," she said:
   "In our own hands for gain or loss: 110
Shall not the Sevenfold Sacred Fire
    Suffice to purge our dross?

"Too short a century of dreams,
   One day of work sufficient length:
Why should not you, why should not I   115
    Attain heroic strength?

"Our life is given us as a blank;
   Ourselves must make it blest or curst:
Who dooms me I shall only be
    The second, not the first?   120

"Learn from old Homer, if you will,
   Such wisdom as his books have said:
In one the acts of Ajax shine,
    In one of Diomed.

125 "Honoured all heroes whose high deeds
        Thro' life, thro' death, enlarge their span:
    Only Achilles in his rage
        And sloth is less than man."

    "Achilles only less than man?
130   He less than man who, half a god,
    Discomfited all Greece with rest,
        Cowed Ilion with a nod?

    "He offered vengeance, lifelong grief
        To one dear ghost, uncounted price:
135 Beasts, Trojans, adverse gods, himself,
        Heaped up the sacrifice.

    "Self-immolated to his friend,
        Shrined in world's wonder, Homer's page,
    Is this the man, the less than men
140   Of this degenerate age?"

    "Gross from his acorns, tusky boar
        Does memorable acts like his;
    So for her snared offended young
        Bleeds the swart lioness."

145 But here she paused; our eyes had met,
        And I was whitening with the jeer;
    She rose: "I went too far," she said;
        Spoke low: "Forgive me, dear.

    "To me our days seem pleasant days,
150   Our home a haven of pure content;
    Forgive me if I said too much,
        So much more than I meant.

"Homer, tho' greater than his gods,
   With rough-hewn virtues was sufficed
And rough-hewn men: but what are such   155
   To us who learn of Christ?"

The much-moved pathos of her voice,
   Her almost tearful eyes, her cheek
Grown pale, confessed the strength of love
   Which only made her speak: 160

For mild she was, of few soft words,
   Most gentle, easy to be led,
Content to listen when I spoke
   And reverence what I said;

I elder sister by six years;   165
   Not half so glad, or wise, or good:
Her words rebuked my secret self
   And shamed me where I stood.

She never guessed her words reproved
   A silent envy nursed within,   170
A selfish, souring discontent
   Pride-born, the devil's sin.

I smiled, half bitter, half in jest:
   "The wisest man of all the wise
Left for his summary of life   175
   'Vanity of vanities.'

"Beneath the sun there's nothing new:
   Men flow, men ebb, mankind flows on:
If I am wearied of my life,
   Why so was Solomon.   180

"Vanity of vanities he preached
    Of all he found, of all he sought:
Vanity of vanities, the gist
    Of all the words he taught.

185   "This in the wisdom of the world,
        In Homer's page, in all, we find:
    As the sea is not filled, so yearns
        Man's universal mind.

    "This Homer felt, who gave his men
190   With glory but a transient state:
    His very Jove could not reverse
        Irrevocable fate.

    "Uncertain all their lot save this—
        Who wins must lose, who lives must die:
195   All trodden out into the dark
        Alike, all vanity."

    She scarcely answered when I paused,
        But rather to herself said: "One
    Is here," low-voiced and loving, "Yea,
200   Greater than Solomon."

    So both were silent, she and I:
        She laid her work aside, and went
    Into the garden-walks, like spring,
        All gracious with content;

205   A little graver than her wont,
        Because her words had fretted me;
    Not warbling quite her merriest tune
        Bird-like from tree to tree.

I chose a book to read and dream:
    Yet half the while with furtive eyes   210
Marked how she made her choice of flowers
    Intuitively wise,

And ranged them with instinctive taste
    Which all my books had failed to teach;
Fresh rose herself, and daintier   215
    Than blossom of the peach.

By birthright higher than myself,
    Tho' nestling of the selfsame nest:
No fault of hers, no fault of mine,
    But stubborn to digest.   220

I watched her, till my book unmarked
    Slid noiseless to the velvet floor;
Till all the opulent summer-world
    Looked poorer than before.

Just then her busy fingers ceased,   225
    Her fluttered colour went and came;
I knew whose step was on the walk,
    Whose voice would name her name.

       *   *   *

Well, twenty years have passed since then:
    My sister now, a stately wife   230
Still fair, looks back in peace and sees
    The longer half of life—

The longer half of prosperous life,
    With little grief, or fear, or fret:
She, loved and loving long ago,   235
    Is loved and loving yet.

A husband honourable, brave,
　　Is her main wealth in all the world:
And next to him one like herself,
240　　　　One daughter golden-curled;

Fair image of her own fair youth,
　　As beautiful and as serene,
With almost such another love
　　As her own love has been.

245　　Yet, tho' of world-wide charity,
　　And in her home most tender dove,
Her treasure and her heart are stored
　　In the home-land of love:

She thrives, God's blessed husbandry;
250　　　　Most like a vine which full of fruit
Doth cling and lean and climb toward heaven
　　While earth still binds its root.

I sit and watch my sister's face:
　　How little altered since the hours
255　　When she, a kind, light-hearted girl,
　　Gathered her garden flowers;

Her song just mellowed by regret
　　For having teased me with her talk;
Then all-forgetful as she heard
260　　　　One step upon the walk.

While I? I sat alone and watched;
　　My lot in life, to live alone
In mine own world of interests,
　　Much felt but little shown.

Not to be first: how hard to learn 265
   That lifelong lesson of the past;
Line graven on line and stroke on stroke;
   But, thank God, learned at last.

So now in patience I possess
   My soul year after tedious year, 270
Content to take the lowest place,
   The place assigned me here.

Yet sometimes, when I feel my strength
   Most weak, and life most burdensome,
I lift mine eyes up to the hills 275
   From whence my help shall come:

Yea, sometimes still I lift my heart
   To the Archangelic trumpet-burst,
When all deep secrets shall be shown,
   And many last be first. 280

A TRIAD.

Three sang of love together: one with lips
   Crimson, with cheeks and bosom in a glow,
Flushed to the yellow hair and finger tips;
   And one there sang who soft and smooth as snow
   Bloomed like a tinted hyacinth at a show; 5
And one was blue with famine after love,
   Who like a harpstring snapped rang harsh and low
The burden of what those were singing of.
One shamed herself in love; one temperately
   Grew gross in soulless love, a sluggish wife; 10
One famished died for love. Thus two of three
   Took death for love and won him after strife;
One droned in sweetness like a fattened bee:
   All on the threshold, yet all short of life.

LOVE FROM THE NORTH.

I had a love in soft south land,
    Beloved thro' April far in May;
He waited on my lightest breath,
    And never dared to say me nay.

5   He saddened if my cheer was sad,
    But gay he grew if I was gay;
We never differed on a hair,
    My yes his yes, my nay his nay.

The wedding hour was come, the aisles
10   Were flushed with sun and flowers that day;
I pacing balanced in my thoughts:
    "It's quite too late to think of nay."—

My bridegroom answered in his turn,
    Myself had almost answered "yea:"
15   When thro' the flashing nave I heard
    A struggle and resounding "nay".

Bridemaids and bridegroom shrank in fear,
    But I stood high who stood at bay:
"And if I answer yea, fair Sir,
20   What man art thou to bar with nay?"

He was a strong man from the north,
    Light-locked, with eyes of dangerous grey:
"Put yea by for another time
    In which I will not say thee nay."

25   He took me in his strong white arms,
    He bore me on his horse away
O'er crag, morass, and hairbreadth pass,
    But never asked me yea or nay.

He made me fast with book and bell,
  With links of love he makes me stay;   30
Till now I've neither heart nor power
  Nor will nor wish to say him nay.

In an Artist's Studio.

One face looks out from all his canvasses,
  One selfsame figure sits or walks or leans;
  We found her hidden just behind those screens,
That mirror gave back all her loveliness.
A queen in opal or in ruby dress,   5
  A nameless girl in freshest summer greens,
  A saint, an angel;—every canvass means
The same one meaning, neither more nor less.
He feeds upon her face by day and night,
  And she with true kind eyes looks back on him   10
Fair as the moon and joyful as the light:
  Not wan with waiting, not with sorrow dim;
Not as she is, but was when hope shone bright;
  Not as she is, but as she fills his dream.

A BETTER RESURRECTION.

I have no wit, no words, no tears;
  My heart within me like a stone
Is numbed too much for hopes or fears;
  Look right, look left, I dwell alone;
I lift mine eyes, but dimmed with grief   5
  No everlasting hills I see;
My life is in the falling leaf:
      O Jesus, quicken me.

My life is like a faded leaf,
   My harvest dwindled to a husk;
Truly my life is void and brief
   And tedious in the barren dusk;
My life is like a frozen thing,
   No bud nor greenness can I see:
Yet rise it shall—the sap of Spring;
   O Jesus, rise in me.

My life is like a broken bowl,
   A broken bowl that cannot hold
One drop of water for my soul
   Or cordial in the searching cold;
Cast in the fire the perished thing,
   Melt and remould it, till it be
A royal cup for Him my King:
   O Jesus, drink of me.

"Whatsoever is right, that shall ye receive."

When all the overwork of life
   Is finished once, and fallen asleep
We shrink no more beneath the knife,
   But having sown prepare to reap;
Delivered from the crossway rough,
   Delivered from the thorny scourge,
   Delivered from the tossing surge,
Then shall we find—(please God!)—it is enough?

Not in this world of hope deferred,
   This world of perishable stuff;
Eye hath not seen, nor ear hath heard,
   Nor heart conceived that full "enough":
Here moans the separating sea,
   Here harvests fail, here breaks the heart;
   There God shall join and no man part,
All one in Christ, so one—(please God!)—with me.

"The heart knoweth its own bitterness."

When all the over-work of life
   Is finished once, and fast asleep
We swerve no more beneath the knife
   But taste that silence cool and deep;
Forgetful of the highways rough,   5
   Forgetful of the thorny scourge,
   Forgetful of the tossing surge,
Then shall we find it is enough?—

How can we say 'enough' on earth;
   'Enough' with such a craving heart: 10
I have not found it since my birth
   But still have bartered part for part.
I have not held and hugged the whole,
   But paid the old to gain the new;
   Much have I paid, yet much is due,   15
Till I am beggared sense and soul.

I used to labour, used to strive
   For pleasure with a restless will:
Now if I save my soul alive
   All else what matters, good or ill?   20
I used to dream alone, to plan
   Unspoken hopes and days to come:—
   Of all my past this is the sum:
I will not lean on child of man.

To give, to give, not to receive,   25
   I long to pour myself, my soul.
Not to keep back or count or leave
   But king with king to give the whole:
I long for one to stir my deep—
   I have had enough of help and gift—   30
   I long for one to search and sift
Myself, to take myself and keep.

You scratch my surface with your pin;
    You stroke me smooth with hushing breath;—
35   Nay pierce, nay probe, nay dig within,
    Probe my quick core and sound my depth.
You call me with a puny call,
    You talk, you smile, you nothing do;
    How should I spend my heart on you,
40   My heart that so outweighs you all?

Your vessels are by much too strait;
    Were I to pour you could not hold,
Bear with me: I must bear to wait
    A fountain sealed thro' heat and cold.
45   Bear with me days or months or years;
    Deep must call deep until the end
    When friend shall no more envy friend
Nor vex his friend at unawares.

Not in this world of hope deferred,
50   This world of perishable stuff;—
Eye hath not seen, nor ear hath heard,
    Nor heart conceived that full 'enough':
Here moans the separating sea,
    Here harvests fail, here breaks the heart;
55   There God shall join and no man part,
I full of Christ and Christ of me.

A BIRTHDAY.

My heart is like a singing bird
    Whose nest is in a watered shoot;
My heart is like an apple tree
    Whose boughs are bent with thickset fruit;
5   My heart is like a rainbow shell
    That paddles in a halcyon sea;
My heart is gladder than all these
    Because my love is come to me.

Raise me a dais of silk and down;
   Hang it with vair and purple dyes; 10
Carve it in doves and pomegranates,
   And peacocks with a hundred eyes;
Work it in gold and silver grapes,
   In leaves and silver fleurs-de-lys;
Because the birthday of my life 15
   Is come, my love is come to me.

AN APPLE-GATHERING.

I plucked pink blossoms from mine apple tree
   And wore them all that evening in my hair:
Then in due season when I went to see
   I found no apples there.

With dangling basket all along the grass 5
   As I had come I went the selfsame track:
My neighbours mocked me while they saw me pass
   So empty-handed back.

Lilian and Lilias smiled in trudging by,
   Their heaped-up basket teazed me like a jeer; 10
Sweet-voiced they sang beneath the sunset sky,
   Their mother's home was near.

Plump Gertrude passed me with her basket full,
   A stronger hand than hers helped it along;
A voice talked with her thro' the shadows cool 15
   More sweet to me than song.

Ah Willie, Willie, was my love less worth
   Than apples with their green leaves piled above?
I counted rosiest apples on the earth
   Of far less worth than love. 20

So once it was with me you stooped to talk
    Laughing and listening in this very lane:
To think that by this way we used to walk
    We shall not walk again!

25   I let my neighbours pass me, ones and twos
        And groups; the latest said the night grew chill,
    And hastened: but I loitered, while the dews
        Fell fast I loitered still.

WINTER: MY SECRET.

I tell my secret? No indeed, not I:
Perhaps some day, who knows?
But not today; it froze, and blows, and snows,
And you're too curious: fie!
5   You want to hear it? well:
Only, my secret's mine, and I won't tell.

Or, after all, perhaps there's none:
Suppose there is no secret after all,
But only just my fun.
10   Today's a nipping day, a biting day;
In which one wants a shawl,
A veil, a cloak, and other wraps:
I cannot ope to every one who taps,
And let the draughts come whistling thro' my hall;
15   Come bounding and surrounding me,
Come buffeting, astounding me,
Nipping and clipping thro' my wraps and all.
I wear my mask for warmth: who ever shows
His nose to Russian snows
20   To be pecked at by every wind that blows?
You would not peck? I thank you for good will,
Believe, but leave that truth untested still.

Spring's an expansive time: yet I don't trust
March with its peck of dust,
Nor April with its rainbow-crowned brief showers, 25
Nor even May, whose flowers
One frost may wither thro' the sunless hours.

Perhaps some languid summer day,
When drowsy birds sing less and less,
And golden fruit is ripening to excess, 30
If there's not too much sun nor too much cloud,
And the warm wind is neither still nor loud,
Perhaps my secret I may say,
Or you may guess.

MAUDE CLARE.

Out of the church she followed them
   With a lofty step and mien:
His bride was like a village maid,
   Maude Clare was like a queen.

"Son Thomas," his lady mother said, 5
   With smiles, almost with tears:
"May Nell and you but live as true
   As we have done for years;

"Your father thirty years ago
   Had just your tale to tell; 10
But he was not so pale as you,
   Nor I so pale as Nell."

My lord was pale with inward strife,
   And Nell was pale with pride;
My lord gazed long on pale Maude Clare 15
   Or ever he kissed the bride.

"Lo, I have brought my gift, my lord,
    Have brought my gift," she said:
"To bless the hearth, to bless the board,
20   To bless the marriage-bed.

"Here's my half of the golden chain
    You wore about your neck,
That day we waded ankle-deep
    For lilies in the beck:

25 "Here's my half of the faded leaves
    We plucked from budding bough,
With feet amongst the lily leaves,—
    The lilies are budding now."

He strove to match her scorn with scorn,
30   He faltered in his place:
"Lady," he said,—"Maude Clare," he said,—
    "Maude Clare:"—and hid his face.

She turn'd to Nell: "My Lady Nell,
    I have a gift for you;
35 Tho', were it fruit, the bloom were gone,
    Or, were it flowers, the dew.

"Take my share of a fickle heart,
    Mine of a paltry love:
Take it or leave it as you will,
40   I wash my hands thereof."

"And what you leave," said Nell, "I'll take,
    And what you spurn, I'll wear;
For he's my lord for better and worse,
    And him I love, Maude Clare.

"Yea, tho' you're taller by the head, 45
  More wise, and much more fair;
I'll love him till he loves me best,
  Me best of all, Maude Clare."

AT HOME.

When I was dead, my spirit turned
  To seek the much frequented house:
I passed the door, and saw my friends
  Feasting beneath green orange boughs;
From hand to hand they pushed the wine, 5
  They sucked the pulp of plum and peach;
They sang, they jested, and they laughed,
  For each was loved of each.

I listened to their honest chat:
  Said one: "Tomorrow we shall be 10
Plod plod along the featureless sands
  And coasting miles and miles of sea."
Said one: "Before the turn of tide
  We will achieve the eyrie-seat."
Said one: "Tomorrow shall be like 15
  Today, but much more sweet."

"Tomorrow," said they, strong with hope,
  And dwelt upon the pleasant way:
"Tomorrow," cried they one and all,
  While no one spoke of yesterday. 20
Their life stood full at blessed noon;
  I, only I, had passed away:
"Tomorrow and today," they cried;
  I was of yesterday.

25   I shivered comfortless, but cast
          No chill across the tablecloth;
      I all-forgotten shivered, sad
          To stay and yet to part how loth:
      I passed from the familiar room,
30   I who from love had passed away,
      Like the remembrance of a guest
              That tarrieth but a day.

UP-HILL.

Does the road wind up-hill all the way?
    Yes, to the very end.
Will the day's journey take the whole long day?
    From morn to night, my friend.

5   But is there for the night a resting-place?
          A roof for when the slow dark hours begin.
      May not the darkness hide it from my face?
          You cannot miss that inn.

      Shall I meet other wayfarers at night?
10   Those who have gone before.
      Then must I knock, or call when just in sight?
          They will not keep you standing at that door.

      Shall I find comfort, travel-sore and weak?
          Of labour you shall find the sum.
15   Will there be beds for me and all who seek?
          Yea, beds for all who come.

THE CONVENT THRESHOLD.

There's blood between us, love, my love,
There's father's blood, there's brother's blood;
And blood's a bar I cannot pass:
I choose the stairs that mount above,
Stair after golden skyward stair,   5
To city and to sea of glass.
My lily feet are soiled with mud,
With scarlet mud which tells a tale
Of hope that was, of guilt that was,
Of love that shall not yet avail;   10
Alas, my heart, if I could bare
My heart, this selfsame stain is there:
I seek the sea of glass and fire
To wash the spot, to burn the snare;
Lo, stairs are meant to lift us higher: 15
Mount with me, mount the kindled stair.

Your eyes look earthward, mine look up.
I see the far-off city grand,
Beyond the hills a watered land,
Beyond the gulf a gleaming strand   20
Of mansions where the righteous sup;
Who sleep at ease among their trees,
Or wake to sing a cadenced hymn
With Cherubim and Seraphim;
They bore the Cross, they drained the cup,   25
Racked, roasted, crushed, wrenched limb from limb,
They the offscouring of the world:
The heaven of starry heavens unfurled,
The sun before their face is dim.

You looking earthward, what see you?   30
Milk-white, wine-flushed among the vines,
Up and down leaping, to and fro,
Most glad, most full, made strong with wines,

Blooming as peaches pearled with dew,
Their golden windy hair afloat,
Love-music warbling in their throat,
Young men and women come and go.

You linger, yet the time is short:
Flee for your life, gird up your strength
To flee; the shadows stretched at length
Show that day wanes, that night draws nigh;
Flee to the mountain, tarry not.
Is this a time for smile and sigh,
For songs among the secret trees
Where sudden blue birds nest and sport?
The time is short and yet you stay:
Today while it is called today
Kneel, wrestle, knock, do violence, pray;
Today is short, tomorrow nigh:
Why will you die? why will you die?

You sinned with me a pleasant sin:
Repent with me, for I repent.
Woe's me the lore I must unlearn!
Woe's me that easy way we went,
So rugged when I would return!
How long until my sleep begin,
How long shall stretch these nights and days?
Surely, clean Angels cry, she prays;
She laves her soul with tedious tears:
How long must stretch these years and years?

I turn from you my cheeks and eyes,
My hair which you shall see no more—
Alas for joy that went before,
For joy that dies, for love that dies.
Only my lips still turn to you,
My livid lips that cry, Repent.
Oh weary life, Oh weary Lent,
Oh weary time whose stars are few.

How should I rest in Paradise,
Or sit on steps of heaven alone?   70
If Saints and Angels spoke of love
Should I not answer from my throne:
Have pity upon me, ye my friends,
For I have heard the sound thereof:
Should I not turn with yearning eyes,   75
Turn earthwards with a pitiful pang?
Oh save me from a pang in heaven.
By all the gifts we took and gave,
Repent, repent, and be forgiven:
This life is long, but yet it ends;   80
Repent and purge your soul and save:
No gladder song the morning stars
Upon their birthday morning sang
Than Angels sing when one repents.

I tell you what I dreamed last night: 85
A spirit with transfigured face
Fire-footed clomb an infinite space.
I heard his hundred pinions clang,
Heaven-bells rejoicing rang and rang,
Heaven-air was thrilled with subtle scents,   90
Worlds spun upon their rushing cars:
He mounted shrieking: "Give me light."
Still light was poured on him, more light;
Angels, Archangels he outstripped
Exultant in exceeding might,   95
And trod the skirts of Cherubim.
Still "Give me light," he shrieked; and dipped
His thirsty face, and drank a sea,
Athirst with thirst it could not slake.
I saw him, drunk with knowledge, take   100
From aching brows the aureole crown—
His locks writhed like a cloven snake—
He left his throne to grovel down

And lick the dust of Seraphs' feet:
105 For what is knowledge duly weighed?
Knowledge is strong, but love is sweet;
Yea all the progress he had made
Was but to learn that all is small
Save love, for love is all in all.

110 I tell you what I dreamed last night:
It was not dark, it was not light,
Cold dews had drenched my plenteous hair
Thro' clay; you came to seek me there.
And "Do you dream of me?" you said.
115 My heart was dust that used to leap
To you; I answered half asleep:
"My pillow is damp, my sheets are red,
There's a leaden tester to my bed:
Find you a warmer playfellow,
120 A warmer pillow for your head,
A kinder love to love than mine."
You wrung your hands; while I like lead
Crushed downwards thro' the sodden earth:
You smote your hands but not in mirth,
125 And reeled but were not drunk with wine.

For all night long I dreamed of you:
I woke and prayed against my will,
Then slept to dream of you again.
At length I rose and knelt and prayed:
130 I cannot write the words I said,
My words were slow, my tears were few;
But thro' the dark my silence spoke
Like thunder. When this morning broke,
My face was pinched, my hair was grey,
135 And frozen blood was on the sill
Where stifling in my struggle I lay.

If now you saw me you would say:
Where is the face I used to love?
And I would answer: Gone before;
It tarries veiled in paradise. 140
When once the morning star shall rise,
When earth with shadow flees away
And we stand safe within the door,
Then you shall lift the veil thereof.
Look up, rise up: for far above 145
Our palms are grown, our place is set;
There we shall meet as once we met
And love with old familiar love.

"What good shall my life do me?"

Have dead men long to wait?—

There is a certain term
For their bodies to the worm
And their souls at heaven gate.
Dust to dust, clod to clod, 5
These precious things of God,
Trampled underfoot by man
And beast the appointed years.—

Their longest life was but a span
For change and smiles and tears. 10
Is it worth while to live,
Rejoice and grieve,
Hope, fear, and die?
Man with man, truth with lie,
The slow show dwindles by: 15
At last what shall we have
Besides a grave?—

Lies and shows no more,
No fear, no pain,
20 But after hope and sleep
Dear joys again.
Those who sowed shall reap:
Those who bore
The Cross shall wear the Crown:
25 Those who clomb the steep
There shall sit down.
The Shepherd of the sheep
Feeds His flock there,
In watered pastures fair
30 They rest and leap.
"Is it worth while to live?"
Be of good cheer:
Love casts out fear:
Rise up, achieve.

WINTER RAIN.

Every valley drinks,
    Every dell and hollow:
Where the kind rain sinks and sinks,
    Green of Spring will follow.

5 Yet a lapse of weeks
    Buds will burst their edges,
Strip their wool-coats, glue-coats, streaks,
    In the woods and hedges;

Weave a bower of love
10   For birds to meet each other,
Weave a canopy above
    Nest and egg and mother.

But for fattening rain
   We should have no flowers,
Never a bud or leaf again   15
   But for soaking showers;

Never a mated bird
   In the rocking tree-tops,
Never indeed a flock or herd
   To graze upon the lea-crops.   20

Lambs so woolly white,
   Sheep the sun-bright leas on,
They could have no grass to bite
   But for rain in season.

We should find no moss   25
   In the shadiest places,
Find no waving meadow grass
   Pied with broad-eyed daisies:

But miles of barren sand,
   With never a son or daughter,   30
Not a lily on the land,
   Or lily on the water.

L.E.L.

"Whose heart was breaking for a little love."

Downstairs I laugh, I sport and jest with all:
   But in my solitary room above
I turn my face in silence to the wall;
   My heart is breaking for a little love.
      Tho' winter frosts are done,   5
      And birds pair every one,
And leaves peep out, for springtide is begun.

I feel no spring, while spring is wellnigh blown,
   I find no nest, while nests are in the grove:
10 Woe's me for mine own heart that dwells alone,
   My heart that breaketh for a little love.
     While golden in the sun
     Rivulets rise and run,
   While lilies bud, for springtide is begun.

15 All love, are loved, save only I; their hearts
   Beat warm with love and joy, beat full thereof:
They cannot guess, who play the pleasant parts,
   My heart is breaking for a little love.
     While beehives wake and whirr,
20   And rabbit thins his fur,
In living spring that sets the world astir.

I deck myself with silks and jewelry,
   I plume myself like any mated dove:
They praise my rustling show, and never see
25   My heart is breaking for a little love.
     While sprouts green lavender
     With rosemary and myrrh,
For in quick spring the sap is all astir.

Perhaps some saints in glory guess the truth,
30   Perhaps some angels read it as they move,
And cry one to another full of ruth,
   "Her heart is breaking for a little love."
     Tho' other things have birth,
     And leap and sing for mirth,
When springtime wakes and clothes and feeds the
35   earth.

Yet saith a saint: "Take patience for thy scathe;"
   Yet saith an angel: "Wait, for thou shalt prove
True best is last, true life is born of death,
   O thou, heart-broken for a little love.

Then love shall fill thy girth,   40
  And love make fat thy dearth,
 When new spring builds new heaven and clean
  new earth."

GOBLIN MARKET.

  Morning and evening
  Maids heard the goblins cry:
  "Come buy our orchard fruits,
  Come buy, come buy:
  Apples and quinces,   5
  Lemons and oranges,
  Plump unpecked cherries,
  Melons and raspberries,
  Bloom-down-cheeked peaches,
  Swart-headed mulberries,   10
  Wild free-born cranberries,
  Crab-apples, dewberries,
  Pine-apples, blackberries,
  Apricots, strawberries;—
  All ripe together   15
  In summer weather,—
  Morns that pass by,
  Fair eves that fly;
  Come buy, come buy:
  Our grapes fresh from the vine,   20
  Pomegranates full and fine,
  Dates and sharp bullaces,
  Rare pears and greengages,
  Damsons and bilberries,
  Taste them and try: 25
  Currants and gooseberries,
  Bright-fire-like barberries,
  Figs to fill your mouth,
  Citrons from the South,
  Sweet to tongue and sound to eye;   30
  Come buy, come buy."

Evening by evening
Among the brookside rushes,
Laura bowed her head to hear,
35 Lizzie veiled her blushes:
Crouching close together
In the cooling weather,
With clasping arms and cautioning lips,
With tingling cheeks and finger tips.
40 "Lie close," Laura said,
Pricking up her golden head:
"We must not look at goblin men,
We must not buy their fruits:
Who knows upon what soil they fed
45 Their hungry thirsty roots?"
"Come buy," call the goblins
Hobbling down the glen.
"Oh," cried Lizzie, "Laura, Laura,
You should not peep at goblin men."
50 Lizzie covered up her eyes,
Covered close lest they should look;
Laura reared her glossy head,
And whispered like the restless brook:
"Look, Lizzie, look, Lizzie,
55 Down the glen tramp little men.
One hauls a basket,
One bears a plate,
One lugs a golden dish
Of many pounds weight.
60 How fair the vine must grow
Whose grapes are so luscious;
How warm the wind must blow
Thro' those fruit bushes."
"No," said Lizzie: "No, no, no;
65 Their offers should not charm us,
Their evil gifts would harm us."

She thrust a dimpled finger
In each ear, shut eyes and ran:
Curious Laura chose to linger
Wondering at each merchant man. 70
One had a cat's face,
One whisked a tail,
One tramped at a rat's pace,
One crawled like a snail,
One like a wombat prowled obtuse and furry, 75
One like a ratel tumbled hurry skurry.
She heard a voice like voice of doves
Cooing all together:
They sounded kind and full of loves
In the pleasant weather. 80

Laura stretched her gleaming neck
Like a rush-imbedded swan,
Like a lily from the beck,
Like a moonlit poplar branch,
Like a vessel at the launch 85
When its last restraint is gone.

Backwards up the mossy glen
Turned and trooped the goblin men,
With their shrill repeated cry,
"Come buy, come buy." 90
When they reached where Laura was
They stood stock still upon the moss,
Leering at each other,
Brother with queer brother;
Signalling each other, 95
Brother with sly brother.
One set his basket down,
One reared his plate;
One began to weave a crown

100 Of tendrils, leaves and rough nuts brown
     (Men sell not such in any town);
     One heaved the golden weight
     Of dish and fruit to offer her:
     "Come buy, come buy," was still their cry.
105 Laura stared but did not stir,
     Longed but had no money:
     The whisk-tailed merchant bade her taste
     In tones as smooth as honey,
     The cat-faced purr'd,
110 The rat-paced spoke a word
     Of welcome, and the snail-paced even was heard;
     One parrot-voiced and jolly
     Cried "Pretty Goblin" still for "Pretty Polly;"—
     One whistled like a bird.

115 But sweet-tooth Laura spoke in haste:
     "Good folk, I have no coin;
     To take were to purloin:
     I have no copper in my purse,
     I have no silver either,
120 And all my gold is on the furze
     That shakes in windy weather
     Above the rusty heather."
     "You have much gold upon your head,"
     They answered all together:
125 "Buy from us with a golden curl."
     She clipped a precious golden lock,
     She dropped a tear more rare than pearl,
     Then sucked their fruit globes fair or red:
     Sweeter than honey from the rock.
130 Stronger than man-rejoicing wine,
     Clearer than water flowed that juice;
     She never tasted such before,
     How should it cloy with length of use?
     She sucked and sucked and sucked the more
135 Fruits which that unknown orchard bore;
     She sucked until her lips were sore;

Then flung the emptied rinds away
But gathered up one kernel-stone,
And knew not was it night or day
As she turned home alone.   140

Lizzie met her at the gate
Full of wise upbraidings:
"Dear, you should not stay so late,
Twilight is not good for maidens;
Should not loiter in the glen   145
In the haunts of goblin men.
Do you not remember Jeanie,
How she met them in the moonlight,
Took their gifts both choice and many,
Ate their fruits and wore their flowers   150
Plucked from bowers
Where summer ripens at all hours?
But ever in the noonlight
She pined and pined away;
Sought them by night and day,   155
Found them no more but dwindled and grew
     grey;
Then fell with the first snow,
While to this day no grass will grow
Where she lies low:
I planted daisies there a year ago   160
That never blow.
You should not loiter so."
"Nay, hush," said Laura:
"Nay, hush, my sister:
I ate and ate my fill,   165
Yet my mouth waters still;
Tomorrow night I will
Buy more:" and kissed her:
"Have done with sorrow;
I'll bring you plums tomorrow   170

Fresh on their mother twigs,
Cherries worth getting;
You cannot think what figs
My teeth have met in,
175 What melons icy-cold
Piled on a dish of gold
Too huge for me to hold,
What peaches with a velvet nap,
Pellucid grapes without one seed:
180 Odorous indeed must be the mead
Whereon they grow, and pure the wave they drink
With lilies at the brink,
And sugar-sweet their sap."

Golden head by golden head,
185 Like two pigeons in one nest
Folded in each other's wings,
They lay down in their curtained bed:
Like two blossoms on one stem,
Like two flakes of new-fall'n snow,
190 Like two wands of ivory
Tipped with gold for awful kings.
Moon and stars gazed in at them,
Wind sang to them lullaby,
Lumbering owls forbore to fly,
195 Not a bat flapped to and fro
Round their rest:
Cheek to cheek and breast to breast
Locked together in one nest.

Early in the morning
200 When the first cock crowed his warning,
Neat like bees, as sweet and busy,
Laura rose with Lizzie:
Fetched in honey, milked the cows,
Aired and set to rights the house,
205 Kneaded cakes of whitest wheat,
Cakes for dainty mouths to eat,

Next churned butter, whipped up cream,
Fed their poultry, sat and sewed;
Talked as modest maidens should:
Lizzie with an open heart,   210
Laura in an absent dream,
One content, one sick in part;
One warbling for the mere bright day's delight,
One longing for the night.

At length slow evening came: 215
They went with pitchers to the reedy brook;
Lizzie most placid in her look,
Laura most like a leaping flame.
They drew the gurgling water from its deep;
Lizzie plucked purple and rich golden flags,   220
Then turning homewards said: "The sunset
     flushes
Those furthest loftiest crags;
Come, Laura, not another maiden lags,
No wilful squirrel wags,
The beasts and birds are fast asleep."   225
But Laura loitered still among the rushes
And said the bank was steep.

And said the hour was early still,
The dew not fall'n, the wind not chill:
Listening ever, but not catching   230
The customary cry,
"Come buy, come buy,"
With its iterated jingle
Of sugar-baited words:
Not for all her watching   235
Once discerning even one goblin
Racing, whisking, tumbling, hobbling;
Let alone the herds
That used to tramp along the glen,
In groups or single,   240
Of brisk fruit-merchant men.

Till Lizzie urged, "O Laura, come;
I hear the fruit-call but I dare not look:
You should not loiter longer at this brook:
245   Come with me home.
The stars rise, the moon bends her arc,
Each glowworm winks her spark,
Let us get home before the night grows dark:
For clouds may gather
250   Tho' this is summer weather,
Put out the lights and drench us thro';
Then if we lost our way what should we do?"

Laura turned cold as stone
To find her sister heard that cry alone,
255   That goblin cry,
"Come buy our fruits, come buy."
Must she then buy no more such dainty fruit?
Must she no more such succous pasture find,
Gone deaf and blind?
260   Her tree of life drooped from the root:
She said not one word in her heart's sore ache;
But peering thro' the dimness, nought discerning,
Trudged home, her pitcher dripping all the way;
So crept to bed, and lay
265   Silent till Lizzie slept;
Then sat up in a passionate yearning,
And gnashed her teeth for baulked desire, and wept
As if her heart would break.

Day after day, night after night,
270   Laura kept watch in vain
In sullen silence of exceeding pain.
She never caught again the goblin cry:
"Come buy, come buy;"—
She never spied the goblin men
275   Hawking their fruits along the glen:
But when the noon waxed bright

Her hair grew thin and gray;
She dwindled, as the fair full moon doth turn
To swift decay and burn
Her fire away.   280

One day remembering her kernel-stone
She set it by a wall that faced the south;
Dewed it with tears, hoped for a root,
Watched for a waxing shoot,
But there came none;   285
It never saw the sun,
It never felt the trickling moisture run:
While with sunk eyes and faded mouth
She dreamed of melons, as a traveller sees
False waves in desert drouth   290
With shade of leaf-crowned trees,
And burns the thirstier in the sandful breeze.

She no more swept the house,
Tended the fowls or cows,
Fetched honey, kneaded cakes of wheat,   295
Brought water from the brook:
But sat down listless in the chimney-nook
And would not eat.

Tender Lizzie could not bear
To watch her sister's cankerous care   300
Yet not to share.
She night and morning
Caught the goblins' cry:
"Come buy our orchard fruits,
Come buy, come buy;"—   305
Beside the brook, along the glen,
She heard the tramp of goblin men,
The voice and stir
Poor Laura could not hear;
Longed to buy fruit to comfort her,   310
But feared to pay too dear.

She thought of Jeanie in her grave,
Who should have been a bride;
But who for joys brides hope to have
315   Fell sick and died
In her gay prime,
In earliest Winter time,
With the first glazing rime,
With the first snow-fall of crisp Winter time.

320   Till Laura dwindling
Seemed knocking at Death's door:
Then Lizzie weighed no more
Better and worse;
But put a silver penny in her purse,
Kissed Laura, crossed the heath with clumps
     of furze
325   At twilight, halted by the brook:
And for the first time in her life
Began to listen and look.

Laughed every goblin
330   When they spied her peeping:
Came towards her hobbling,
Flying, running, leaping,
Puffing and blowing,
Chuckling, clapping, crowing,
335   Clucking and gobbling,
Mopping and mowing,
Full of airs and graces,
Pulling wry faces,
Demure grimaces,
340   Cat-like and rat-like,
Ratel- and wombat-like,
Snail-paced in a hurry,
Parrot-voiced and whistler,
Helter skelter, hurry skurry,
345   Chattering like magpies,
Fluttering like pigeons,

Gliding like fishes,—
Hugged her and kissed her,
Squeezed and caressed her:
Stretched up their dishes,   350
Panniers, and plates:
"Look at our apples
Russet and dun,
Bob at our cherries,
Bite at our peaches,   355
Citrons and dates,
Grapes for the asking,
Pears red with basking
Out in the sun,
Plums on their twigs;   360
Pluck them and suck them,
Pomegranates, figs."—

"Good folk," said Lizzie,
Mindful of Jeanie:
"Give me much and many:"—   365
Held out her apron,
Tossed them her penny.
"Nay, take a seat with us,
Honour and eat with us,"
They answered grinning: 370
"Our feast is but beginning.
Night yet is early,
Warm and dew-pearly,
Wakeful and starry:
Such fruits as these   375
No man can carry;
Half their bloom would fly,
Half their dew would dry,
Half their flavour would pass by.
Sit down and feast with us,   380
Be welcome guest with us,
Cheer you and rest with us."—

"Thank you," said Lizzie: "But one waits
At home alone for me:
385 So without further parleying,
If you will not sell me any
Of your fruits tho' much and many,
Give me back my silver penny
I tossed you for a fee."—
390 They began to scratch their pates,
No longer wagging, purring,
But visibly demurring,
Grunting and snarling.
One called her proud,
395 Cross-grained, uncivil;
Their tones waxed loud,
Their looks were evil.
Lashing their tails
They trod and hustled her,
400 Elbowed and jostled her,
Clawed with their nails,
Barking, mewing, hissing, mocking,
Tore her gown and soiled her stocking,
Twitched her hair out by the roots,
405 Stamped upon her tender feet,
Held her hands and squeezed their fruits
Against her mouth to make her eat.

White and golden Lizzie stood,
Like a lily in a flood,—
410 Like a rock of blue-veined stone
Lashed by tides obstreperously,—
Like a beacon left alone
In a hoary roaring sea,
Sending up a golden fire,—
415 Like a fruit-crowned orange-tree
White with blossoms honey-sweet
Sore beset by wasp and bee,—

Like a royal virgin town
Topped with gilded dome and spire
Close beleaguered by a fleet   420
Mad to tug her standard down.

One may lead a horse to water,
Twenty cannot make him drink.
Tho' the goblins cuffed and caught her,
Coaxed and fought her,   425
Bullied and besought her,
Scratched her, pinched her black as ink,
Kicked and knocked her,
Mauled and mocked her,
Lizzie uttered not a word;   430
Would not open lip from lip
Lest they should cram a mouthful in:
But laughed in heart to feel the drip
Of juice that syrupped all her face,
And lodged in dimples of her chin,   435
And streaked her neck which quaked like
     curd.
At last the evil people
Worn out by her resistance
Flung back her penny, kicked their fruit
Along whichever road they took,   440
Not leaving root or stone or shoot;
Some writhed into the ground,
Some dived into the brook
With ring and ripple,
Some scudded on the gale without a sound,   445
Some vanished in the distance.

In a smart, ache, tingle,
Lizzie went her way;
Knew not was it night or day;
Sprang up the bank, tore thro' the furze,   450
Threaded copse and dingle,
And heard her penny jingle

Bouncing in her purse,
Its bounce was music to her ear.
455 She ran and ran
As if she feared some goblin man
Dogged her with gibe or curse
Or something worse:
But not one goblin skurried after,
460 Nor was she pricked by fear;
The kind heart made her windy-paced
That urged her home quite out of breath with
        haste
And inward laughter.

She cried "Laura," up the garden,
465 "Did you miss me?
Come and kiss me.
Never mind my bruises,
Hug me, kiss me, suck my juices
Squeezed from goblin fruits for you,
470 Goblin pulp and goblin dew.
Eat me, drink me, love me;
Laura, make much of me:
For your sake I have braved the glen
And had to do with goblin merchant men."

475 Laura started from her chair,
Flung her arms up in the air,
Clutched her hair:
"Lizzie, Lizzie, have you tasted
For my sake the fruit forbidden?
480 Must your light like mine be hidden,
Your young life like mine be wasted,
Undone in mine undoing
And ruined in my ruin,
Thirsty, cankered, goblin-ridden?"—

She clung about her sister, 485
Kissed and kissed and kissed her:
Tears once again
Refreshed her shrunken eyes,
Dropping like rain
After long sultry drouth; 490
Shaking with aguish fear, and pain,
She kissed and kissed her with a hungry mouth.

Her lips began to scorch,
That juice was wormwood to her tongue,
She loathed the feast: 495
Writhing as one possessed she leaped and
    sung,
Rent all her robe, and wrung
Her hands in lamentable haste,
And beat her breast.
Her locks streamed like the torch 500
Borne by a racer at full speed,
Or like the mane of horses in their flight,
Or like an eagle when she stems the light
Straight toward the sun,
Or like a caged thing freed, 505
Or like a flying flag when armies run.

Swift fire spread thro' her veins, knocked at
    her heart,
Met the fire smouldering there
And overbore its lesser flame;
She gorged on bitterness without a name: 510
Ah! fool, to choose such part
Of soul-consuming care!
Sense failed in the mortal strife:
Like the watch-tower of a town
Which an earthquake shatters down, 515
Like a lightning-stricken mast,

Like a wind-uprooted tree
Spun about,
Like a foam-topped waterspout
520   Cast down headlong in the sea,
She fell at last;
Pleasure past and anguish past,
Is it death or is it life?

Life out of death.
525   That night long Lizzie watched by her,
Counted her pulse's flagging stir,
Felt for her breath,
Held water to her lips, and cooled her face
With tears and fanning leaves:
530   But when the first birds chirped about their eaves,
And early reapers plodded to the place
Of golden sheaves,
And dew-wet grass
Bowed in the morning winds so brisk to pass,
535   And new buds with new day
Opened of cup-like lilies on the stream,
Laura awoke as from a dream,
Laughed in the innocent old way,
Hugged Lizzie but not twice or thrice;
540   Her gleaming locks showed not one thread of grey,
Her breath was sweet as May
And light danced in her eyes.

Days, weeks, months, years
Afterwards, when both were wives
545   With children of their own;
Their mother-hearts beset with fears,
Their lives bound up in tender lives;
Laura would call the little ones
And tell them of her early prime,
550   Those pleasant days long gone
Of not-returning time:

Would talk about the haunted glen,
The wicked, quaint fruit-merchant men,
Their fruits like honey to the throat
But poison in the blood;   555
(Men sell not such in any town:)
Would tell them how her sister stood
In deadly peril to do her good,
And win the fiery antidote:
Then joining hands to little hands   560
Would bid them cling together,
"For there is no friend like a sister
In calm or stormy weather;
To cheer one on the tedious way,
To fetch one if one goes astray,   565
To lift one if one totters down,
To strengthen whilst one stands."

"NO, THANK YOU, JOHN."

I never said I loved you, John:
   Why will you teaze me day by day,
And wax a weariness to think upon
    With always "do" and "pray"?

You know I never loved you, John;   5
   No fault of mine made me your toast:
Why will you haunt me with a face as wan
    As shows an hour-old ghost?

I dare say Meg or Moll would take
   Pity upon you, if you'd ask: 10
And pray don't remain single for my sake
    Who can't perform that task.

I have no heart?—Perhaps I have not;
   But then you're mad to take offence
15 That I don't give you what I have not got:
    Use your own common sense.

Let bygones be bygones:
   Don't call me false, who owed not to be true:
I'd rather answer "No" to fifty Johns
20   Than answer "Yes" to you.

Let's mar our pleasant days no more,
   Song-birds of passage, days of youth:
Catch at today, forget the days before:
    I'll wink at your untruth.

25 Let us strike hands as hearty friends;
   No more, no less; and friendship's good:
Only don't keep in view ulterior ends,
    And points not understood

In open treaty. Rise above
30   Quibbles and shuffling off and on:
Here's friendship for you if you like; but love,—
    No, thank you, John.

"Out of the deep."

Have mercy, Thou my God; mercy, my God;
   For I can hardly bear life day by day:
   Be I here or there I fret myself away:
Lo for Thy staff I have but felt Thy rod
5 Along this tedious desert path long trod.
   When will Thy judgement judge me, Yea or Nay?
   I pray for grace; but then my sins unpray
My prayer: on holy ground I fool stand shod.
While still Thou haunts't me, faint upon the cross,
10   A sorrow beyond sorrow in Thy look,

Unutterable craving for my soul.
All faithful Thou, Lord: I, not Thou, forsook
    Myself; I traitor slunk back from the goal:
Lord, I repent; help Thou my helpless loss.

THE QUEEN OF HEARTS.

How comes it, Flora, that, whenever we
Play cards together, you invariably,
    However the pack parts,
    Still hold the Queen of Hearts?

I've scanned you with a scrutinizing gaze,   5
Resolved to fathom these your secret ways:
    But, sift them as I will,
    Your ways are secret still.

I cut and shuffle; shuffle, cut, again;
But all my cutting, shuffling, proves in vain: 10
    Vain hope, vain forethought too;
    That Queen still falls to you.

I dropped her once, prepense; but, ere the deal
Was dealt, your instinct seemed her loss to feel:
    "There should be one card more,"   15
    You said, and searched the floor.

I cheated once; I made a private notch
In Heart-Queen's back, and kept a lynx-eyed
        watch;
    Yet such another back
    Deceived me in the pack: 20

The Queen of Clubs assumed by arts unknown
An imitative dint that seemed my own;
    This notch, not of my doing,
    Misled me to my ruin.

25   It baffles me to puzzle out the clue,
    Which must be skill, or craft, or luck in you:
            Unless, indeed, it be
            Natural affinity.

CONSIDER.

        Consider
The lilies of the field whose bloom is brief:—
            We are as they;
            Like them we fade away,
5   As doth a leaf.

        Consider
The sparrows of the air of small account:
            Our God doth view
Whether they fall or mount,—
10   He guards us too.

        Consider
The lilies that do neither spin nor toil,
            Yet are most fair:—
            What profits all this care
15   And all this coil?

        Consider
The birds that have no barn nor harvest-weeks;
            God gives them food:—
Much more our Father seeks
20   To do us good.

THE LOWEST PLACE.

Give me the lowest place: not that I dare
   Ask for that lowest place, but Thou hast died
That I might live and share
   Thy glory by Thy side.

Give me the lowest place: or if for me   5
   That lowest place too high, make one more low
Where I may sit and see
   My God and love Thee so.

BEAUTY IS VAIN.

While roses are so red,
   While lilies are so white,
Shall a woman exalt her face
   Because it gives delight?
She's not so sweet as a rose,   5
   A lily's straighter than she,
And if she were as red or white
   She'd be but one of three.

Whether she flush in love's summer
   Or in its winter grow pale,   10
Whether she flaunt her beauty
   Or hide it away in a veil,
Be she red or white,
   And stand she erect or bowed,
Time will win the race he runs with her   15
   And hide her away in a shroud.

WHAT WOULD I GIVE?

What would I give for a heart of flesh to warm me thro',
Instead of this heart of stone ice-cold whatever I do;
Hard and cold and small, of all hearts the worst of all.

What would I give for words, if only words would
        come;
5   But now in its misery my spirit has fallen dumb:
O merry friends, go your way, I have never a word to
        say.

What would I give for tears, not smiles but scalding tears,
To wash the black mark clean, and to thaw the frost of
        years,
To wash the stain ingrain and to make me clean again.

WHO SHALL DELIVER ME?

God strengthen me to bear myself;
That heaviest weight of all to bear,
Inalienable weight of care.

All others are outside myself;
5   I lock my door and bar them out,
The turmoil, tedium, gad-about.

I lock my door upon myself,
And bar them out; but who shall wall
Self from myself, most loathed of all?

10 If I could once lay down myself,
And start self-purged upon the race
That all must run! Death runs apace.

If I could set aside myself,
And start with lightened heart upon
The road by all men overgone!   15

God harden me against myself,
This coward with pathetic voice
Who craves for ease, and rest, and joys:

Myself, arch-traitor to myself;
My hollowest friend, my deadliest foe,   20
My clog whatever road I go.

Yet One there is can curb myself,
Can roll the strangling load from me,
Break off the yoke and set me free.

TWICE.

I took my heart in my hand
    (O my love, O my love),
I said: Let me fall or stand,
    Let me live or die,
But this once hear me speak—   5
    (O my love, O my love)—
Yet a woman's words are weak;
    You should speak, not I.

You took my heart in your hand
    With a friendly smile,   10
With a critical eye you scanned,
    Then set it down,
And said: It is still unripe,
    Better wait awhile;
Wait while the skylarks pipe,   15
    Till the corn grows brown.

As you set it down it broke—
    Broke, but I did not wince;
I smiled at the speech you spoke,
    At your judgment that I heard:
But I have not often smiled
    Since then, nor questioned since,
Nor cared for corn-flowers wild,
    Nor sung with the singing bird.

I take my heart in my hand,
    O my God, O my God,
My broken heart in my hand:
    Thou hast seen, judge Thou.
My hope was written on sand,
    O my God, O my God;
Now let Thy judgment stand—
    Yea, judge me now.

This contemned of a man,
    This marred one heedless day,
This heart take Thou to scan
    Both within and without:
Refine with fire its gold,
    Purge Thou its dross away—
Yea hold it in Thy hold,
    Whence none can pluck it out.

I take my heart in my hand—
    I shall not die, but live—
Before Thy face I stand;
    I, for Thou callest such:
All that I have I bring,
    All that I am I give,
Smile Thou and I shall sing,
    But shall not question much.

JESSIE CAMERON.

"Jessie, Jessie Cameron,
   Hear me but this once," quoth he.
"Good luck go with you, neighbour's son,
   But I'm no mate for you," quoth she.
Day was verging toward the night   5
   There beside the moaning sea,
Dimness overtook the light
   There where the breakers be.
"O Jessie, Jessie Cameron,
   I have loved you long and true."—   10
"Good luck go with you, neighbour's son,
   But I'm no mate for you."

She was a careless, fearless girl,
   And made her answer plain,
Outspoken she to earl or churl,   15
   Kindhearted in the main,
But somewhat heedless with her tongue
   And apt at causing pain;
A mirthful maiden she and young,
   Most fair for bliss or bane.   20
"Oh long ago I told you so,
   I tell you so today:
Go you your way, and let me go
   Just my own free way."

The sea swept in with moan and foam   25
   Quickening the stretch of sand;
They stood almost in sight of home;
   He strove to take her hand.
"Oh can't you take your answer then,
   And won't you understand?   30
For me you're not the man of men,
   I've other plans are planned.

You're good for Madge, or good for Cis,
   Or good for Kate, may be:
35 But what's to me the good of this
   While you're not good for me?"

They stood together on the beach,
   They two alone,
And louder waxed his urgent speech,
40   His patience almost gone:
"Oh say but one kind word to me,
   Jessie, Jessie Cameron."—
"I'd be too proud to beg," quoth she,
   And pride was in her tone.
45 And pride was in her lifted head,
   And in her angry eye,
And in her foot, which might have fled,
   But would not fly.

Some say that he had gipsy blood,
50   That in his heart was guile:
Yet he had gone thro' fire and flood
   Only to win her smile.
Some say his grandam was a witch,
   A black witch from beyond the Nile,
55 Who kept an image in a niche
   And talked with it the while.
And by her hut far down the lane
   Some say they would not pass at night,
Lest they should hear an unked strain
60   Or see an unked sight.

Alas for Jessie Cameron!—
   The sea crept moaning, moaning nigher:
She should have hastened to begone,—
   The sea swept higher, breaking by her:

She should have hastened to her home 65
  While yet the west was flushed with fire,
But now her feet are in the foam,
  The sea-foam sweeping higher.
O mother, linger at your door,
  And light your lamp to make it plain; 70
But Jessie she comes home no more,
  No more again.

They stood together on the strand,
  They only each by each;
Home, her home, was close at hand, 75
  Utterly out of reach.
Her mother in the chimney nook
  Heard a startled sea-gull screech,
But never turned her head to look
  Towards the darkening beach: 80
Neighbours here and neighbours there
  Heard one scream, as if a bird
Shrilly screaming cleft the air:—
  That was all they heard.

Jessie she comes home no more, 85
  Comes home never;
Her lover's step sounds at his door
  No more for ever.
And boats may search upon the sea
  And search along the river, 90
But none know where the bodies be:
  Sea-winds that shiver,
Sea-birds that breast the blast,
  Sea-waves swelling,
Keep the secret first and last 95
  Of their dwelling.

Whether the tide so hemmed them round
   With its pitiless flow,
That when they would have gone they found
100   No way to go;
Whether she scorned him to the last
   With words flung to and fro,
Or clung to him when hope was past,
   None will ever know:
105 Whether he helped or hindered her,
   Threw up his life or lost it well,
The troubled sea for all its stir
   Finds no voice to tell.

Only watchers by the dying
110   Have thought they heard one pray
Wordless, urgent; and replying
   One seem to say him nay:
And watchers by the dead have heard
   A windy swell from miles away,
115 With sobs and screams, but not a word
   Distinct for them to say:
And watchers out at sea have caught
   Glimpse of a pale gleam here or there,
Come and gone as quick as thought,
120   Which might be hand or hair.

THE PRINCE'S PROGRESS.

Till all sweet gums and juices flow,
Till the blossom of blossoms blow,
The long hours go and come and go,
   The bride she sleepeth, waketh, sleepeth,
5 Waiting for one whose coming is slow:—
     Hark! the bride weepeth.

"How long shall I wait, come heat come rime?"—
"Till the strong Prince comes, who must come in
    time"
(Her women say), "there's a mountain to climb,
  A river to ford. Sleep, dream and sleep: 10
Sleep" (they say): "we've muffled the chime,
    Better dream than weep."

In his world-end palace the strong Prince sat,
Taking his ease on cushion and mat,
Close at hand lay his staff and his hat. 15
  "When wilt thou start? the bride waits,
      O youth."—
"Now the moon's at full; I tarried for that,
    Now I start in truth.

"But tell me first, true voice of my doom,
Of my veiled bride in her maiden bloom; 20
Keeps she watch thro' glare and thro' gloom,
  Watch for me asleep and awake?"—
"Spell-bound she watches in one white room,
    And is patient for thy sake.

"By her head lilies and rosebuds grow; 25
The lilies droop, will the rosebuds blow?
The silver slim lilies hang the head low;
  Their stream is scanty, their sunshine rare;
Let the sun blaze out, and let the stream flow,
    They will blossom and wax fair. 30

"Red and white poppies grow at her feet,
The blood-red wait for sweet summer heat,
Wrapped in bud-coats hairy and neat;
  But the white buds swell, one day they will
      burst,
Will open their death-cups drowsy and sweet— 35
    Which will open the first?"

Then a hundred sad voices lifted a wail,
And a hundred glad voices piped on the gale:
"Time is short, life is short," they took up the tale:
 "Life is sweet, love is sweet, use today while you
40   may;
Love is sweet, and tomorrow may fail;
  Love is sweet, use today."

While the song swept by, beseeching and meek,
Up rose the Prince with a flush on his cheek,
45 Up he rose to stir and to seek,
 Going forth in the joy of his strength;
Strong of limb if of purpose weak,
  Starting at length.

Forth he set in the breezy morn,
50 Across green fields of nodding corn,
As goodly a Prince as ever was born,
 Carolling with the carolling lark;—
Sure his bride will be won and worn,
  Ere fall of the dark.

55 So light his step, so merry his smile,
A milkmaid loitered beside a stile,
Set down her pail and rested awhile,
 A wave-haired milkmaid, rosy and white;
The Prince, who had journeyed at least a mile,
60   Grew athirst at the sight.

"Will you give me a morning draught?"—
"You're kindly welcome," she said, and laughed.
He lifted the pail, new milk he quaffed;
 Then wiping his curly black beard like silk:
65 "Whitest cow that ever was calved
  Surely gave you this milk."

Was it milk now, or was it cream?
Was she a maid, or an evil dream?
Her eyes began to glitter and gleam;
   He would have gone, but he stayed instead;   70
Green they gleamed as he looked in them:
      "Give me my fee," she said.—

"I will give you a jewel of gold."—
"Not so; gold is heavy and cold."—
"I will give you a velvet fold   75
   Of foreign work your beauty to deck."—
"Better I like my kerchief rolled
      Light and white round my neck."—

"Nay," cried he, "but fix your own fee."—
She laughed, "You may give the full moon to me;   80
Or else sit under this apple-tree
   Here for one idle day by my side;
After that I'll let you go free,
      And the world is wide."

Loth to stay, yet to leave her slack,   85
He half turned away, then he quite turned back:
For courtesy's sake he could not lack
   To redeem his own royal pledge;
Ahead too the windy heaven lowered black
      With a fire-cloven edge.   90

So he stretched his length in the apple-tree shade,
Lay and laughed and talked to the maid,
Who twisted her hair in a cunning braid
   And writhed it in shining serpent-coils,
And held him a day and night fast laid   95
      In her subtle toils.

At the death of night and the birth of day,
When the owl left off his sober play,
And the bat hung himself out of the way,
100   Woke the song of mavis and merle,
And heaven put off its hodden grey
      For mother-o'-pearl.

Peeped up daisies here and there,
Here, there, and everywhere;
105   Rose a hopeful lark in the air,
    Spreading out towards the sun his breast;
While the moon set solemn and fair
      Away in the West.

"Up, up, up," called the watchman lark,
110   In his clear réveillée: "Hearken, oh hark!
Press to the high goal, fly to the mark.
    Up, O sluggard, new morn is born;
If still asleep when the night falls dark,
      Thou must wait a second morn."

115   "Up, up, up," sad glad voices swelled:
"So the tree falls and lies as it's felled.
Be thy bands loosed, O sleeper, long held
    In sweet sleep whose end is not sweet.
Be the slackness girt and the softness quelled
120   And the slowness fleet."

Off he set. The grass grew rare,
A blight lurked in the darkening air,
The very moss grew hueless and spare,
    The last daisy stood all astunt;
125   Behind his back the soil lay bare,
      But barer in front.

A land of chasm and rent, a land
Of rugged blackness on either hand:
If water trickled its track was tanned
   With an edge of rust to the chink;   130
If one stamped on stone or on sand
     It returned a clink.

A lifeless land, a loveless land,
Without lair or nest on either hand:
Only scorpions jerked in the sand,   135
   Black as black iron, or dusty pale;
From point to point sheer rock was manned
     By scorpions in mail.

A land of neither life nor death,
Where no man buildeth or fashioneth,   140
Where none draws living or dying breath;
   No man cometh or goeth there,
No man doeth, seeketh, saith,
     In the stagnant air.

Some old volcanic upset must   145
Have rent the crust and blackened the crust;
Wrenched and ribbed it beneath its dust
   Above earth's molten centre at seethe,
Heaved and heaped it by huge upthrust
     Of fire beneath.   150

Untrodden before, untrodden since:
Tedious land for a social Prince;
Halting, he scanned the outs and ins,
   Endless, labyrinthine, grim,
Of the solitude that made him wince,   155
     Laying wait for him.

By bulging rock and gaping cleft,
Even of half mere daylight reft,
Rueful he peered to right and left,
　　Muttering in his altered mood:
"The fate is hard that weaves my weft,
　　　Tho' my lot be good."

Dim the changes of day to night,
Of night scarce dark to day not bright.
Still his road wound towards the right,
　　Still he went, and still he went,
Till one night he spied a light,
　　　In his discontent.

Out it flashed from a yawn-mouthed cave,
Like a red-hot eye from a grave.
No man stood there of whom to crave
　　Rest for wayfarer plodding by:
Tho' the tenant were churl or knave
　　　The Prince might try.

In he passed and tarried not,
Groping his way from spot to spot,
Towards where the cavern flare glowed hot:—
　　An old, old mortal, cramped and double,
Was peering into a seething-pot,
　　　In a world of trouble.

The veriest atomy he looked,
With grimy fingers clutching and crooked,
Tight skin, a nose all bony and hooked,
　　And a shaking, sharp, suspicious way;
Blinking, his eyes had scarcely brooked
　　　The light of day.

Stared the Prince, for the sight was new;
Stared, but asked without more ado:
"May a weary traveller lodge with you,
    Old father, here in your lair?   190
In your country the inns seem few,
        And scanty the fare."

The head turned not to hear him speak;
The old voice whistled as thro' a leak
(Out it came in a quavering squeak):   195
    "Work for wage is a bargain fit:
If there's aught of mine that you seek
        You must work for it.

"Buried alive from light and air
This year is the hundredth year,   200
I feed my fire with a sleepless care,
    Watching my potion wane or wax:
Elixir of Life is simmering there,
        And but one thing lacks.

"If you're fain to lodge here with me,   205
Take that pair of bellows you see—
Too heavy for my old hands they be—
    Take the bellows and puff and puff:
When the steam curls rosy and free
        The broth's boiled enough.   210

"Then take your choice of all I have;
I will give you life if you crave.
Already I'm mildewed for the grave,
    So first myself I must drink my fill:
But all the rest may be yours, to save   215
        Whomever you will."

"Done," quoth the Prince, and the bargain stood.
First he piled on resinous wood,
Next plied the bellows in hopeful mood;
    Thinking, "My love and I will live.
If I tarry, why life is good,
    And she may forgive."

The pot began to bubble and boil;
The old man cast in essence and oil,
He stirred all up with a triple coil
    Of gold and silver and iron wire,
Dredged in a pinch of virgin soil,
    And fed the fire.

But still the steam curled watery white;
Night turned to day and day to night;
One thing lacked, by his feeble sight
    Unseen, unguessed by his feeble mind:
Life might miss him, but Death the blight
    Was sure to find.

So when the hundredth year was full
The thread was cut and finished the school.
Death snapped the old worn-out tool,
    Snapped him short while he stood and stirred
(Tho' stiff he stood as a stiff-necked mule)
    With never a word.

Thus at length the old crab was nipped.
The dead hand slipped, the dead finger dipped
In the broth as the dead man slipped,—
    That same instant, a rosy red
Flushed the steam, and quivered and clipped
    Round the dead old head.

The last ingredient was supplied
(Unless the dead man mistook or lied).
Up started the Prince, he cast aside
   The bellows plied thro' the tedious trial,   250
Made sure that his host had died,
     And filled a phial.

"One night's rest," thought the Prince: "This
     done,
Forth I speed with the rising sun:
With the morrow I rise and run,   255
   Come what will of wind or of weather.
This draught of Life when my Bride is won
     We'll drink together."

Thus the dead man stayed in his grave,
Self-chosen, the dead man in his cave;   260
There he stayed, were he fool or knave,
   Or honest seeker who had not found:
While the Prince outside was prompt to crave
     Sleep on the ground.

"If she watches, go bid her sleep;   265
Bid her sleep, for the road is steep:
He can sleep who holdeth her cheap,
   Sleep and wake and sleep again.
Let him sow, one day he shall reap,
     Let him sow the grain.   270

"When there blows a sweet garden rose,
Let it bloom and wither if no man knows:
But if one knows when the sweet thing blows,
   Knows, and lets it open and drop,
If but a nettle his garden grows   275
     He hath earned the crop."

Thro' his sleep the summons rang,
Into his ears it sobbed and it sang.
Slow he woke with a drowsy pang,
    Shook himself without much debate,
280   Turned where he saw green branches hang,
        Started tho' late.

For the black land was travelled o'er,
He should see the grim land no more.
285   A flowering country stretched before
    His face when the lovely day came back:
He hugged the phial of Life he bore,
        And resumed his track.

By willow courses he took his path,
290   Spied what a nest the kingfisher hath,
Marked the fields green to aftermath,
    Marked where the red-brown field-mouse ran,
Loitered awhile for a deep-stream bath,
        Yawned for a fellow-man.

295   Up on the hills not a soul in view,
In the vale not many nor few;
Leaves, still leaves, and nothing new.
    It's oh for a second maiden, at least,
To bear the flagon, and taste it too,
300   And flavour the feast.

Lagging he moved, and apt to swerve;
Lazy of limb, but quick of nerve,
At length the water-bed took a curve,
    The deep river swept its bankside bare;
305   Waters streamed from the hill-reserve—
        Waters here, waters there.

High above, and deep below,
Bursting, bubbling, swelling the flow,
Like hill-torrents after the snow,—
    Bubbling, gurgling, in whirling strife,   310
Swaying, sweeping, to and fro,—
    He must swim for his life.

Which way?—which way?—his eyes grew dim
With the dizzying whirl—which way to swim?
The thunderous downshoot deafened him;   315
    Half he choked in the lashing spray:
Life is sweet, and the grave is grim—
    Which way?—which way?

A flash of light, a shout from the strand:
"This way—this way; here lies the land!"   320
His phial clutched in one drowning hand;
    He catches—misses—catches a rope;
His feet slip on the slipping sand:
    Is there life?—is there hope?

Just saved, without pulse or breath,—   325
Scarcely saved from the gulp of death;
Laid where a willow shadoweth—
    Laid where a swelling turf is smooth.
(O Bride! but the Bridegroom lingereth
    For all thy sweet youth.)   330

Kind hands do and undo,
Kind voices whisper and coo:
"I will chafe his hands"—"And I"—"And you
    Raise his head, put his hair aside."
(If many laugh, one well may rue: 335
    Sleep on, thou Bride.)

So the Prince was tended with care:
One wrung foul ooze from his clustered hair;
Two chafed his hands, and did not spare;
   But one propped his head that drooped awry:
Till his eyes oped, and at unaware
     They met eye to eye.

Oh a moon face in a shadowy place,
And a light touch and a winsome grace,
And a thrilling tender voice which says:
   "Safe from waters that seek the sea—
Cold waters by rugged ways—
     Safe with me."

While overhead bird whistles to bird,
And round about plays a gamesome herd:
"Safe with us"—some take up the word—
   "Safe with us, dear lord and friend:
All the sweeter if long deferred
     Is rest in the end."

Had he stayed to weigh and to scan,
He had been more or less than a man:
He did what a young man can,
   Spoke of toil and an arduous way—
Toil tomorrow, while golden ran
     The sands of today.

Slip past, slip fast,
Uncounted hours from first to last,
Many hours till the last is past,
   Many hours dwindling to one—
One hour whose die is cast,
     One last hour gone.

Come, gone—gone for ever—
Gone as an unreturning river—
Gone as to death the merriest liver—
 Gone as the year at the dying fall—   370
Tomorrow, today, yesterday, never—
  Gone once for all.

Came at length the starting-day,
With last words, and last, last words to say,
With bodiless cries from far away—   375
 Chiding wailing voices that rang
Like a trumpet-call to the tug and fray;
  And thus they sang:

"Is there life?—the lamp burns low;
Is there hope?—the coming is slow: 380
The promise promised so long ago,
 The long promise, has not been kept.
Does she live?—does she die?—she slumbers so
  Who so oft has wept.

"Does she live?—does she die?—she
    languisheth   385
As a lily drooping to death,
As a drought-worn bird with failing breath,
 As a lovely vine without a stay,
As a tree whereof the owner saith,
  'Hew it down today.'"   390

Stung by that word the Prince was fain
To start on his tedious road again.
He crossed the stream where a ford was plain,
 He clomb the opposite bank tho' steep,
And swore to himself to strain and attain   395
  Ere he tasted sleep.

Huge before him a mountain frowned
With foot of rock on the valley ground,
And head with snows incessant crowned,
    And a cloud mantle about its strength,
And a path which the wild goat hath not found
      In its breadth and length.

But he was strong to do and dare:
If a host had withstood him there,
He had braved a host with little care
    In his lusty youth and his pride,
Tough to grapple tho' weak to snare.
      He comes, O Bride.

Up he went where the goat scare clings,
Up where the eagle folds her wings,
Past the green line of living things,
    Where the sun cannot warm the cold,—
Up he went as a flame enrings
      Where there seems no hold.

Up a fissure barren and black,
Till the eagles tired upon his track,
And the clouds were left behind his back,
    Up till the utmost peak was past.
Then he gasped for breath and his strength fell
      slack;
      He paused at last.

Before his face a valley spread
Where fatness laughed, wine, oil, and bread,
Where all fruit-trees their sweetness shed,
    Where all birds made love to their kind,
Where jewels twinkled, and gold lay red
      And not hard to find.

Midway down the mountain side
(On its green slope the path was wide)
Stood a house for a royal bride,
   Built all of changing opal stone,   430
The royal palace, till now descried
    In his dreams alone.

Less bold than in days of yore,
Doubting now tho' never before,
Doubting he goes and lags the more: 435
   Is the time late? does the day grow dim?
Rose, will she open the crimson core
    Of her heart to him?

Above his head a tangle glows
Of wine-red roses, blushes, snows,   440
Closed buds and buds that unclose,
   Leaves, and moss, and prickles too;
His hand shook as he plucked a rose,
    And the rose dropped dew.

Take heart of grace! the potion of Life   445
May go far to woo him a wife:
If she frown, yet a lover's strife
   Lightly raised can be laid again:
A hasty word is never the knife
    To cut love in twain.   450

Far away stretched the royal land,
Fed by dew, by a spice-wind fanned:
Light labour more, and his foot would stand
   On the threshold, all labour done;
Easy pleasure laid at his hand,   455
    And the dear Bride won.

His slackening steps pause at the gate—
Does she wake or sleep?—the time is late—
Does she sleep now, or watch and wait?
   She has watched, she has waited long,
Watching athwart the golden grate
     With a patient song.

Fling the golden portals wide,
The Bridegroom comes to his promised Bride;
Draw the gold-stiff curtains aside,
   Let them look on each other's face,
She in her meekness, he in his pride—
     Day wears apace.

Day is over, the day that wore.
What is this that comes thro' the door,
The face covered, the feet before?
   This that coming takes his breath;
This Bride not seen, to be seen no more
     Save of Bridegroom Death?

Veiled figures carrying her
Sweep by yet make no stir;
There is a smell of spice and myrrh,
   A bride-chant burdened with one name;
The bride-song rises steadier
     Than the torches' flame:

"Too late for love, too late for joy,
   Too late, too late!
You loitered on the road too long,
   You trifled at the gate:
The enchanted dove upon her branch
   Died without a mate;
The enchanted princess in her tower
   Slept, died, behind the grate;
Her heart was starving all this while
   You made it wait.

"Ten years ago, five years ago,
   One year ago,
Even then you had arrived in time,
   Tho' somewhat slow;
Then you had known her living face   495
   Which now you cannot know:
The frozen fountain would have leaped,
   The buds gone on to blow,
The warm south wind would have awaked
   To melt the snow.   500

"Is she fair now as she lies?
   Once she was fair;
Meet queen for any kingly king,
   With gold-dust on her hair.
Now these are poppies in her locks,   505
   White poppies she must wear;
Must wear a veil to shroud her face
   And the want graven there:
Or is the hunger fed at length,
   Cast off the care?   510

"We never saw her with a smile
   Or with a frown;
Her bed seemed never soft to her,
   Tho' tossed of down;
She little heeded what she wore,   515
   Kirtle, or wreath, or gown;
We think her white brows often ached
   Beneath her crown,
Till silvery hairs showed in her locks
   That used to be so brown.   520

"We never heard her speak in haste:
   Her tones were sweet,
And modulated just so much
   As it was meet:

525   Her heart sat silent thro' the noise
      And concourse of the street.
There was no hurry in her hands,
      No hurry in her feet;
There was no bliss drew nigh to her,
530   That she might run to greet.

"You should have wept her yesterday,
      Wasting upon her bed:
But wherefore should you weep today
      That she is dead?
535   Lo, we who love weep not today,
      But crown her royal head.
Let be these poppies that we strew,
      Your roses are too red:
Let be these poppies, not for you
540   Cut down and spread."

MEMORY.

I

I nursed it in my bosom while it lived,
    I hid it in my heart when it was dead;
In joy I sat alone, even so I grieved
    Alone and nothing said.

5   I shut the door to face the naked truth,
    I stood alone—I faced the truth alone,
Stripped bare of self-regard or forms or ruth
    Till first and last were shown.

I took the perfect balances and weighed;
10   No shaking of my hand disturbed the poise;
Weighed, found it wanting: not a word I said,
    But silent made my choice.

None know the choice I made; I make it still.
  None know the choice I made and broke my
      heart,
Breaking mine idol: I have braced my will   15
  Once, chosen for once my part.

I broke it at a blow, I laid it cold,
  Crushed in my deep heart where it used to live.
My heart dies inch by inch; the time grows old,
  Grows old in which I grieve.   20

II

I have a room whereinto no one enters
  Save I myself alone:
  There sits a blessed memory on a throne,
There my life centres;

While winter comes and goes—oh tedious
      comer!—   25
  And while its nip-wind blows;
  While bloom the bloodless lily and warm rose
Of lavish summer.

If any should force entrance he might see there
  One buried yet not dead,   30
  Before whose face I no more bow my head
Or bend my knee there;

But often in my worn life's autumn weather
  I watch there with clear eyes,
  And think how it will be in Paradise   35
When we're together.

AMOR MUNDI.

"Oh where are you going with your love-locks flowing
   On the west wind blowing along this valley track?"
"The downhill path is easy, come with me an it please ye,
   We shall escape the uphill by never turning back."

5 So they two went together in glowing August weather,
   The honey-breathing heather lay to their left and
      right;
And dear she was to doat on, her swift feet seemed to
      float on
   The air like soft twin pigeons too sportive to alight.

"Oh what is that in heaven where grey cloud-flakes are
      seven,
   Where blackest clouds hang riven just at the rainy
10   skirt?"
"Oh that's a meteor sent us, a message dumb,
      portentous,
   An undeciphered solemn signal of help or hurt."

"Oh what is that glides quickly where velvet flowers
      grow thickly,
   Their scent comes rich and sickly?"—"A scaled and
      hooded worm."
"Oh what's that in the hollow, so pale I quake to
15   follow?"
   "Oh that's a thin dead body which waits the eternal
      term."

"Turn again, O my sweetest,—turn again, false and
      fleetest:
   This beaten way thou beatest I fear is hell's own
      track."

"Nay, too steep for hill-mounting; nay, too late for
    cost-counting:
  This downhill path is easy, but there's no turning
    back."   20

"THE INIQUITY OF THE FATHERS UPON THE CHILDREN"

Oh the rose of keenest thorn!
One hidden summer morn
Under the rose I was born.

I do not guess his name
Who wrought my Mother's shame,   5
And gave me life forlorn,
But my Mother, Mother, Mother,
I know her from all other.
My Mother pale and mild,
Fair as ever was seen,   10
She was but scarce sixteen,
Little more than a child,
When I was born
To work her scorn.
With secret bitter throes,   15
In a passion of secret woes,
She bore me under the rose.

One who my Mother nursed
Took me from the first:—
"O nurse, let me look upon   20
This babe that costs so dear;
Tomorrow she will be gone:
Other mothers may keep
Their babes awake and asleep,
But I must not keep her here."—   25
Whether I know or guess,
I know this not the less.

So I was sent away
That none might spy the truth:
30 And my childhood waxed to youth
And I left off childish play.
I never cared to play.
With the village boys and girls;
And I think they thought me proud,
35 I found so little to say
And kept so from the crowd:
But I had the longest curls
And I had the largest eyes,
And my teeth were small like pearls;
40 The girls might flout and scout me,
But the boys would hang about me
In sheepish mooning wise.

Our one-street village stood
A long mile from the town,
45 A mile of windy down
And bleak one-sided wood,
With not a single house.
Our town itself was small,
With just the common shops,
50 And throve in its small way.
Our neighbouring gentry reared
The good old-fashioned crops,
And made old-fashioned boasts
Of what John Bull would do
55 If Frenchman Frog appeared,
And drank old-fashioned toasts,
And made old-fashioned bows
To my Lady at the Hall.

My Lady at the Hall
60 Is grander than they all:
Hers is the oldest name
In all the neighbourhood;

But the race must die with her
Tho' she's a lofty dame,
For she's unmarried still.   65
Poor people say she's good
And has an open hand
As any in the land,
And she's the comforter
Of many sick and sad;   70
My nurse once said to me
That everything she had
Came of my Lady's bounty:
"Tho' she's greatest in the county
She's humble to the poor,   75
No beggar seeks her door
But finds help presently.
I pray both night and day
For her, and you must pray:
But she'll never feel distress   80
If needy folk can bless."

I was a little maid
When here we came to live
From somewhere by the sea.
Men spoke a foreign tongue   85
There where we used to be
When I was merry and young,
Too young to feel afraid;
The fisher-folk would give
A kind strange word to me,   90
There by the foreign sea:
I don't know where it was,
But I remember still
Our cottage on a hill,
And fields of flowering grass   95
On that fair foreign shore.

I liked my old home best,
But this was pleasant too:
So here we made our nest
100 And here I grew.
And now and then my Lady
In riding past our door
Would nod to Nurse and speak,
Or stoop and pat my cheek;
105 And I was always ready
To hold the field-gate wide
For my Lady to go thro';
My Lady in her veil
So seldom put aside,
110 My Lady grave and pale.

I often sat to wonder
Who might my parents be,
For I knew of something under
My simple-seeming state.
115 Nurse never talked to me
Of mother or of father,
But watched me early and late
With kind suspicious cares:
Or not suspicious, rather
120 Anxious, as if she knew
Some secret I might gather
And smart for unawares.
Thus I grew.

But Nurse waxed old and grey,
125 Bent and weak with years.
There came a certain day
That she lay upon her bed
Shaking her palsied head,
With words she gasped to say
130 Which had to stay unsaid.
Then with a jerking hand
Held out so piteously

She gave a ring to me
Of gold wrought curiously,
A ring which she had worn   135
Since the day that I was born,
She once had said to me:
I slipped it on my finger;
Her eyes were keen to linger
On my hand that slipped it on;   140
Then she sighed one rattling sigh
And stared on with sightless eyes:—
The one who loved me was gone.

How long I stayed alone
With the corpse, I never knew,   145
For I fainted dead as stone:
When I came to life once more
I was down upon the floor,
With neighbours making ado
To bring me back to life.   150
I heard the sexton's wife
Say: "Up, my lad, and run
To tell it at the Hall;
She was my Lady's nurse,
And done can't be undone.   155
I'll watch by this poor lamb.
I guess my Lady's purse
Is always open to such:
I'd run up on my crutch
A cripple as I am,"   160
(For cramps had vexed her much)
"Rather than this dear heart
Lack one to take her part."

For days day after day
On my weary bed I lay   165
Wishing the time would pass;
Oh, so wishing that I was
Likely to pass away:

For the one friend whom I knew
Was dead, I knew no other,
Neither father nor mother;
And I, what should I do?

One day the sexton's wife
Said: "Rouse yourself, my dear:
My Lady has driven down
From the Hall into the town,
And we think she's coming here.
Cheer up, for life is life."

But I would not look or speak,
Would not cheer up at all.
My tears were like to fall,
So I turned round to the wall
And hid my hollow cheek
Making as if I slept,
As silent as a stone,
And no one knew I wept.
What was my Lady to me,
The grand lady from the Hall?
She might come, or stay away,
I was sick at heart that day:
The whole world seemed to be
Nothing, just nothing to me,
For aught that I could see.

Yet I listened where I lay:
A bustle came below,
A clear voice said: "I know;
I will see her first alone,
It may be less of a shock
If she's so weak today:"—
A light hand turned the lock,
A light step crossed the floor,
One sat beside my bed:
But never a word she said.

For me, my shyness grew
Each moment more and more: 205
So I said never a word
And neither looked nor stirred;
I think she must have heard
My heart go pit-a-pat:
Thus I lay, my Lady sat,   210
More than a mortal hour—
(I counted one and two
By the house-clock while I lay):
I seemed to have no power
To think of a thing to say,   215
Or do what I ought to do,
Or rouse myself to a choice.

At last she said: "Margaret,
Won't you even look at me?"
A something in her voice   220
Forced my tears to fall at last,
Forced sobs from me thick and fast;
Something not of the past,
Yet stirring memory;
A something new, and yet   225
Not new, too sweet to last,
Which I never can forget.

I turned and stared at her:
Her cheek showed hollow-pale;
Her hair like mine was fair,   230
A wonderful fall of hair
That screened her like a veil;
But her height was statelier,
Her eyes had depth more deep;
I think they must have had   235
Always a something sad,
Unless they were asleep.

While I stared, my Lady took
My hand in her spare hand
Jewelled and soft and grand,
And looked with a long long look
Of hunger in my face;
As if she tried to trace
Features she ought to know,
And half hoped, half feared, to find.
Whatever was in her mind
She heaved a sigh at last,
And began to talk to me.

"Your nurse was my dear nurse,
And her nursling's dear," said she:
"No one told me a word
Of her getting worse and worse,
Till her poor life was past"
(Here my Lady's tears dropped fast):
"I might have been with her,
I might have promised and heard,
But she had no comforter.
She might have told me much
Which now I shall never know,
Never never shall know."
She sat by me sobbing so,
And seemed so woe-begone,
That I laid one hand upon
Hers with a timid touch,
Scarce thinking what I did,
Not knowing what to say:
That moment her face was hid
In the pillow close by mine,
Her arm was flung over me,
She hugged me, sobbing so
As if her heart would break,
And kissed me where I lay.

After this she often came
To bring me fruit or wine,
Or sometimes hothouse flowers.   275
And at nights I lay awake
Often and often thinking
What to do for her sake.
Wet or dry it was the same:
She would come in at all hours,   280
Set me eating and drinking
And say I must grow strong;
At last the day seemed long
And home seemed scarcely home
If she did not come.   285

Well, I grew strong again:
In time of primroses,
I went to pluck them in the lane;
In time of nestling birds,
I heard them chirping round the house;   290
And all the herds
Were out at grass when I grew strong,
And days were waxen long,
And there was work for bees
Among the May-bush boughs,   295
And I had shot up tall,
And life felt after all
Pleasant, and not so long
When I grew strong.

I was going to the Hall   300
To be my Lady's maid:
"Her little friend," she said to me,
"Almost her child,"
She said and smiled
Sighing painfully;   305
Blushing, with a second flush
As if she blushed to blush.

Friend, servant, child: just this
My standing at the Hall;
310   The other servants call me "Miss,"
My Lady calls me "Margaret,"
With her clear voice musical.
She never chides when I forget
This or that; she never chides.
315   Except when people come to stay,
(And that's not often) at the Hall,
I sit with her all day
And ride out when she rides.
She sings to me and makes me sing;
320   Sometimes I read to her,
Sometimes we merely sit and talk.
She noticed once my ring
And made me tell its history:
That evening in our garden walk
325   She said she should infer
The ring had been my father's first,
Then my mother's, given for me
To the nurse who nursed
My mother in her misery,
330   That so quite certainly
Some one might know me, who . . .
Then she was silent, and I too.

I hate when people come:
The women speak and stare
335   And mean to be so civil.
This one will stroke my hair,
That one will pat my cheek
And praise my Lady's kindness,
Expecting me to speak;
340   I like the proud ones best
Who sit as struck with blindness,

As if I wasn't there.
But if any gentleman
Is staying at the Hall
(Tho' few come prying here),   345
My Lady seems to fear
Some downright dreadful evil,
And makes me keep my room
As closely as she can:
So I hate when people come,   350
It is so troublesome.
In spite of all her care,
Sometimes to keep alive
I sometimes do contrive
To get out in the grounds   355
For a whiff of wholesome air,
Under the rose you know:
It's charming to break bounds,
Stolen waters are sweet,
And what's the good of feet   360
If for days they mustn't go?
Give me a longer tether,
Or I may break from it.

Now I have eyes and ears
And just some little wit: 365
"Almost my Lady's child;"
I recollect she smiled,
Sighed and blushed together;
Then her story of the ring
Sounds not improbable,   370
She told it me so well
It seemed the actual thing:—
Oh, keep your counsel close,
But I guess under the rose,
In long past summer weather   375
When the world was blossoming,

And the rose upon its thorn:
I guess not who he was
Flawed honour like a glass
380 And made my life forlorn,
But my Mother, Mother, Mother,
Oh, I know her from all other.

My Lady, you might trust
Your daughter with your fame.
385 Trust me, I would not shame
Our honourable name,
For I have noble blood
Tho' I was bred in dust
And brought up in the mud.
390 I will not press my claim,
Just leave me where you will:
But you might trust your daughter,
For blood is thicker than water
And you're my mother still.

395 So my Lady holds her own
With condescending grace,
And fills her lofty place
With an untroubled face
As a queen may fill a throne.
400 While I could hint a tale—
(But then I am her child)—
Would make her quail;
Would set her in the dust,
Lorn with no comforter,
405 Her glorious hair defiled
And ashes on her cheek:
The decent world would thrust
Its finger out at her,
Not much displeased I think
410 To make a nine days' stir;
The decent world would sink
Its voice to speak of her.

Now this is what I mean
To do, no more, no less:
Never to speak, or show   415
Bare sign of what I know.
Let the blot pass unseen;
Yea, let her never guess
I hold the tangled clue
She huddles out of view.   420
Friend, servant, almost child,
So be it and nothing more
On this side of the grave.
Mother, in Paradise,
You'll see with clearer eyes;   425
Perhaps in this world even
When you are like to die
And face to face with Heaven
You'll drop for once the lie:
But you must drop the mask, not I.   430

My Lady promises
Two hundred pounds with me
Whenever I may wed
A man she can approve:
And since besides her bounty   435
I'm fairest in the county
(For so I've heard it said,
Tho' I don't vouch for this),
Her promised pounds may move
Some honest man to see   440
My virtues and my beauties;
Perhaps the rising grazier,
Or temperance publican,
May claim my wifely duties.
Meanwhile I wait their leisure   445
And grace-bestowing pleasure,
I wait the happy man;
But if I hold my head
And pitch my expectations

450 Just higher than their level,
They must fall back on patience:
I may not mean to wed,
Yet I'll be civil.

Now sometimes in a dream
455 My heart goes out of me
To build and scheme,
Till I sob after things that seem
So pleasant in a dream:
A home such as I see
460 My blessed neighbours live in
With father and with mother,
All proud of one another,
Named by one common name
From baby in the bud
465 To full-blown workman father;
It's little short of Heaven.
I'd give my gentle blood
To wash my special shame
And drown my private grudge;
470 I'd toil and moil much rather
The dingiest cottage drudge
Whose mother need not blush,
Than live here like a lady
And see my Mother flush
475 And hear her voice unsteady
Sometimes, yet never dare
Ask to share her care.

Of course the servants sneer
Behind my back at me;
480 Of course the village girls,
Who envy me my curls
And gowns and idleness,
Take comfort in a jeer;

Of course the ladies guess
Just so much of my history   485
As points the emphatic stress
With which they laud my Lady;
The gentlemen who catch
A casual glimpse of me
And turn again to see,   490
Their valets on the watch
To speak a word with me,
All know and sting me wild;
Till I am almost ready
To wish that I were dead,   495
No faces more to see,
No more words to be said,
My Mother safe at last
Disburdened of her child,
And the past past.   500

"All equal before God"—
Our Rector has it so,
And sundry sleepers nod:
It may be so; I know
All are not equal here,   505
And when the sleepers wake
They make a difference.
"All equal in the grave"—
That shows an obvious sense:
Yet something which I crave   510
Not death itself brings near;
How should death half atone
For all my past; or make
The name I bear my own?

I love my dear old Nurse   515
Who loved me without gains;
I love my mistress even,
Friend, Mother, what you will:
But I could almost curse

520 My Father for his pains;
And sometimes at my prayer
Kneeling in sight of Heaven
I almost curse him still:
Why did he set his snare
525 To catch at unaware
My Mother's foolish youth;
Load me with shame that's hers,
And her with something worse,
A lifelong lie for truth?

530 I think my mind is fixed
On one point and made up:
To accept my lot unmixed;
Never to drug the cup
But drink it by myself.
535 I'll not be wooed for pelf;
I'll not blot out my shame
With any man's good name;
But nameless as I stand,
My hand is my own hand,
540 And nameless as I came
I go to the dark land.

"All equal in the grave"—
I bide my time till then:
"All equal before God"—
545 Today I feel His rod,
Tomorrow He may save:
            Amen.

A DAUGHTER OF EVE.

A fool I was to sleep at noon,
    And wake when night is chilly
Beneath the comfortless cold moon;
A fool to pluck my rose too soon,
    A fool to snap my lily.   5

My garden-plot I have not kept;
    Faded and all-forsaken,
I weep as I have never wept:
Oh it was summer when I slept,
    It's winter now I waken.   10

Talk what you please of future Spring
    And sun-warmed sweet tomorrow:—
Stripped bare of hope and everything,
No more to laugh, no more to sing,
    I sit alone with sorrow.   15

A SMILE AND A SIGH.

A smile because the nights are short!
    And every morning brings such pleasure
Of sweet love-making, harmless sport:
    Love that makes and finds its treasure;
    Love, treasure without measure.   5

A sigh because the days are long!
    Long long these days that pass in sighing,
A burden saddens every song:
    While time lags which should be flying,
    We live who would be dying.   10

AUTUMN VIOLETS.

Keep love for youth, and violets for the spring:
   Or if these bloom when worn-out autumn grieves,
   Let them lie hid in double shade of leaves,
Their own, and others dropped down withering;
5 For violets suit when home birds build and sing,
   Not when the outbound bird a passage cleaves;
   Not with dry stubble of mown harvest sheaves,
But when the green world buds to blossoming.
Keep violets for the spring, and love for youth,
10 Love that should dwell with beauty, mirth, and hope:
   Or if a later sadder love be born,
   Let this not look for grace beyond its scope,
But give itself, nor plead for answering truth—
   A grateful Ruth tho' gleaning scanty corn.

"THEY DESIRE A BETTER COUNTRY."

I.

I would not if I could undo my past,
   Tho' for its sake my future is a blank;
   My past for which I have myself to thank,
For all its faults and follies first and last.
5 I would not cast anew the lot once cast,
   Or launch a second ship for one that sank,
   Or drug with sweets the bitterness I drank,
Or break by feasting my perpetual fast.
I would not if I could: for much more dear
10 Is one rememberance than a hundred joys,
   More than a thousand hopes in jubilee;
   Dearer the music of one tearful voice
   That unforgotten calls and calls to me,
"Follow me here, rise up, and follow here."

II.

What seekest thou, far in the unknown land?   15
  In hope I follow joy gone on before;
  In hope and fear persistent more and more,
As the dry desert lengthens out its sand.
Whilst day and night I carry in my hand
  The golden key to ope the golden door   20
  Of golden home; yet mine eye weepeth sore,
For long the journey is that makes no stand.
And who is this that veiled doth walk with thee?
  Lo, this is Love that walketh at my right;
    One exile holds us both, and we are bound   25
  To selfsame home-joys in the land of light.
Weeping thou walkest with him; weepeth he?—
    Some sobbing weep, some weep and make no
      sound.

III.

A dimness of a glory glimmers here
  Thro' veils and distance from the space
      remote,   30
  A faintest far vibration of a note
Reaches to us and seems to bring us near;
Causing our face to glow with braver cheer,
  Making the serried mist to stand afloat,
  Subduing languor with an antidote,   35
And strengthening love almost to cast out fear:
Till for one moment golden city walls
  Rise looming on us, golden walls of home,
Light of our eyes until the darkness falls;
  Then thro' the outer darkness burdensome   40
I hear again the tender voice that calls,
  "Follow me hither, follow, rise, and come."

A CHRISTMAS CAROL.

In the bleak mid-winter
  Frosty wind made moan,
Earth stood hard as iron,
  Water like a stone;
Snow had fallen, snow on snow,
  Snow on snow,
In the bleak mid-winter
  Long ago.

Our God, Heaven cannot hold Him
  Nor earth sustain;
Heaven and earth shall flee away
  When He comes to reign:
In the bleak mid-winter
  A stable-place sufficed
The Lord God Almighty
  Jesus Christ.

Enough for Him whom cherubim
  Worship night and day,
A breastful of milk
  And a mangerful of hay;
Enough for Him whom angels
  Fall down before,
The ox and ass and camel
  Which adore.

Angels and archangels
  May have gathered there,
Cherubim and seraphim
  Throng'd the air,
But only His mother
  In her maiden bliss
Worshipped the Beloved
  With a kiss.

What can I give Him,
   Poor as I am?
If I were a shepherd   35
   I would bring a lamb,
If I were a wise man
   I would do my part,—
Yet what I can I give Him,
   Give my heart.   40

Love me,—I love you,
   Love me, my baby;
Sing it high, sing it low,
   Sing it as may be.

Mother's arms under you,   5
   Her eyes above you;
Sing it high, sing it low,
   Love me,—I love you.

A city plum is not a plum;
A dumb-bell is no bell, though dumb;
A party rat is not a rat;
A sailor's cat is not a cat;
A soldier's frog is not a frog;   5
A captain's log is not a log.

A baby's cradle with no baby in it,
   A baby's grave where autumn leaves drop sere;
The sweet soul gathered home to Paradise,
   The body waiting here.

Hope is like a harebell trembling from its birth,
Love is like a rose the joy of all the earth;
Faith is like a lily lifted high and white,
Love is like a lovely rose the world's delight;
Harebells and sweet lilies show a thornless growth,
But the rose with all its thorns excels them both.

A linnet in a gilded cage,—
    A linnet on a bough,—
In frosty winter one might doubt
    Which bird is luckier now.

But let the trees burst out in leaf,
    And nests be on the bough,
Which linnet is the luckier bird,
    Oh who could doubt it now?

If all were rain and never sun,
    No bow could span the hill;
If all were sun and never rain,
    There'd be no rainbow still.

If I were a Queen,
    What would I do?
I'd make you King,
    And I'd wait on you.

If I were a King,
    What would I do?
I'd make you Queen,
    For I'd marry you.

What are heavy? sea-sand and sorrow:
What are brief? today and tomorrow:
What are frail? Spring blossoms and youth:
What are deep? the ocean and truth.

Brown and furry
Caterpillar in a hurry,
Take your walk
To the shady leaf, or stalk,
Or what not,   5
Which may be the chosen spot.
No toad spy you,
Hovering bird of prey pass by you;
Spin and die,
To live again a butterfly.   10

A toadstool comes up in a night,—
    Learn the lesson, little folk:—
An oak grows on a hundred years,
    But then it is an oak.

If a pig wore a wig,
    What could we say?

Treat him as a gentleman,
    And say "Good day."

If his tail chanced to fail,   5
    What could we do?—
Send him to the tailoress
    To get one new.

How many seconds in a minute?
Sixty, and no more in it.

How many minutes in an hour?
Sixty for sun and shower.

5   How many hours in a day?
Twenty-four for work and play.

How many days in a week?
Seven both to hear and speak.

How many weeks in a month?
10   Four, as the swift moon runn'th.

How many months in a year?
Twelve the almanack makes clear.

How many years in an age?
One hundred says the sage.

15   How many ages in time?
No one knows the rhyme.

What is pink? a rose is pink
By the fountain's brink.
What is red? a poppy's red
In its barley bed.
5   What is blue? the sky is blue
Where the clouds float thro'.
What is white? a swan is white
Sailing in the light.
What is yellow? pears are yellow,
10   Rich and ripe and mellow.
What is green? the grass is green,

With small flowers between.
What is violet? clouds are violet
In the summer twilight.
What is orange? why, an orange,   15
Just an orange!

A pin has a head, but has no hair;
A clock has a face, but no mouth there;
Needles have eyes, but they cannot see;
A fly has a trunk without lock or key;
A timepiece may lose, but cannot win;   5
A corn-field dimples without a chin;
A hill has no leg, but has a foot;
A wine-glass a stem, but not a root;
A watch has hands, but no thumb or finger;
A boot has a tongue, but is no singer;   10
Rivers run, though they have no feet;
A saw has teeth, but it does not eat;
Ash-trees have keys, yet never a lock;
And baby crows, without being a cock.

When fishes set umbrellas up
    If the rain-drops run,
Lizards will want their parasols
    To shade them from the sun.

The peacock has a score of eyes,
    With which he cannot see;
The cod-fish has a silent sound,
    However that may be;

₅ No dandelions tell the time,
    Although they turn to clocks;
  Cat's-cradle does not hold the cat,
    Nor foxglove fit the fox.

The wind has such a rainy sound
  Moaning through the town,
The sea has such a windy sound,—
  Will the ships go down?

₅ The apples in the orchard
  Tumble from their tree.—
Oh will the ships go down, go down,
  In the windy sea?

Who has seen the wind?
  Neither I nor you:
But when the leaves hang trembling
  The wind is passing thro'.

₅ Who has seen the wind?
  Neither you nor I:
But when the trees bow down their heads
  The wind is passing by.

When a mounting skylark sings
  In the sunlit summer morn,
I know that heaven is up on high,
  And on earth are fields of corn.

But when a nightingale sings 5
   In the moonlit summer even,
I know not if earth is merely earth,
   Only that heaven is heaven.

An emerald is as green as grass;
   A ruby red as blood;
A sapphire shines as blue as heaven;
   A flint lies in the mud.

A diamond is a brilliant stone, 5
   To catch the world's desire;
An opal holds a fiery spark;
   But a flint holds fire.

What does the bee do?
   Bring home honey.
And what does Father do?
   Bring home money.
And what does Mother do? 5
   Lay out the money.
And what does baby do?
   Eat up the honey.

I caught a little ladybird
   That flies far away;
I caught a little lady wife
   That is both staid and gay.

Come back, my scarlet ladybird, 5
   Back from far away;
I weary of my dolly wife,
   My wife that cannot play.

She's such a senseless wooden thing
    She stares the livelong day;
Her wig of gold is stiff and cold
    And cannot change to grey.

Baby lies so fast asleep
    That we cannot wake her:
Will the Angels clad in white
    Fly from heaven to take her?

Baby lies so fast asleep
    That no pain can grieve her;
Put a snowdrop in her hand,
    Kiss her once and leave her.

CONFLUENTS.

As rivers seek the sea,
    Much more deep than they,
So my soul seeks thee
    Far away:
As running rivers moan
On their course alone,
    So I moan
    Left alone.

As the delicate rose
    To the sun's sweet strength
Doth herself unclose,
    Breadth and length;
So spreads my heart to thee
Unveiled utterly,
    I to thee
    Utterly.

As morning dew exhales
   Sunwards pure and free,
So my spirit fails
   After thee: 20
As dew leaves not a trace
On the green earth's face;
   I, no trace
   On thy face.

Its goal the river knows, 25
   Dewdrops find a way,
Sunlight cheers the rose
   In her day:
Shall I, lone sorrow past,
Find thee at the last? 30
   Sorrow past,
   Thee at last?

"Yet a little while."

Heaven is not far, tho' far the sky
   Overarching earth and main.
It takes not long to live and die,
   Die, revive, and rise again.
Not long: how long? Oh, long re-echoing
     song! 5
O Lord, how long?

MONNA INNOMINATA.
A SONNET OF SONNETS.

Beatrice, immortalized by "altissimo poeta . . . cotanto amante";
Laura, celebrated by a great tho' an inferior bard,—have alike
paid the exceptional penalty of exceptional honour, and have
come down to us resplendent with charms, but (at least, to my
apprehension) scant of attractiveness.

These heroines of world-wide fame were preceded by a bevy of unnamed ladies "donne innominate" sung by a school of less conspicuous poets; and in that land and that period which gave simultaneous birth to Catholics, to Albigenses, and to Trouba-dours, one can imagine many a lady as sharing her lover's poetic aptitude, while the barrier between them might be one held sacred by both, yet not such as to render mutual love incompatible with mutual honour.

Had such a lady spoken for herself, the portrait left us might have appeared more tender, if less dignified, than any drawn even by a devoted friend. Or had the Great Poetess of our own day and nation only been unhappy instead of happy, her circum-stances would have invited her to bequeath to us, in lieu of the "Portuguese Sonnets," an inimitable "donna innominata" drawn not from fancy but from feeling, and worthy to occupy a niche beside Beatrice and Laura.

I.

"Lo dì che han detto a' dolci amici addio."—DANTE.
"Amor, con quanto sforzo oggi mi vinci!"—PETRARCA.

Come back to me, who wait and watch for you:—
   Or come not yet, for it is over then,
   And long it is before you come again,
So far between my pleasures are and few.
5 While, when you come not, what I do I do
   Thinking "Now when he comes," my sweetest
     "when:"
   For one man is my world of all the men
This wide world holds; O love, my world is you.
Howbeit, to meet you grows almost a pang
10 Because the pang of parting comes so soon;
   My hope hangs waning, waxing, like a moon
    Between the heavenly days on which we meet:
Ah me, but where are now the songs I sang
   When life was sweet because you called them
    sweet?

2.

"Era già l'ora che volge il desio."—DANTE.
"Ricorro al tempo ch'io vi vidi prima."—PETRARCA.

I wish I could remember that first day,
   First hour, first moment of your meeting me,
   If bright or dim the season, it might be
Summer or Winter for aught I can say;
So unrecorded did it slip away,   5
   So blind was I to see and to foresee,
   So dull to mark the budding of my tree
That would not blossom yet for many a May.
If only I could recollect it, such
   A day of days! I let it come and go   10
   As traceless as a thaw of bygone snow;
It seemed to mean so little, meant so much;
If only now I could recall that touch,
   First touch of hand in hand—Did one but know!

3.

"O ombre vane, fuor che ne l'aspetto!"—DANTE.
"Immaginata guida la conduce."—PETRARCA.

I dream of you to wake: would that I might
   Dream of you and not wake but slumber on;
   Nor find with dreams the dear companion gone,
As Summer ended Summer birds take flight.
In happy dreams I hold you full in sight,   5
   I blush again who waking look so wan;
   Brighter than sunniest day that ever shone,
In happy dreams your smile makes day of night.
Thus only in a dream we are at one,
   Thus only in a dream we give and take   10
     The faith that maketh rich who take or give;
If thus to sleep is sweeter than to wake,
    To die were surely sweeter than to live,
Tho' there be nothing new beneath the sun.

4.

"Poca favilla gran fiamma seconda."—DANTE.
"Ogni altra cosa, ogni pensier va fore,
E sol ivi con voi rimansi amore."—PETRARCA.

I loved you first: but afterwards your love
    Outsoaring mine, sang such a loftier song
As drowned the friendly cooings of my dove.
    Which owes the other most? my love was long,
5   And yours one moment seemed to wax more strong;
I loved and guessed at you, you construed me
And loved me for what might or might not be—
    Nay, weights and measures do us both a wrong.
For verily love knows not "mine" or "thine;"
10   With separate "I" and "thou" free love has done,
     For one is both and both are one in love:
Rich love knows nought of "thine that is not mine;"
    Both have the strength and both the length
        thereof,
    Both of us, of the love which makes us one.

5.

"Amor che a nulla amato amar perdona."—DANTE.
"Amor m'addusse in sì gioiosa spene."—PETRARCA.

O my heart's heart, and you who are to me
    More than myself myself, God be with you,
    Keep you in strong obedience leal and true
To Him whose noble service setteth free,
5   Give you all good we see or can foresee,
    Make your joys many and your sorrows few,
    Bless you in what you bear and what you do,
Yea, perfect you as He would have you be.
So much for you; but what for me, dear friend?
10   To love you without stint and all I can
Today, tomorrow, world without an end;

To love you much and yet to love you more,
As Jordan at his flood sweeps either shore;
Since woman is the helpmeet made for man.

6.

"Or puoi la quantitate
Comprender de l'amor che a te mi scalda."—DANTE.
"Non vo'che da tal nodo amor mi scioglia."—PETRARCA.

Trust me, I have not earned your dear rebuke,
  I love, as you would have me, God the most;
   Would lose not Him, but you, must one be lost,
Nor with Lot's wife cast back a faithless look
Unready to forego what I forsook;   5
  This say I, having counted up the cost,
  This, tho' I be the feeblest of God's host,
The sorriest sheep Christ shepherds with His crook.
Yet while I love my God the most, I deem
  That I can never love you overmuch;   10
   I love Him more, so let me love you too;
  Yea, as I apprehend it, love is such
I cannot love you if I love not Him,
   I cannot love Him if I love not you.

7.

"Qui primavera sempre ed ogni frutto."—DANTE.
"Ragionando con meco ed io con lui."—PETRARCA.

"Love me, for I love you"—and answer me,
  "Love me, for I love you"—so shall we stand
  As happy equals in the flowering land
Of love, that knows not a dividing sea.
Love builds the house on rock and not on sand,   5
  Love laughs what while the winds rave desperately;
And who hath found love's citadel unmanned?
  And who hath held in bonds love's liberty?

My heart's a coward tho' my words are brave—
10   We meet so seldom, yet we surely part
       So often; there's a problem for your art!
          Still I find comfort in his Book, who saith,
Tho' jealousy be cruel as the grave,
          And death be strong, yet love is strong as death.

                         8.

"Come dicesse a Dio: D'altro non calme."—DANTE.
"Spero trovar pietà non che perdono."—PETRARCA.

"I, if I perish, perish"—Esther spake:
       And bride of life or death she made her fair
       In all the lustre of her perfumed hair
And smiles that kindle longing but to slake.
5   She put on pomp of loveliness, to take
       Her husband thro' his eyes at unaware;
       She spread abroad her beauty for a snare,
Harmless as doves and subtle as a snake.
She trapped him with one mesh of silken hair,
10   She vanquished him by wisdom of her wit,
          And built her people's house that it should
             stand:—
          If I might take my life so in my hand,
And for my love to Love put up my prayer,
       And for love's sake by Love be granted it!

                         9.

"O dignitosa coscienza e netta!"—DANTE.
"Spirto più acceso di virtuti ardenti."—PETRARCA.

Thinking of you, and all that was, and all
       That might have been and now can never be,
       I feel your honoured excellence, and see
Myself unworthy of the happier call:

For woe is me who walk so apt to fall,   5
   So apt to shrink afraid, so apt to flee,
   Apt to lie down and die (ah, woe is me!)
Faithless and hopeless turning to the wall.
And yet not hopeless quite nor faithless quite,
Because not loveless; love may toil all night,   10
   But take at morning; wrestle till the break
      Of day, but then wield power with God and
      man:—
   So take I heart of grace as best I can,
Ready to spend and be spent for your sake.

10.

"Con miglior corso e con migliore stella."—DANTE.
"La vita fugge e non s'arresta un' ora."—PETRARCA.

Time flies, hope flags, life plies a wearied wing;
   Death following hard on life gains ground apace;
   Faith runs with each and rears an eager face,
Outruns the rest, makes light of everything,
Spurns earth, and still finds breath to pray and sing;   5
   While love ahead of all uplifts his praise,
   Still asks for grace and still gives thanks for grace,
Content with all day brings and night will bring.
Life wanes; and when love folds his wings above
   Tired hope, and less we feel his conscious pulse,   10
      Let us go fall asleep, dear friend, in peace:
      A little while, and age and sorrow cease;
   A little while, and life reborn annuls
Loss and decay and death, and all is love.

11.

"Vien dietro a me e lascia dir le genti."—DANTE.
"Contando i casi della vita nostra."—PETRARCA.

Many in aftertimes will say of you
   "He loved her"—while of me what will they say?
   Not that I loved you more than just in play.
For fashion's sake as idle women do.
5 Even let them prate; who know not what we knew
   Of love and parting in exceeding pain,
   Of parting hopeless here to meet again,
Hopeless on earth, and heaven is out of view.
But by my heart of love laid bare to you,
10   My love that you can make not void nor vain,
Love that foregoes you but to claim anew
    Beyond this passage of the gate of death,
   I charge you at the Judgment make it plain
    My love of you was life and not a breath.

12.

"Amor, che ne la mente mi ragiona."—DANTE.
"Amor vien nel bel viso di costei."—PETRARCA.

If there be any one can take my place
   And make you happy whom I grieve to grieve,
   Think not that I can grudge it, but believe
I do commend you to that nobler grace,
5 That readier wit than mine, that sweeter face;
   Yea, since your riches make me rich, conceive
   I too am crowned, while bridal crowns I weave,
And thread the bridal dance with jocund pace.
For if I did not love you, it might be
10   That I should grudge you some one dear delight;
    But since the heart is yours that was mine own,
   Your pleasure is my pleasure, right my right,
Your honourable freedom makes me free,
    And you companioned I am not alone.

13.

"E drizzeremo glí occhi al Primo Amore."—DANTE.
"Ma trovo peso non da le mie braccia."—PETRARCA.

If I could trust mine own self with your fate,
   Shall I not rather trust it in God's hand?
   Without Whose Will one lily doth not stand,
Nor sparrow fall at his appointed date;
   Who numbereth the innumerable sand,   5
Who weighs the wind and water with a weight,
To Whom the world is neither small nor great,
   Whose knowledge foreknew every plan we planned.
Searching my heart for all that touches you,
   I find there only love and love's goodwill   10
Helpless to help and impotent to do,
      Of understanding dull, of sight most dim;
      And therefore I commend you back to Him
   Whose love your love's capacity can fill.

14.

"E la Sua Volontade è nostra pace."—DANTE.
"Sol con questi pensier, con altre chiome."—PETRARCA.

Youth gone, and beauty gone if ever there
   Dwelt beauty in so poor a face as this;
   Youth gone and beauty, what remains of bliss?
I will not bind fresh roses in my hair,
To shame a cheek at best but little fair,—   5
   Leave youth his roses, who can bear a thorn,—
I will not seek for blossoms anywhere,
   Except such common flowers as blow with corn.
Youth gone and beauty gone, what doth remain?
   The longing of a heart pent up forlorn,   10
      A silent heart whose silence loves and longs;
      The silence of a heart which sang its songs
   While youth and beauty made a summer morn,
Silence of love that cannot sing again.

Sonnets are full of love, and this my tome
   Has many sonnets: so here now shall be
   One sonnet more, a love sonnet, from me
To her whose heart is my heart's quiet home,
5   To my first Love, my Mother, on whose knee
I learnt love-lore that is not troublesome;
   Whose service is my special dignity,
And she my loadstar while I go and come.
And so because you love me, and because
10   I love you, Mother, I have woven a wreath
     Of rhymes wherewith to crown your honoured
       name:
     In you not fourscore years can dim the flame
Of love, whose blessed glow transcends the laws
   Of time and change and mortal life and death.

THE KEY-NOTE.

Where are the songs I used to know,
   Where are the notes I used to sing?
   I have forgotten everything
I used to know so long ago;
5   Summer has followed after Spring;
   Now Autumn is so shrunk and sere,
I scarcely think a sadder thing
   Can be the Winter of my year.

Yet Robin sings thro' Winter's rest,
10   When bushes put their berries on;
   While they their ruddy jewels don,
He sings out of a ruddy breast;
The hips and haws and ruddy breast
   Make one spot warm where snowflakes lie,
15   They break and cheer the unlovely rest
   Of Winter's pause—and why not I?

HE AND SHE.

"Should one of us remember,
  And one of us forget,
I wish I knew what each will do—
  But who can tell as yet?"

"Should one of us remember,   5
  And one of us forget,
I promise you what I will do—
And I'm content to wait for you,
  And not be sure as yet."

DE PROFUNDIS.

Oh why is heaven built so far,
  Oh why is earth set so remote?
I cannot reach the nearest star
    That hangs afloat.

I would not care to reach the moon,   5
  One round monotonous of change;
Yet even she repeats her tune
    Beyond my range.

I never watch the scattered fire
  Of stars, or sun's far-trailing train,   10
But all my heart is one desire,
    And all in vain:

For I am bound with fleshly bands,
  Joy, beauty, lie beyond my scope;
I strain my heart, I stretch my hands,   15
    And catch at hope.

"HOLLOW-SOUNDING AND MYSTERIOUS."

There's no replying
To the Wind's sighing,
Telling, foretelling,
Dying, undying,
5   Dwindling and swelling,
Complaining, droning,
Whistling and moaning,
Ever beginning,
Ending, repeating,
10   Hinting and dinning,
Lagging and fleeting—
We've no replying
Living or dying
To the Wind's sighing.
15   What are you telling,
Variable Wind-tone?
What would be teaching,
O sinking, swelling,
Desolate Wind-moan?
20   Ever for ever
Teaching and preaching,
Never, ah never
Making us wiser—
The earliest riser
25   Catches no meaning,
The last who hearkens
Garners no gleaning
Of wisdom's treasure,
While the world darkens:—
30   Living or dying,
In pain, in pleasure,
We've no replying
To wordless flying
Wind's sighing.

AT LAST.

Many have sung of love a root of bane:
  While to my mind a root of balm it is,
  For love at length breeds love; sufficient bliss
For life and death and rising up again.
Surely when light of Heaven makes all things plain,   5
  Love will grow plain with all its mysteries;
  Nor shall we need to fetch from over seas
Wisdom or wealth or pleasure safe from pain.
Love in our borders, love within our heart,
  Love all in all, we then shall bide at rest,   10
  Ended for ever life's unending quest,
    Ended for ever effort, change and fear:
Love all in all;—no more that better part
    Purchased, but at the cost of all things here.

MARIANA.

Not for me marring or making,
Not for me giving or taking;
  I love my Love and he loves not me,
I love my Love and my heart is breaking.

Sweet is Spring in its lovely showing,   5
Sweet the violet veiled in blowing,
  Sweet it is to love and be loved;
Ah, sweet knowledge beyond my knowing!

Who sighs for love sighs but for pleasure,
Who wastes for love hoards up a treasure;   10
  Sweet to be loved and take no count,
Sweet it is to love without measure.

Sweet my Love whom I loved to try for,
Sweet my Love whom I love and sigh for,
    Will you once love me and sigh for me,
You my Love whom I love and die for?

PASSING AND GLASSING.

All things that pass
    Are woman's looking-glass;
They show her how her bloom must fade,
And she herself be laid
With withered roses in the shade;
    With withered roses and the fallen peach,
    Unlovely, out of reach
        Of summer joy that was.

All things that pass
    Are woman's tiring-glass;
The faded lavender is sweet,
Sweet the dead violet
Culled and laid by and cared for yet;
    The dried-up violets and dried lavender
    Still sweet, may comfort her,
        Nor need she cry Alas!

All things that pass
    Are wisdom's looking-glass;
Being full of hope and fear, and still
Brimful of good or ill,
According to our work and will;
    For there is nothing new beneath the sun;
    Our doings have been done,
        And that which shall be was.

THE THREAD OF LIFE.

1.

The irresponsive silence of the land,
   The irresponsive sounding of the sea,
   Speak both one message of one sense to me:—
Aloof, aloof, we stand aloof, so stand
Thou too aloof bound with the flawless band   5
   Of inner solitude; we bind not thee;
   But who from thy self-chain shall set thee free?
What heart shall touch thy heart? what hand thy
      hand?—
And I am sometimes proud and sometimes meek,
   And sometimes I remember days of old   10
When fellowship seemed not so far to seek
   And all the world and I seemed much less cold,
   And at the rainbow's foot lay surely gold,
And hope felt strong and life itself not weak.

2.

Thus am I mine own prison. Everything
   Around me free and sunny and at ease:
   Or if in shadow, in a shade of trees
Which the sun kisses, where the gay birds sing
And where all winds make various murmuring;   5
   Where bees are found, with honey for the bees;
   Where sounds are music, and where silences
Are music of an unlike fashioning.
Then gaze I at the merrymaking crew.
   And smile a moment and a moment sigh   10
Thinking: Why can I not rejoice with you?
   But soon I put the foolish fancy by:
I am not what I have nor what I do;
   But what I was I am, I am even I.

3.

Therefore myself is that one only thing
   I hold to use or waste, to keep or give;
   My sole possession every day I live,
And still mine own despite Time's winnowing.
5 Ever mine own, while moons and seasons bring
   From crudeness ripeness mellow and sanative;
   Ever mine own, till Death shall ply his sieve;
And still mine own, when saints break grave and sing.
And this myself as king unto my King
10 I give, to Him Who gave Himself for me;
Who gives Himself to me, and bids me sing
   A sweet new song of His redeemed set free;
He bids me sing: O death, where is thy sting?
   And sing: O grave, where is thy victory?

TOUCHING "NEVER."

Because you never yet have loved me, dear,
   Think you you never can nor ever will?
   Surely while life remains hope lingers still,
Hope the last blossom of life's dying year.
5 Because the season and mine age grow sere,
   Shall never Spring bring forth her daffodil,
   Shall never sweeter Summer feast her fill
Of roses with the nightingales they hear?
If you had loved me, I not loving you,
10 If you had urged me with the tender plea
Of what our unknown years to come might do
   (Eternal years, if Time should count too few),
   I would have owned the point you pressed on me,
Was possible, or probable, or true.

AN OLD-WORLD THICKET.

... "Una selva oscura."—DANTE.

Awake or sleeping (for I know not which)
   I was or was not mazed within a wood
   Where every mother-bird brought up her brood
     Safe in some leafy niche
Of oak or ash, of cypress or of beech,   5

Of silvery aspen trembling delicately,
   Of plane or warmer-tinted sycomore,
   Of elm that dies in secret from the core,
     Of ivy weak and free,
Of pines, of all green lofty things that be.   10

Such birds they seemed as challenged each desire;
   Like spots of azure heaven upon the wing,
   Like downy emeralds that alight and sing,
     Like actual coals on fire,
Like anything they seemed, and everything.   15

Such mirth they made, such warblings and such chat
   With tongue of music in a well-tuned beak,
   They seemed to speak more wisdom than we speak,
     To make our music flat
And all our subtlest reasonings wild or weak.   20

Their meat was nought but flowers like butterflies,
   With berries coral-coloured or like gold;
   Their drink was only dew, which blossoms hold
     Deep where the honey lies;
Their wings and tails were lit by sparkling eyes.   25

The shade wherein they revelled was a shade
    That danced and twinkled to the unseen sun;
    Branches and leaves cast shadows one by one,
        And all their shadows swayed
30 In breaths of air that rustled and that played.

A sound of waters neither rose nor sank,
    And spread a sense of freshness through the air;
    It seemed not here or there, but everywhere,
        As if the whole earth drank,
35 Root fathom deep and strawberry on its bank.

But I who saw such things as I have said,
    Was overdone with utter weariness;
    And walked in care, as one whom fears oppress
        Because above his head
40 Death hangs, or damage, or the dearth of bread.

Each sore defeat of my defeated life
    Faced and outfaced me in that bitter hour;
    And turned to yearning palsy all my power,
        And all my peace to strife,
45 Self stabbing self with keen lack-pity knife.

Sweetness of beauty moved me to despair,
    Stung me to anger by its mere content,
    Made me all lonely on that way I went,
        Piled care upon my care,
50 Brimmed full my cup, and stripped me empty and bare:

For all that was but showed what all was not,
    But gave clear proof of what might never be;
    Making more destitute my poverty,
        And yet more blank my lot,
55 And me much sadder by its jubilee.

Therefore I sat me down: for wherefore walk?
  And closed mine eyes: for wherefore see or hear?
  Alas, I had no shutter to mine ear,
    And could not shun the talk
  Of all rejoicing creatures far or near.   60

Without my will I hearkened and I heard
  (Asleep or waking, for I know not which),
  Till note by note the music changed its pitch;
    Bird ceased to answer bird,
And every wind sighed softly if it stirred.   65

The drip of widening waters seemed to weep,
  All fountains sobbed and gurgled as they sprang,
Somewhere a cataract cried out in its leap
    Sheer down a headlong steep;
  High over all cloud-thunders gave a clang.   70

Such universal sound of lamentation
  I heard and felt, fain not to feel or hear;
  Nought else there seemed but anguish far and near;
    Nought else but all creation
  Moaning and groaning wrung by pain or fear,   75

Shuddering in the misery of its doom:
  My heart then rose a rebel against light,
  Scouring all earth and heaven and depth and height,
    Ingathering wrath and gloom,
  Ingathering wrath to wrath and night to night.   80

Ah me, the bitterness of such revolt,
  All impotent, all hateful, and all hate,
That kicks and breaks itself against the bolt
    Of an imprisoning fate,
  And vainly shakes, and cannot shake the gate.   85

Agony to agony, deep called to deep,
   Out of the deep I called of my desire;
    My strength was weakness and my heart was fire;
     Mine eyes that would not weep
90 Or sleep, scaled height and depth, and could not sleep;

The eyes, I mean, of my rebellious soul,
   For still my bodily eyes were closed and dark:
    A random thing I seemed without a mark,
     Racing without a goal,
95   Adrift upon life's sea without an ark.

More leaden than the actual self of lead
   Outer and inner darkness weighed on me.
    The tide of anger ebbed. Then fierce and free
     Surged full above my head
100   The moaning tide of helpless misery.

Why should I breathe, whose breath was but a sigh?
   Why should I live, who drew such painful breath?
   Oh weary work, the unanswerable why!—
    Yet I, why should I die,
105   Who had no hope in life, no hope in death?

Grasses and mosses and the fallen leaf
   Make peaceful bed for an indefinite term;
    But underneath the grass there gnaws a worm—
     Haply, there gnaws a grief—
110 Both, haply always; not, as now, so brief.

The pleasure I remember, it is past;
   The pain I feel, is passing passing by;
    Thus all the world is passing, and thus I:
     All things that cannot last
115   Have grown familiar, and are born to die.

And being familiar, have so long been borne
   That habit trains us not to break but bend:
Mourning grows natural to us who mourn
     In foresight of an end,
   But that which ends not who shall brave or
       mend?   120

Surely the ripe fruits tremble on their bough,
   They cling and linger trembling till they drop:
I, trembling, cling to dying life; for how
     Face the perpetual Now?
   Birthless, and deathless, void of start or stop,   125

Void of repentance, void of hope and fear,
   Of possibility, alternative,
   Of all that ever made us bear to live
     From night to morning here,
   Of promise even which has no gift to give.   130

The wood, and every creature of the wood,
   Seemed mourning with me in an undertone;
   Soft scattered chirpings and a windy moan,
     Trees rustling where they stood
And shivered, showed, compassion for my mood.   135

Rage to despair; and now despair had turned
   Back to self-pity and mere weariness,
With yearnings like a smouldering fire that burned,
     And might grow more or less,
   And might die out or wax to white excess.   140

Without, within me, music seemed to be;
   Something not music, yet most musical,
Silence and sound in heavenly harmony;
     At length a pattering fall
   Of feet, a bell, and bleatings, broke through all.   145

Then I looked up. The wood lay in a glow
    From golden sunset and from ruddy sky;
    The sun had stooped to earth though once so high;
      Had stooped to earth, in slow
150   Warm dying loveliness brought near and low.

Each water drop made answer to the light,
    Lit up a spark and showed the sun his face;
    Soft purple shadows paved the grassy space
      And crept from height to height,
155   From height to loftier height crept up apace.

While opposite the sun a gazing moon
    Put on his glory for her coronet,
Kindling her luminous coldness to its noon,
      As his great splendour set;
160   One only star made up her train as yet.

Each twig was tipped with gold, each leaf was edged
    And veined with gold from the gold-flooded west;
Each mother-bird, and mate-bird, and unfledged
      Nestling, and curious nest,
165   Displayed a gilded moss or beak or breast.

And filing peacefully between the trees,
    Having the moon behind them, and the sun
Full in their meek mild faces, walked at ease
      A homeward flock, at peace
170   With one another and with every one.

A patriarchal ram with tinkling bell
    Led all his kin; sometimes one browsing sheep
Hung back a moment, or one lamb would leap
      And frolic in a dell;
175   Yet still they kept together, journeying well,

And bleating, one or other, many or few,
  Journeying together toward the sunlit west;
  Mild face by face, and woolly breast by breast,
    Patient, sun-brightened too,
  Still journeying toward the sunset and their rest.   180

LATER LIFE: A DOUBLE SONNET
OF SONNETS.

1.

Before the mountains were brought forth, before
  Earth and the world were made, then God was God:
And God will still be God, when flames shall roar
  Round earth and heaven dissolving at His nod:
  And this God is our God, even while His rod   5
Of righteous wrath falls on us smiting sore:
And this God is our God for evermore
  Thro' life, thro' death, while clod returns to clod.
For tho' He slay us we will trust in Him;
  We will flock home to Him by divers ways: 10
  Yea, tho' He slay us we will vaunt His praise,
Serving and loving with the Cherubim,
Watching and loving with the Seraphim,
  Our very selves His praise thro' endless days.

2.

Rend hearts and rend not garments for our sins;
  Gird sackcloth not on body but on soul;
  Grovel in dust with faces toward the goal
Nor won, nor neared: he only laughs who wins.
Not neared the goal, the race too late begins;   5
  All left undone, we have yet to do the whole;
  The sun is hurrying west and toward the pole
Where darkness waits for earth with all her kins.
Let us today while it is called today
  Set out, if utmost speed may yet avail—   10
  The shadows lengthen and the light grows pale:

For who thro' darkness and the shadow of death,
Darkness that may be felt, shall find a way,
    Blind-eyed, deaf-eared, and choked with failing
      breath?

3.

Thou Who didst make and knowest whereof we are
    made,
  Oh bear in mind our dust and nothingness,
  Our wordless tearless dumbness of distress:
Bear Thou in mind the burden Thou hast laid
5 Upon us, and our feebleness unstayed
  Except Thou stay us: for the long long race
  Which stretches far and far before our face
Thou knowest,—remember Thou whereof we are made.
If making makes us Thine then Thine we are,
10 And if redemption we are twice Thine own:
If once Thou didst come down from heaven afar
    To seek us and to find us, how not save?
  Comfort us, save us, leave us not alone,
    Thou Who didst die our death and fill our grave.

4.

So tired am I, so weary of today,
  So unrefreshed from foregone weariness,
  So overburdened by foreseen distress,
So lagging and so stumbling on my way,
5 I scarce can rouse myself to watch or pray,
    To hope, or aim, or toil for more or less,—
    Ah, always less and less, even while I press
Forward and toil and aim as best I may.
Half-starved of soul and heartsick utterly,
10 Yet lift I up my heart and soul and eyes
  (Which fail in looking upward) toward the prize:
Me, Lord, Thou seest tho' I see not Thee;
  Me now, as once the Thief in Paradise,
Even me, O Lord my Lord, remember me.

5.

Lord, Thou Thyself art Love and only Thou;
   Yet I who am not love would fain love Thee;
   But Thou alone being Love canst furnish me
With that same love my heart is craving now.
Allow my plea! for if Thou disallow,   5
   No second fountain can I find but Thee;
   No second hope or help is left to me,
No second anything, but only Thou.
O Love accept, according my request;
   O Love exhaust, fulfilling my desire: 10
   Uphold me with the strength that cannot tire,
Nerve me to labour till Thou bid me rest,
   Kindle my fire from Thine unkindled fire,
And charm the willing heart from out my breast.

6.

We lack, yet cannot fix upon the lack:
   Not this, nor that; yet somewhat, certainly.
   We see the things we do not yearn to see
Around us: and what see we glancing back?
Lost hopes that leave our hearts upon the rack,   5
   Hopes that were never ours yet seemed to be,
   For which we steered on life's salt stormy sea
Braving the sunstroke and the frozen pack.
If thus to look behind is all in vain,
   And all in vain to look to left or right,   10
Why face we not our future once again,
Launching with hardier hearts across the main,
   Straining dim eyes to catch the invisible sight,
And strong to bear ourselves in patient pain?

7.

To love and to remember; that is good:
   To love and to forget; that is not well:
   To lapse from love to hatred; that is hell
And death and torment, rightly understood.

5   Soul dazed by love and sorrow, cheer thy mood;
      More blest art thou than mortal tongue can tell:
      Ring not thy funeral but thy marriage bell,
And salt with hope thy life's insipid food.
Love is the goal, love is the way we wend,
10   Love is our parallel unending line
      Whose only perfect Parallel is Christ,
Beginning not begun, End without end:
      For He Who hath the Heart of God sufficed,
      Can satisfy all hearts,—yea, thine and mine.

8.

We feel and see with different hearts and eyes:—
    Ah Christ, if all our hearts could meet in Thee
    How well it were for them and well for me,
Our hearts Thy dear accepted sacrifice.
5   Thou, only Life of hearts and Light of eyes,
    Our life, our light, if once we turn to Thee,
    So be it, O Lord, to them and so to me;
Be all alike Thine own dear sacrifice.
Thou Who by death hast ransomed us from death,
10   Thyself God's sole well-pleasing Sacrifice,
      Thine only sacred Self I plead with Thee:
      Make Thou it well for them and well for me
That Thou hast given us souls and wills and breath,
    And hearts to love Thee, and to see Thee eyes.

9.

Star Sirius and the Pole Star dwell afar
    Beyond the drawings each of other's strength:
    One blazes thro' the brief bright summer's length
Lavishing life-heat from a flaming car;
5   While one unchangeable upon a throne
    Broods o'er the frozen heart of earth alone,
Content to reign the bright particular star
    Of some who wander or of some who groan.
They own no drawings each of other's strength,
10   Nor vibrate in a visible sympathy,

   Nor veer along their courses each toward each:
     Yet are their orbits pitched in harmony
Of one dear heaven, across whose depth and length
     Mayhap they talk together without speech.

10.

Tread softly! all the earth is holy ground.
    It may be, could we look with seeing eyes,
    This spot we stand on is a Paradise
Where dead have come to life and lost been found,
Where Faith has triumphed, Martyrdom been
       crowned,   5
    Where fools have foiled the wisdom of the wise;
    From this same spot the dust of saints may rise,
And the King's prisoners come to light unbound.
O earth, earth, earth, hear thou thy Maker's Word:
    "Thy dead thou shalt give up, nor hide thy
       slain"—   10
    Some who went weeping forth shall come again
     Rejoicing from the east or from the west,
As doves fly to their windows, love's own bird
     Contented and desirous to the nest.*

11.

Lifelong our stumbles, lifelong our regret,
    Lifelong our efforts failing and renewed,
    While lifelong is our witness, "God is good:"
Who bore with us till now, bears with us yet,
Who still remembers and will not forget,   5
    Who gives us light and warmth and daily food;
    And gracious promises half understood,
And glories half unveiled, whereon to set
Our heart of hearts and eyes of our desire;
    Uplifting us to longing and to love,   10

     *"Quali colombe dal disio chiamate
     Con l'ali aperte e ferme al dolce nido
     Volan per l'aer dal voler portate."
                     DANTE.

Luring us upward from this world of mire,
   Urging us to press on and mount above
   Ourselves and all we have had experience of,
Mounting to Him in love's perpetual fire.

12.

A dream there is wherein we are fain to scream,
   While struggling with ourselves we cannot speak:
   And much of all our waking life, as weak
And misconceived, eludes us like the dream.
5 For half life's seemings are not what they seem,
   And vain the laughs we laugh, the shrieks we shriek;
   Yea, all is vain that mars the settled meek
Contented quiet of our daily theme.
When I was young I deemed that sweets are sweet:
10 But now I deem some searching bitters are
   Sweeter than sweets, and more refreshing far,
    And to be relished more, and more desired,
And more to be pursued on eager feet,
   On feet untired, and still on feet tho' tired.

13.

Shame is a shadow cast by sin: yet shame
   Itself may be a glory and a grace,
   Refashioning the sin-disfashioned face;
A nobler bruit than hollow-sounded fame,
5 A new-lit lustre on a tarnished name,
   One virtue pent within an evil place,
   Strength for the fight, and swiftness for the race,
A stinging salve, a life-requickening flame.
A salve so searching we may scarcely live,
10 A flame so fierce it seems that we must die,
   An actual cautery thrust into the heart:
   Nevertheless, men die not of such smart;
And shame gives back what nothing else can give,
   Man to himself,—then sets him up on high.

14.

When Adam and when Eve left Paradise
   Did they love on and cling together still,
   Forgiving one another all that ill
The twain had wrought on such a different wise?
She propped upon his strength, and he in guise   5
   Of lover tho' of lord, girt to fulfil
   Their term of life and die when God should will;
Lie down and sleep, and having slept arise.
Boast not against us, O our enemy!
   Today we fall, but we shall rise again;   10
We grope today, tomorrow we shall see:
      What is today that we should fear today?
      A morrow cometh which shall sweep away
Thee and thy realm of change and death and pain.

15.

Let woman fear to teach and bear to learn,
   Remembering the first woman's first mistake.
   Eve had for pupil the inquiring snake,
Whose doubts she answered on a great concern;
But he the tables so contrived to turn,   5
   It next was his to give and her's to take;
   Till man deemed poison sweet for her sweet sake,
And fired a train by which the world must burn.
Did Adam love his Eve from first to last?
   I think so; as we love who works us ill,   10
   And wounds us to the quick, yet loves us still.
Love pardons the unpardonable past:
Love in a dominant embrace holds fast
   His frailer self, and saves without her will.

16.

Our teachers teach that one and one make two:
   Later, Love rules that one and one make one:
   Abstruse the problems! neither need we shun,
But skilfully to each should yield its due.

5   The narrower total seems to suit the few,
      The wider total suits the common run;
      Each obvious in its sphere like moon or sun;
Both provable by me, and both by you.
Befogged and witless, in a wordy maze
10   A groping stroll perhaps may do us good;
      If cloyed we are with much we have understood,
If tired of half our dusty world and ways,
      If sick of fasting, and if sick of food;—
And how about these long still-lengthening days?

17.

Something this foggy day, a something which
      Is neither of this fog nor of today,
      Has set me dreaming of the winds that play
Past certain cliffs, along one certain beach,
5   And turn the topmost edge of waves to spray:
      Ah pleasant pebbly strand so far away,
So out of reach while quite within my reach,
      As out of reach as India or Cathay!
I am sick of where I am and where I am not,
10   I am sick of foresight and of memory,
      I am sick of all I have and all I see,
        I am sick of self, and there is nothing new;
Oh weary impatient patience of my lot!—
      Thus with myself: how fares it, Friends, with you?

18.

So late in Autumn half the world's asleep,
      And half the wakeful world looks pinched and pale;
      For dampness now, not freshness, rides the gale;
And cold and colourless comes ashore the deep
5   With tides that bluster or with tides that creep;
      Now veiled uncouthness wears an uncouth veil
      Of fog, not sultry haze; and blight and bale
Have done their worst, and leaves rot on the heap.
So late in Autumn one forgets the Spring,
10   Forgets the Summer with its opulence,

The callow birds that long have found a wing,
   The swallows that more lately gat them hence:
Will anything like Spring, will anything
   Like Summer, rouse one day the slumbering sense?

19.

Here now is Winter. Winter, after all,
   Is not so drear as was my boding dream
   While Autumn gleamed its latest watery gleam
On sapless leafage too inert to fall.
Still leaves and berries clothe my garden wall   5
   Where ivy thrives on scantiest sunny beam;
   Still here a bud and there a blossom seem
Hopeful, and robin still is musical.
Leaves, flowers and fruit and one delightful song
   Remain; these days are short, but now the nights   10
   Intense and long, hang out their utmost lights;
Such starry nights are long, yet not too long;
Frost nips the weak, while strengthening still the
        strong
   Against that day when Spring sets all to rights.

20.

A hundred thousand birds salute the day:—
   One solitary bird salutes the night:
Its mellow grieving wiles our grief away,
   And tunes our weary watches to delight;
It seems to sing the thoughts we cannot say,   5
   To know and sing them, and to set them right;
Until we feel once more that May is May,
   And hope some buds may bloom without a blight.
This solitary bird outweighs, outvies,
   The hundred thousand merry-making birds   10
Whose innocent warblings yet might make us wise
Would we but follow when they bid us rise,
   Would we but set their notes of praise to words
And launch our hearts up with them to the skies.

21.

A host of things I take on trust: I take
    The nightingales on trust, for few and far
    Between those actual summer moments are
When I have heard what melody they make.
So chanced it once at Como on the Lake:
    But all things, then, waxed musical; each star
    Sang on its course, each breeze sang on its car,
All harmonies sang to senses wide awake.
All things in tune, myself not out of tune,
    Those nightingales were nightingales indeed:
    Yet truly an owl had satisfied my need,
And wrought a rapture underneath that moon,
    Or simple sparrow chirping from a reed;
For June that night glowed like a doubled June.

22.

The mountains in their overwhelming might
    Moved me to sadness when I saw them first,
And afterwards they moved me to delight;
    Struck harmonies from silent chords which burst
    Out into song, a song by memory nursed;
For ever unrenewed by touch or sight
Sleeps the keen magic of each day or night,
    In pleasure and in wonder then immersed.
All Switzerland behind us on the ascent,
    All Italy before us we plunged down
        St. Gothard, garden of forget-me-not:
        Yet why should such a flower choose such a spot?
Could we forget that way which once we went
    Tho' not one flower had bloomed to weave its
        crown?

23.

Beyond the seas we know, stretch seas unknown
    Blue and bright-coloured for our dim and green;
    Beyond the lands we see, stretch lands unseen
With many-tinted tangle overgrown;

And icebound seas there are like seas of stone,   5
   Serenely stormless as death lies serene;
   And lifeless tracts of sand, which intervene
Betwixt the lands where living flowers are blown.
This dead and living world befits our case
   Who live and die: we live in wearied hope,   10
We die in hope not dead; we run a race
Today, and find no present halting-place;
   All things we see lie far within our scope,
And still we peer beyond with craving face.

24.

The wise do send their hearts before them to
   Dear blessed Heaven, despite the veil between;
   The foolish nurse their hearts within the screen
Of this familiar world, where all we do
Or have is old, for there is nothing new: 5
   Yet elder far that world we have not seen;
   God's Presence antedates what else hath been:
Many the foolish seem, the wise seem few.
Oh foolishest fond folly of a heart
   Divided, neither here nor there at rest!   10
     That hankers after Heaven, but clings to earth;
     That neither here nor there knows thorough
       mirth,
Half-choosing, wholly missing, the good part:—
   Oh fool among the foolish, in thy quest.

25.

When we consider what this life we lead
   Is not, and is: how full of toil and pain,
   How blank of rest and of substantial gain,
Beset by hunger earth can never feed,
And propping half our hearts upon a reed;   5
   We cease to mourn lost treasures, mourned in vain,
   Lost treasures we are fain and yet not fain
To fetch back for a solace of our need.
For who that feel this burden and this strain,

10   This wide vacuity of hope and heart,
     Would bring their cherished well-beloved again:
          To bleed with them and wince beneath the smart,
     To have with stinted bliss such lavish bane,
          To hold in lieu of all so poor a part?

26.

     This Life is full of numbness and of balk,
          Of haltingness and baffled short-coming,
          Of promise unfulfilled, of everything
     That is puffed vanity and empty talk:
5   Its very bud hangs cankered on the stalk,
          Its very song-bird trails a broken wing,
          Its very Spring is not indeed like Spring,
     But sighs like Autumn round an aimless walk.
     This Life we live is dead for all its breath;
10   Death's self it is, set off on pilgrimage,
               Travelling with tottering steps the first short stage:
                    The second stage is one mere desert dust
                    Where Death sits veiled amid creation's rust:—
     Unveil thy face, O Death who art not Death.

27.

     I have dreamed of Death:—what will it be to die
          Not in a dream, but in the literal truth
          With all Death's adjuncts ghastly and uncouth,
     The pang that is the last and the last sigh?
5   Too dulled, it may be, for a last good-bye,
          Too comfortless for any one to soothe,
          A helpless charmless spectacle of ruth
     Thro' long last hours, so long while yet they fly.
     So long to those who hopeless in their fear
10   Watch the slow breath and look for what they dread:
     While I supine with ears that cease to hear,
               With eyes that glaze, with heart pulse running down
          (Alas! no saint rejoicing on her bed),
               May miss the goal at last, may miss a crown.

28.

In life our absent friend is far away:
   But death may bring our friend exceeding near,
   Show him familiar faces long so dear
And lead him back in reach of words we say.
He only cannot utter yea or nay   5
   In any voice accustomed to our ear;
   He only cannot make his face appear
And turn the sun back on our shadowed day.
The dead may be around us, dear and dead;
   The unforgotten dearest dead may be   10
      Watching us with unslumbering eyes and heart;
Brimful of words which cannot yet be said,
    Brimful of knowledge they may not impart,
    Brimful of love for you and love for me.

"Judge nothing before the time."

Love understands the mystery, whereof
   We can but spell a surface history:
Love knows, remembers: let us trust in Love:
   Love understands the mystery.

   Love weighs the event, the long pre-history,   5
Measures the depth beneath, the height above,
   The mystery, with the ante-mystery.

To love and to be grieved befits a dove
   Silently telling her bead-history:
Trust all to Love, be patient and approve: 10
   Love understands the mystery.

Joy is but sorrow,
    While we know
It ends tomorrow:—
    Even so!
Joy with lifted veil
Shows a face as pale
As the fair changing moon so fair and frail.

Pain is but pleasure,
    If we know
It heaps up treasure:—
    Even so!
Turn, transfigured Pain,
Sweetheart, turn again,
For fair thou art as moonrise after rain.

"Redeeming the Time."

A life of hope deferred too often is
A life of wasted opportunities;
A life of perished hope too often is
A life of all-lost opportunities:
Yet hope is but the flower and not the root,
And hope is still the flower and not the fruit;—
Arise and sow and weed: a day shall come
When also thou shalt keep thy harvest home.

"Doeth well . . . doeth better."

My love whose heart is tender said to me,
    "A moon lacks light except her sun befriend her.
Let us keep tryst in heaven, dear Friend," said she,
    My love whose heart is tender.

From such a loftiness no words could bend her: 5
Yet still she spoke of "us" and spoke as "we,"
   Her hope substantial, while my hope grew slender.

Now keeps she tryst beyond earth's utmost sea,
   Wholly at rest, tho' storms should toss and rend her;
And still she keeps my heart and keeps its key,   10
   My love whose heart is tender.

A CASTLE-BUILDER'S WORLD.

"The line of confusion, and the stones of emptiness."

Unripe harvest there hath none to reap it
   From the misty gusty place,
Unripe vineyard there hath none to keep it
   In unprofitable space.
Living men and women are not found there,   5
   Only masks in flocks and shoals;
Flesh-and-bloodless hazy masks surround there,
   Ever wavering orbs and poles;
Flesh-and-bloodless vapid masks abound there,
   Shades of bodies without souls.   10

Piteous my rhyme is
What while I muse of love and pain,
Of love misspent, of love in vain,
Of love that is not loved again:
   And is this all then?   5
   As long as time is,
Love loveth. Time is but a span,
The dalliance space of dying man:
And is this all immortals can?
   The gain were small then.   10

Love loves for ever,
And finds a sort of joy in pain,
And gives with nought to take again,
And loves too well to end in vain:
15   Is the gain small then?
Love laughs at "never,"
Outlives our life, exceeds the span
Appointed to mere mortal man:
All which love is and does and can
20   Is all in all then.

If love is not worth loving, then life is not worth living,
    Nor aught is worth remembering but well forgot;
For store is not worth storing and gifts are not worth
        giving,
    If love is not;

5   And idly cold is death-cold, and life-heat idly hot,
And vain is any offering and vainer our receiving,
    And vanity of vanities is all our lot.
Better than life's heaving heart is death's heart
        unheaving,
    Better than the opening leaves are the leaves that rot,
10 For there is nothing left worth achieving or retrieving,
    If love is not.

Roses on a brier,
    Pearls from out the bitter sea,
Such is earth's desire
    However pure it be.

Neither bud nor brier,   5
   Neither pearl nor brine for me:
Be stilled, my long desire;
   There shall be no more sea.

Be stilled, my passionate heart;
   Old earth shall end, new earth shall be: 10
Be still, and earn thy part
   Where shall be no more sea.

"Called to be Saints."

The lowest place. Ah, Lord, how steep and high
   That lowest place whereon a saint shall sit!
Which of us halting, trembling, pressing nigh,
    Shall quite attain to it?

Yet, Lord, Thou pressest nigh to hail and grace   5
   Some happy soul, it may be still unfit
For Right Hand or for Left Hand, but whose place
    Waits there prepared for it.

Of each sad word which is more sorrowful,
   "Sorrow" or "Disappointment"? I have heard
Subtle inflections baffling subtlest rule,
   Of each sad word.

Sorrow can mourn: and lo! a mourning bird   5
Sings sweetly to sweet echoes of its dule,
   While silent disappointment broods unstirred.

Yet both nurse hope, where Penitence keeps school
　　Who makes fools wise and saints of them that erred:
10   Wise men shape stepping stone, or curb, or tool,
　　　Of each sad word.

　　　　Our heaven must be within ourselves,
　　　　　Our home and heaven the work of faith
　　　All thro' this race of life which shelves
　　　　　　Downward to death.

5　　　So faith shall build the boundary wall,
　　　　　And hope shall plant the secret bower,
　　　That both may show magnifical
　　　　　　With gem and flower.

　　　While over all a dome must spread,
10　　　And love shall be that dome above;
　　　And deep foundations must be laid,
　　　　　　And these are love.

"A HELPMEET FOR HIM."

Woman was made for man's delight;
　　Charm, O woman, be not afraid!
His shadow by day, his moon by night,
　　Woman was made.

5　　Her strength with weakness is overlaid;
　　　Meek compliances veil her might;
Him she stays, by whom she is stayed.

World-wide champion of truth and right,
　　Hope in gloom and in danger aid,
10　Tender and faithful, ruddy and white,
　　Woman was made.

O ye who love today,
Turn away
From Patience with her silver ray:
  For Patience shows a twilight face,
    Like a half-lighted moon   5
  When daylight dies apace.

But ye who love tomorrow
Beg or borrow
Today some bitterness of sorrow:
  For Patience shows a lustrous face,   10
    In depth of night her noon;
  Then to her sun gives place.

Lord, I am feeble and of mean account:
Thou Who dost condescend as well as mount,
  Stoop Thou Thyself to me
  And grant me grace to hear and grace to see.

Lord, if Thou grant me grace to hear and see   5
Thy very Self Who stoopest thus to me,
  I make but slight account
  Of aught beside wherein to sink or mount.

What is the beginning? Love. What the course? Love
  still.
What the goal? The goal is Love on the happy hill.
Is there nothing then but Love, search we sky or earth?
There is nothing out of Love hath perpetual worth:
All things flag but only Love, all things fail or flee;   5
There is nothing left but Love worthy you and me.

As froth on the face of the deep,
 As foam on the crest of the sea,
As dreams at the waking of sleep,
 As gourd of a day and a night,
As harvest that no man shall reap,
 As vintage that never shall be,
Is hope if it cling not aright,
 O my God, unto Thee.

Patience must dwell with Love, for Love and Sorrow
 Have pitched their tent together here:
Love all alone will build a house tomorrow,
 And sorrow not be near.

Today for Love's sake hope, still hope, in sorrow,
 Rest in her shade and hold her dear:
Today she nurses thee; and lo! tomorrow
 Love only will be near.

Hope is the counterpoise of fear
While night enthralls us here.

Fear hath a startled eye that holds a tear:
Hope hath an upward glance, for dawn draws near
With sunshine and with cheer.
Fear gazing earthwards spies a bier;
And sets herself to rear
A lamentable tomb where leaves drop sere,
Bleaching to congruous skeletons austere:
Hope chants a funeral hymn most sweet and clear,
And seems true chanticleer
Of resurrection and of all things dear
In the oncoming endless year.

Fear ballasts hope, hope buoys up fear,
And both befit us here.   15

"Subject to like Passions as we are."

Whoso hath anguish is not dead in sin,
    Whoso hath pangs of utterless desire.
    Like as in smouldering flax which harbours fire,—
Red heat of conflagration may begin,
Melt that hard heart, burn out the dross within,   5
    Permeate with glory the new man entire,
    Crown him with fire, mould for his hands a lyre
Of fiery strings to sound with those who win.
Anguish is anguish, yet potential bliss,
    Pangs of desire are birth-throes of delight;   10
    Those citizens felt such who walk in white,
And meet, but no more sunder, with a kiss;
Who fathom still unfathomed mysteries,
    And love, adore, rejoice, with all their might.

Experience bows a sweet contented face,
    Still setting to her seal that God is true:
    Beneath the sun, she knows, is nothing new;
All things that go return with measured pace,
Winds, rivers, man's still recommencing race:—   5
    While Hope beyond earth's circle strains her view,
    Past sun and moon, and rain and rainbow too,
Enamoured of unseen eternal grace.
Experience saith, "My God doth all things well:"
    And for the morrow taketh little care,   10
        Such peace and patience garrison her soul:—
        While Hope, who never yet hath eyed the goal,
    With arms flung forth, and backward floating hair,
Touches, embraces, hugs the invisible.

"Charity never Faileth."

Such is Love, it comforts in extremity,
   Tho' a tempest rage around and rage above,
Tempest beyond tempest, far as eye can see:
   Such is Love,

5   That it simply heeds its mourning inward Dove;
Dove which craves contented for a home to be
   Set amid the myrtles or an olive grove.

Dove-eyed Love contemplates the Twelve-fruited Tree,
   Marks the bowing palms which worship as they move;
10 Simply sayeth, simply prayeth, "All for me!"
   Such is Love.

Safe where I cannot lie yet,
   Safe where I hope to lie too,
Safe from the fume and the fret;
   You, and you,
5   Whom I never forget.

Safe from the frost and the snow,
   Safe from the storm and the sun,
Safe where the seeds wait to grow
   One by one
10 And to come back in blow.

How great is little man!
   Sun, moon, and stars respond to him,
   Shine or grow dim
Harmonious with his span.

How great is little man!   5
  More changeable that changeful moon,
  Nor half in tune
With Heaven's harmonious plan.

Ah, rich man! ah, poor man!
  Make ready for the testing day   10
  When wastes away
What bears not fire or fan.

Thou heir of all things, man,
  Pursue the saints by heavenward track:
  They looked not back;   15
Run thou, as erst they ran.

Little and great is man:
  Great if he will, or if he will
  A pigmy still;
For what he will he can.   20

"The Greatest of these is Charity."

A moon impoverished amid stars curtailed,
  A sun of its exuberant lustre shorn,
  A transient morning that is scarcely morn,
A lingering night in double dimness veiled.—
Our hands are slackened and our strength has failed: 5
  We born to darkness, wherefore were we born?
  No ripening more for olive, grape, or corn:
Faith faints, hope faints, even love himself has paled.
Nay! love lifts up a face like any rose
  Flushing and sweet above a thorny stem,   10
Softly protesting that the way he knows;
  And as for faith and hope, will carry them
  Safe to the gate of New Jerusalem,
Where light shines full and where the palm-tree blows.

"O Lucifer, Son of the Morning!"

Oh fallen star! a darkened light,
  A glory hurtled from its car,
Self-blasted from the holy height:
    Oh fallen star!

5   Fallen beyond earth's utmost bar,
Beyond return, beyond far sight
  Of outmost glimmering nebular.

Now blackness, which once walked in white;
  Now death, whose life once glowed afar;
10 Oh son of dawn that loved the night,
    Oh fallen star!

Time seems not short:
  If so I call to mind
  Its vast prerogative to loose or bind,
And bear and strike amort
5   All humankind.

Time seems not long:
  If I peer out and see
  Sphere within sphere, time in eternity,
And hear the alternate song
10 Cry endlessly.

Time greatly short,
  O time so briefly long,
  Yea, time sole battle-ground of right and wrong:
Art thou a time for sport
15 And for a song?

"Judge not according to the appearance."

Lord, purge our eyes to see
Within the seed a tree,
  Within the glowing egg a bird,
    Within the shroud a butterfly:

Till taught by such, we see   5
Beyond all creatures Thee,
  And hearken for Thy tender word,
    And hear it, "Fear not: it is I."

ST. PETER.

"Launch out into the deep," Christ spake of old
  To Peter: and he launched into the deep;
  Strengthened should tempest wake which lay
        asleep,
Strengthened to suffer heat or suffer cold.
Thus, in Christ's Prescience: patient to behold   5
  A fall, a rise, a scaling Heaven's high steep;
  Prescience of Love, which deigned to overleap
The mire of human errors manifold.
Lord, Lover of Thy Peter, and of him
  Beloved with craving of a humbled heart   10
    Which eighteen hundred years have satisfied;
Hath he his throne among Thy Seraphim
  Who love? or sits he on a throne apart,
    Unique, near Thee, to love Thee human-eyed?

"Sit down in the lowest room."

Lord, give me grace
To take the lowest place;
Nor even desire,
Unless it be Thy Will, to go up higher.
Except by grace,
I fail of lowest place;
Except desire
Sit low, it aims awry to go up higher.

"Consider the Lilies of the field."

Solomon most glorious in array
    Put not on his glories without care:—
Clothe us as Thy lilies of a day,
    As the lilies Thou accountest fair,
      Lilies of Thy making,
      Of Thy love partaking,
    Filling with free fragrance earth and air:
    Thou Who gatherest lilies, gather us and wear.

Our Mothers, lovely women pitiful;
    Our Sisters, gracious in their life and death;
    To us each unforgotten memory saith:
"Learn as we learned in life's sufficient school,
Work as we worked in patience of our rule,
    Walk as we walked, much less by sight than faith,
    Hope as we hoped, despite our slips and scathe,
Fearful in joy and confident in dule."
I know not if they see us or can see;
    But if they see us in our painful day,

How looking back to earth from Paradise
　　Do tears not gather in those loving eyes?—
Ah, happy eyes! whose tears are wiped away
Whether or not you bear to look on me.

Babylon the Great.

Foul is she and ill-favoured, set askew:
　　Gaze not upon her till thou dream her fair,
　　Lest she should mesh thee in her wanton hair,
Adept in arts grown old yet ever new.
Her heart lusts not for love, but thro' and thro' 　　　5
　　For blood, as spotted panther lusts in lair;
　　No wine is in her cup, but filth is there
Unutterable, with plagues hid out of view.
Gaze not upon her, for her dancing whirl
　　Turns giddy the fixed gazer presently: 　　　　10
　　Gaze not upon her, lest thou be as she
　　　When, at the far end of her long desire,
Her scarlet vest and gold and gem and pearl
　　And she amid her pomp are set on fire.

"Do this, and he doeth it."

Content to come, content to go,
　　Content to wrestle or to race,
Content to know or not to know,
　　　Each in his place;

Lord, grant us grace to love Thee so 　　　　5
　　That glad of heart and glad of face
At last we may sit, high or low,
　　　Each in his place;

Where pleasures flow as rivers flow,
10   And loss has left no barren trace,
And all that are, are perfect so,
          Each in his place.

"Standing afar off for the fear of her torment."

Is this the end? is there no end but this?
     Yea, none beside:
     No other end for pride
And foulness and besottedness.

5   Hath she no friend? hath she no clinging friend?
     Nay, none at all;
     Who stare upon her fall
Quake for themselves with hair on end.

Will she be done away? vanish away?
10   Yea, like a dream;
     Yea, like the shades that seem
Somewhat, and lo! are nought by day.

Alas for her amid man's helpless moan,
     Alas for her!
15   She hath no comforter:
In solitude of fire she sits alone.

VIGIL OF ST. BARTHOLOMEW.

Lord, to Thine own grant watchful hearts and eyes;
     Hearts strung to prayer, awake while eyelids sleep;
     Eyes patient till the end to watch and weep.
So will sleep nourish power to wake and rise
5   With Virgins who keep vigil and are wise,
     To sow among all sowers who shall reap,
     From out man's deep to call Thy vaster deep,
And tread the uphill track to Paradise.

Sweet souls! so patient that they make no moan,
  So calm on journey that they seem at rest,   10
    So rapt in prayer that half they dwell in heaven
    Thankful for all withheld and all things given;
  So lit by love that Christ shines manifest
Transfiguring their aspects to His own.

"Who hath despised the day of small things?"

  As violets so be I recluse and sweet,
    Cheerful as daisies unaccounted rare,
  Still sunward-gazing from a lowly seat,
    Still sweetening wintry air.

  While half-awakened Spring lags incomplete,   5
    While lofty forest trees tower bleak and bare,
  Daisies and violets own remotest heat
    And bloom and make them fair.

Tune me, O Lord, into one harmony
  With Thee, one full responsive vibrant chord;
Unto Thy praise all love and melody,
  Tune me, O Lord.

  Thus need I flee nor death, nor fire, nor sword: 5
A little while these be, then cease to be,
  And sent by Thee not these should be abhorred.

Devil and world, gird me with strength to flee,
  To flee the flesh, and arm me with Thy word:
As Thy Heart is to my heart, unto Thee   10
  Tune me, O Lord.

Notes

In the notes to each poem, the first date given is the poem's composition date, while the second date provided is the date of its first publication in a poetry volume (see the list of editions of Rossetti's works overleaf). The phrase 'First poetry volume', together with a date, is used only if the poem first appeared elsewhere, such as in a journal or magazine. Where no composition date is available, I have given the date of first publication only. For poems which originally appeared in contemporary magazines or in Rossetti's prose-works, the dates of their first publication in a poetry volume are also provided. 'Unpublished', given after a poem's composition date, indicates that the poem remained unpublished until Crump's edition (*The Complete Poems of Christina Rossetti*, Louisiana State University Press, 1979–90).

Following the precedent set by the Betty S. Flowers *Complete Poems*, my notes include William Michael Rossetti's own 'Notes' to his sister's *Poetical Works*. In response to her introduction's call for greater attention to Rossetti's relationship to the Authorized Version of the Bible, I have given special attention to biblical allusions.

Attention has also been given to the ways in which Rossetti uses both the primary and the secondary meanings of the Victorian popular language of flowers. Sources were *The Language of Flowers: An Alphabet of Floral Emblems* (T. Nelson and Sons, 1857) and Henry Phillips, *Floral Emblems* (Saunders and Otley, 1825).

I have depended heavily on the work of Crump, Flowers and on Jan Marsh's biography of Rossetti, and cannot recommend their work highly enough to students and admirers of Christina Rossetti.

ABBREVIATIONS

Rossetti Siblings

CR   Christina Rossetti
DGR   Dante Gabriel Rossetti
MFR   Maria Francesca Rossetti
WMR   William Michael Rossetti

Frequently Mentioned Works

CR   Jan Marsh, *Christina Rossetti: A Literary Biography* (Jonathan Cape, 1994)
FD   *The Face of the Deep: A Devotional Commentary on the Apocalypse* (Society for Promoting Christian Knowledge, 1892 – SPCK hereafter)
Flowers   Betty Flowers, *Christina Rossetti: The Complete Poems* (Penguin, 2001)
Letters   *The Letters of Christina Rossetti*, ed. Antony H. Harrison, 4 vols. (University Press of Virginia, 1997–2004)
'Memoir' WMR's 'Memoir' from *The Poetical Works of Christina Georgina Rossetti* (Macmillan, 1904), pp. xlv–lxxi
'Notes'   WMR's notes on CR's poems from *The Poetical Works*, pp. 459–94
TF   *Time Flies: A Reading Diary* (SPCK, 1885)

Editions of Rossetti's Works

1847 *Verses: Dedicated to her Mother* (privately printed by Gaetano Polidori)
1862 *Goblin Market and Other Poems* (Macmillan)
1866 *The Prince's Progress and Other Poems* (Macmillan)
1870 *Commonplace, and Other Short Stories* (F. S. Ellis)
1872 *Sing-Song: A Nursery Rhyme Book* (Routledge)
1874 *Annus Domini: A Prayer for Each Day of the Year, Founded on a Text of Holy Scripture* (James Parker and Co.)
1875 *Goblin Market, The Prince's Progress, and Other Poems* (Macmillan)
1881 *A Pageant and Other Poems* (Macmillan)
1881 *Called to be Saints: The Minor Festivals Devotionally Studied* (SPCK)

1885 *Time Flies: A Reading Diary* (SPCK)
1892 *The Face of the Deep: A Devotional Commentary on the Apoca-lypse* (SPCK)
1893 *Verses. Reprinted from "Called to be Saints," "Time Flies," "The Face of the Deep"* (SPCK)
1896 *New Poems, Hitherto Unpublished or Uncollected*, ed. WMR (Macmillan)
1897 *Maude: A Story for Girls* (James Bowdon)
1904 *The Poetical Works of Christina Georgina Rossetti, with Memoir and Notes by William Michael Rossetti* (Macmillan)

On Albina

Composed June 1844. First published 1896.

4.   *painted* applied make-up.

Forget Me Not

Composed 19 August 1844. First published 1896.

Charade

Composed 3 December 1845. Unpublished. The solution to this poem's 'charade' is 'a sonnet'.

Hope in Grief

Composed 3 December 1845. Unpublished.

14.   *pall* a cloth used to drape a coffin, bier or tomb.
19–21. *Say not, vain . . . its toil* 'Vanity of vanities, saith the Preacher, vanity of vanities; all is vanity' (Ecclesiastes 1:2).

On the Death of a Cat

Composed 14 March 1846. First published 1896. According to WMR, 'This cat belonged to our aunt, Eliza Harriet Polidori' ('Notes' 465). CR was very close to her Aunt Eliza, a formidable woman who won a Turkish medal for her service as a Nightingale Nurse in Scutari during the Crimean War. Eliza, who died at the age of eighty-three, survived all her siblings, including CR's mother, Frances.

14. *Grimalkin* a faery cat in Scottish legend, its name (from 'grey', the colour, and *malkin*, an old word for 'cat') became associated with witches' cats in the Middle Ages; it is also the name of the Witches' cat in William Shakespeare's *Macbeth*.

21. *reft* broken or torn apart, plundered (from *reave*, to break or tear apart, take away by force).

Sappho

Composed 11 September 1846. First published 1847.

Title. Sappho was a seventh-century Greek poet whose work survives only in fragments yet has an ongoing influence on Western poetry. Famous nowadays for her bisexuality, Sappho was most noted in CR's time for her dramatic suicide: she plunged from a cliff to her death for unrequited love.

5–6. *Oh! It were better ... mourn and sigh* see ll. 55–6 of John Keats's 'Ode to a Nightingale' (1819): 'Now more than ever seems it rich to die / To cease upon the midnight with no pain'.

13–14. *Living unloved ... untended and alone* see ll. 11–12 of Alfred Lord Tennyson's 'Mariana in the South' (1833): 'And "Ah," she sang, "to be all alone, / To live forgotten, and love forlorn." '

Heart's Chill Between

Composed 22 September 1847. First published in *The Athenaeum* 1095 (21 October 1848), 1056. First poetry volume 1904. WMR writes that the poem's original title was 'The Last Hope' and that it 'was the first poem by Christina that got published'. Yet he thought 'it ought to have been better than it is, and was hardly good enough for re-publication'. WMR ultimately included it in his volume because Mackenzie Bell's biography of CR had revived interest in the poem ('Notes' 467).

8. *restive* restless.

38. *stupified* dazed, with senses dulled.

Death's Chill Between

Composed 29 September 1847. First published in *The Athenaeum* 1094 (14 October 1848), 1032. First poetry volume 1904. WMR writes that this poem's title 'was originally *Anne of Warwick*, and was intended to represent (in a rather "young-ladyish" form) the dolorous emotions and flitting frenzy of Anne, when widowed of her youthful husband, the Prince of Wales'. He further notes that 'this poem was offered to *The Athenaeum* at the same time as *Heart's Chill Between*; and my brother [DGR] then substituted these titles for the original ones' ('Notes' 467).

Lines / given with a Penwiper

Composed 20 November 1847. Unpublished. Jan Marsh notes that this poem is about Rossetti's father, whose declining health meant that Christina had to care for him at home (*CR* 78).

3.   *Brussels web* a type of rug.

A Pause of Thought

Composed 14 February 1848. First published in *The Germ* 2 (February 1850), 57. First poetry volume 1862.

2.   *hope deferred made my heart sick* 'Hope deferred maketh the heart sick: but when the desire cometh, it is a tree of life' (Proverbs 13:12).

Song ['*She sat and sang alway*']

Composed 26 November 1848. First published 1862. See Emily Dickinson's 'I died for beauty, but was scarce' (1862).

Song ['*When I am dead, my dearest*']

Composed 12 December 1848. First published 1862. WMR writes that this poem 'has been oftener quoted, and certainly oftener set to music, than anything else by Christina Rossetti' ('Notes' 477–8).

3.   *roses at my head* a crown of roses signifies a reward of virtue.
4.   *cypress* emblem of death, mourning, despair.
11.   *nightingale* see John Keats's 'Ode to a Nightingale' (1819).

Some ladies dress in muslin full and white

Composed between 1848 and 1849. First published 1896. Written during the Rossetti siblings' *bouts-rimés* sonnet competitions (see the Introduction). Also included in *Maude: A Story for Girls* (1897). Both story and poem remained unpublished during CR's lifetime.

Title. 'Vanity Fair' was added by WMR as the title in *New Poems* (1896).

3.   *dog-cart* a two-wheeled vehicle drawn by one horse; *hack* a hackney coach for hire.

4.   *clarence* a closed, four-wheeled carriage.

14. *Bason* (or *basin*) reservoir. In *Maude*, a character explains that 'everyone will understand the Bason to mean the one in St James's Park' (p. 23). The basin was built to provide water for St James's Palace in the eighteenth century, on the orders of Queen Caroline, wife of George II.

On Keats

Composed 18 January 1849. First published 1896. CR wrote this poem on St Agnes's Eve to commemorate John Keats's poem 'The Eve of St Agnes' (1820).

3.   *strong man grown weary of a race* 'Which is as a bridegroom coming out of his chamber, and rejoiceth as a strong man to run a race' (Psalms 19:5).

4–5. *Unto him a goodly lot ... there thorns are not* This refers to Christ's parable of the sower, which appears in different versions in Matthew 13, Mark 4 and Luke 8. In this parable, a sower plants seeds, some of which do not grow because they 'fell by the way side', 'upon a rock', 'among thorns', while others 'fell on good ground, and sprang up, and bare fruit an hundredfold' (Luke 8:5, 6, 7, 8). The seeds which fall on thorny ground represent the rejection of God's word, while those which fall on good ground represent 'they, which in an honest and good heart, having heard the word, keep it, and bring forth fruit with patience' (Luke 8:15). This parable of conversion is an odd choice here, as Keats was not religious, neither personally nor as a poet.

6.   *daisies* emblems of innocence. Daisies feature frequently in Keats's poems.

10–11. *Here lies one whose name was writ / In water* Keats's epi-
taph.
12. *basil* alludes to Keats's 'Isabella and the Pot of Basil' (1820).

Song ['*Oh roses for the flush of youth*']

Composed 6 February 1849. First published 1862. The manuscript
version begins with two additional stanzas describing the death of a
young girl. The original title of the poem was 'A Song in a Song'.

1. *roses* emblems of love and beauty; here also with their secondary
meaning of pride and danger.
2. *laurel* associated with Apollo, and, along with bay (l. 6), sym-
bolizes poetic glory.
3. *ivy* emblem of faith and tenacity.
5. *violets* emblems of innocence and modesty.
6. *bay* signifies (poetic) glory.
7. *withered leaves* symbolize melancholy, here possibly book
leaves.

Have you forgotten?

Composed 7 February 1849. Unpublished.

Sweet Death

Composed 9 February 1849. First published in *The Germ* 2 (March
1850), 177. First poetry volume 1862.

16. *grass* emblem of utility, submission. Biblical symbol of mortality.
24. *glean with Ruth* the widowed Ruth marries Boaz after he sees
her gleaning (gathering or collecting what was left by the
reapers) in his cornfield. Their union begins the earthly lineage
of Christ (Ruth 2–3). See also ll. 65–7 of John Keats's 'Ode to a
Nightingale' (1819): 'Perhaps the self-same song that found a
path / Through the sad heart of Ruth, when, sick for home, / She
stood in tears amid the alien corn'.

An End

Composed 5 March 1849. First published in *The Germ* 1 (January
1850), 48. First poetry volume 1862.

1.   *Love, strong as Death* 'Set me as a seal upon thine heart, as a seal upon thine arm: for love is strong as death; jealousy is cruel as the grave: the coals thereof are coals of fire, which hath a most vehement flame' (Song of Solomon 8:6).

Dream-Land

Composed April 1849. First published in *The Germ* 1 (January 1850), 20.

Title. See S. T. Coleridge's 'Kubla Khan, or, A Vision in a Dream, a Fragment' (1816).

5.   *Led by a single star* in Matthew 2:9–12, the wise men are led by a star to the newly born Christ child.

10. *corn* signifies riches.

15–16. *And hears the nightingale / That sadly sings* see John Keats's 'Ode to a Nightingale' (1819).

Remember

Composed 25 July 1849. First published 1862.

Three Nuns

Part 2 composed 12 February 1849; parts 1 and 3 composed 10 May 1850. First published 1896. English translations of the Italian epigraphs are all from WMR ('Notes' 460).

I

Epigraph. 'This heart sighs, and I know not wherefore.'

3.   *pall* see note for l. 14 of 'Hope in Grief'.

17. *vesper bell* calls worshippers to evening church service.

18. CR's footnote refers to l. 8 ('Sweetest eyes were ever seen') of Elizabeth Barrett Browning's 'Catarina to Camoens' (1838), a poem written in the voice of Catarina de Ataíde, lover and muse of the Portuguese poet Luis Vas de Camões (1524–80), who died while Camões was away in Africa.

39. *matins* morning church service; also called 'Morning Prayers'.

46. *clematis* represent mental beauty.

47. *hyacinths* symbolize sport, play.

56. *water-lilies* signify silence.

60. *lilies* symbolize purity.

2

Epigraph. 'It may be sighing for love, but to me it says not so.'

69.   *Throw the first stone* 'So when they continued asking him, he lifted up himself, and said unto them, He that is without sin among you, let him first cast a stone at her' (John 8:7); *Pharisee* a self-righteous or hypocritical person (originally a member of a strictly religious ancient Jewish sect).

88.   *sweet is death* see l. 12 of 'Sweet Death': 'Sweet life, but sweeter death that passeth by'.

96.   *cordial* in this case, of or pertaining to the heart.

99.   *exceeding great reward* 'After these things the word of the Lord came unto Abram in a vision, saying, Fear not, Abram: I am thy shield, and thy exceeding great reward' (Genesis 15:1).

101.   *palm* emblem of victory.

122.   *Faithful is He Who promiseth* 'Let us hold fast the profession of our faith without wavering; (for he is faithful that promised)' (Hebrews 10:23).

3

Epigraph. 'Answer me, my heart, wherefore sighest thou? It answers: I want God – I sigh for Jesus.'

124.   *My heart is as a freeborn bird* see l. 1 of 'A Birthday': 'My heart is like a singing bird'.

138.   *True Vine* 'I am the true vine, and my Father is the husbandman' (John 15:1).

140.   *Tree of Life* the tree of life grew in the Garden of Eden: 'And out of the ground made the Lord God to grow every tree that is pleasant to the sight, and good for food: the tree of life also in the midst of the garden, and the tree of knowledge of good and evil' (Genesis 2:9); 'In the midst of the street of it, and on either side of the river, was there the tree of life, which bare twelve manner of fruits, and yielded her fruit every month: and the leaves of the tree were for the healing of the nations' (Revelation 22:2). See also note for l. 2 of 'A Pause of Thought'.

142.   *Growing beside the Living Well* from John 14:11–15, where Jesus says that a man who drinks water from an earthly well will be thirsty again, but a man who drinks 'the water that I shall give him shall never thirst, and that there will be in him a well of water springing up into everlasting life'.

147.   *the Shadow of the Rock* 'And a man shall be as an hiding place from the wind, and a covert from the tempest; as rivers of water

in a dry place, as the shadow of a great rock in a weary land'
(Isaiah 32:2).

161. *City builded without hands* 'For we know that if our earthly
house of this tabernacle were dissolved, we have a building of
God, an house not made with hands, eternal in the heavens'
(2 Corinthians 5:1).

163. *the rest is but vanity* see ll. 19–21 of 'Hope in Grief'. 'Say not
. . . fears are vain'.

170. *Red roses* represent love.

177. *New Jerusalem* 'Him that overcometh will I make a pillar in the
temple of my God, and he shall go no more out: and I will write
upon him the name of my God, and the name of the city of my
God, which is new Jerusalem, which cometh down out of heaven
from my God: and I will write upon him my new name' (Revela-
tion 3:12). See also Revelation 21:2 and the note for l. 37 of
' "They Desire a Better Country" '.

204. *Hope deferred seems to numb* see l. 2 of 'A Pause of Thought':
'And hope deferred made my heart sick in truth'.

207. *"The Spirit and the Bride say, Come"* 'And the Spirit and the
bride say, Come. And let him that heareth say, Come. And let
him that is athirst come. And whosoever will, let him take the
water of life freely' (Revelation 22:17).

Portraits

Composed 9 May 1853. First published 1896. WMR writes that the
first stanza is about him and the second portrays himself and DGR.
He reveals that 'There used to be a second stanza characterizing *him*
[DGR]; it is torn out (by his rather arbitrary hand, beyond a doubt).'
He adds: 'A laudatory phrase or two regarding myself ought possibly
to have induced me to exclude the verse, but I cannot make up my
mind to do that' ('Notes' 491).

'Consider the Lilies of the Field'
['Flowers preach to us if we will hear']

Composed 21 October 1853. First published 1862. See also ' "Con-
sider the Lilies of the field" ' ('Solomon, most glorious in array') and
'Consider'.

Title. Christ's parable of the lilies is a recurring theme of CR's poetry.
'And why take ye thought for raiment? Consider the lilies of the

field, how they grow; they toil not, neither do they spin: And yet I say unto you, That even Solomon in all his glory was not arrayed like one of these' (Matthew 6:28-9). See also Luke 12:27.

2. *rose* see note for l. 1 of 'Song' ('Oh roses for the flush of youth').

6. *The poppy saith amid the corn* poppies in general are emblems of evanescent pleasure, but scarlet poppies specifically signify fantastic extravagance, and red poppies consolation. For corn, see note for l. 10 of 'Dream-Land'.

11. *lilies* see note for l. 60 of 'Three Nuns'.

13. *violets* see note for l. 5 of 'Song' ('Oh roses for the flush of youth').

19. *grass* see note for l. 16 of 'Sweet Death'.

21. *Lichen and moss* lichen symbolizes dejection and solitude, while moss is both an emblem of a recluse and of maternal love.

The P.R.B.

Composed 10 November 1853. First published in WMR's *Dante Gabriel Rossetti: His Family-Letters With A Memoir*, 2 vols. (Ellis and Elvey, 1895), vol. I, p. 138. First poetry volume 1904.

Title. The Pre-Raphaelite Brotherhood. Everyone mentioned in the poem was a member.

2. *Woolner in Australia* sculptor Thomas Woolner (1825-92) moved briefly to Australia to search for gold.

3. *Hunt . . . Cheops* the painter Holman Hunt (1827-1910) was preparing for a painting trip to Egypt (home to Cheops, the pharaoh believed to have built the Great Pyramid of Giza) and Palestine.

4. *shuns the vulgar optic* DGR, stung by bad reviews of his work, was refusing to exhibit publicly.

5-6. *William M. Rossetti . . . Coptic* 'It means that I, as art-critic of *The Spectator*, abused in that paper my fellows in the Præ-raphaelite Brotherhood, and that no one heeded my reviews. This joke was not historically true . . .' ('Notes' 491). Coptic was the extinct, liturgical language of the Coptic Church.

7. *Stephens* F. G. Stephens (1828-1907), an art critic 'who had scarcely come forward as an exhibiting artist at all' ('Notes' 491).

9. *Millais* the painter John Everett Millais (1829-96).

11. *A.R.A.* Millais was made an Associate of the Royal Academy of Art.

The Bourne

Composed 17 February 1854. First published in *Macmillan's Magazine* 7 (March 1863), 382. First poetry volume 1866.

Title. Commonly a small stream or brook, but also an archaic word meaning a boundary or limit.

The World

Composed 27 June 1854. First published 1862. WMR writes that CR had 'a horror of "the world" in the sense which that term bears in the New Testament; its power to blur all the great traits of character, to dead all lofty aims, to clog all the impulses of the soul aspiring to unseen Truth' ('Notes' 470). See also John Keats's 'La Belle Dame Sans Merci' (1820) for a similar changeling creature who enthrals and dooms the unwary.

4.   *subtle serpents gliding in her hair* allusion to the snake-haired gorgon Medusa whose looks turn men to stone.
14. *Till my feet, cloven too, take hold on hell?* 'For the lips of a strange woman drop as an honeycomb, and her mouth is smoother than oil: but her end is bitter as wormwood, sharp as a two-edged sword. Her feet go down to death; her steps take hold on hell' (Proverbs 5:3–5). CR discusses this proverb in *FD* 401.

From the Antique

Composed 28 June 1854. Unpublished.

Title. In art, the practice of drawing plaster casts made from classical figurative sculpture in order to learn anatomy.

1.   *It's a weary life* see the refrain of Alfred Lord Tennyson's 'Mariana' (1830): 'She said, "I am aweary, aweary, / I would that I were dead!"'
9.   *wag* to go along, proceed.

Three Stages

Composed in 'three stages', from 1848 to 1854. First published as a whole by WMR in 1904.

I

Composed 14 February 1848. First published as 'A Pause of Thought' in *The Germ* 2 (February 1850), 57. See notes for 'A Pause of Thought'.

2

Composed 18 April 1849. First published as 'The End of the First Part', 1896.

9.   *I must pull down my palace that I built* see l. 293 of Alfred Lord Tennyson's 'The Palace of Art' (1832): 'Yet pull not down my palace towers . . .'.
26. *sweet-briar* an emblem of poetry; *thyme* symbolizes activity.

3

Composed 25 July 1854. Lines 9–12 were published in 1893 as part of the poem 'Heaven's chimes are slow, but sure to strike at last'.

3.   *fret* cause corrosion.
7.   *poppied wheat* wheat represents prosperity; for poppies, see note for l. 6 of ' "Consider the Lilies of the Field" ' ('Flowers preach to us if we will hear').
10. *This sand is slow, but surely droppeth thro'* refers to an hourglass.
16. *counterpoise* an equal or counterbalancing weight.
31–40. *Alas, I cannot build . . . What once I gave, again* see sonnet 14 of 'Monna Innominata'.

Echo

Composed 18 December 1854. First published 1862.

My Dream

Composed 9 March 1855. First published 1862.

15. *waxed* grew in size.
16. *girdle* a belt or sash worn around the waist.
48. *appropriate tears* 'crocodile' tears.
49–50. *What can it mean? . . . myself must echo, What?* see ll. 33–4 of 'Winter: My Secret': 'Perhaps my secret I may say, / or you may guess.'

May

Composed 20 November 1855. First published 1862.

5. *poppies* see note for l. 6 of ' "Consider the Lilies of the Field" '
   ('Flowers preach to us if we will hear').
6. *corn* see note for l. 10 of 'Dream-Land'.

Shut Out

Composed 21 January 1856. Published 1862. WMR tells us that the
manuscript poem 'bears the too significant title, *What happened to
Me*' ('Notes' 480).

4. *pied* having sections or patches of different colours.
25. *violet* see note for l. 5 of 'Song' ('Oh roses for the flush of youth').

Amen

Composed 20 April 1856. First published 1862.

5. *wheat* see note for l. 5, stanza 3 of 'Three Stages'.
6. *It is finished* 'When Jesus therefore had received the vinegar, he
   said, It is finished: and he bowed his head, and gave up the ghost'
   (John 19:30).
9. *fallow field left unsown* 'For thus saith the Lord to the men of
   Judah and Jerusalem, Break up your fallow ground, and sow not
   among thorns' (Jeremiah 4:3).
14. *Roses* see note for l. 1 of 'Song' ('Oh roses for the flush of youth');
    bramble signifies lowliness, envy, remorse.

The Hour and the Ghost

Composed 11 September 1856. First published 1862.

The Lowest Room

Composed 30 September 1856. First published in *Macmillan's Maga-
zine* 9 (March 1864), 436–9. First poetry volume 1875. WMR tells
us that DGR accused the poem of having 'a modern vicious style' and
a 'falsetto muscularity', similar to that of Elizabeth Barrett Browning.
WMR disagrees. The original title was 'A Fight Over the Body of
Homer' ('Notes' 460).

Title. Refers to Christ's parable of the lowest room, which advises his followers to show humility by voluntary taking the 'lowest place' so that they can be invited to 'go up higher'. The aspiration to the 'lowest place' is a frequent theme of CR's poetry and prose. See Luke 14:7–14. See also 'The Lowest Place' and ' "Sit down in the lowest room" '.

22. *Hector* Trojan prince.

23. *Aeacides* a family name referring to descendants of Aeacus, a son of Zeus and grandfather of Achilles and Ajax.

24. *Homer* Greek poet, author of the *Iliad* and the *Odyssey*.

31. *Ajax* Greek warrior who never receives help from the gods. His *red right hand* is possibly an allusion to John Milton's *Paradise Lost* II.173–4: 'Should intermitted vengeance arm again / His red right hand to plague us?'

32. *Juno* Roman queen of the gods, wife of Jupiter, associated with Greek goddess Hera.

36. *dross* worthless, commonplace or trivial matter, waste.

77. *dim Dian's face* Diana, Roman goddess of the moon.

111. *Sevenfold Sacred Fire* 'Moreover the light of the moon shall be as the light of the sun, and the light of the sun shall be sevenfold, as the light of seven days, in the day that the Lord bindeth up the breach of his people, and healeth the stroke of their wound' (Isaiah 30:26).

117. *Our life is given us as a blank* see l. 2 of 'From the Antique': 'Doubly blank is a woman's lot'.

124. *Diomed* Greek hero of Trojan war.

127. *Achilles in his rage* greatest warrior of the *Iliad*, the only mortal to experience all-consuming rage (*menis*).

132. *Ilion* site of the Trojan War.

133–7. *He offered . . . to his friend* refer to Achilles' vengeful desire at the death of his friend Patroclus.

135. *Trojans* citizens of Troy, seized by the Greeks.

144. *swart* dark.

174. *The wisest man* Solomon (presumed to be the writer of Ecclesiastes).

176. *Vanity of vanities* see note for ll. 19–21 of 'Hope in Grief'.

187. *As the sea is not filled* 'All the rivers run into the sea; yet the sea is not full; unto the place from whence the rivers come, thither they return again' (Ecclesiastes 1:7).

191. *Jove* Jupiter, chief Roman god, husband of Juno.

200. *Greater than Solomon* refers to Christ. See Matthew 12:42 and Luke 11:31.

215. *rose* see note for l. 1 of 'Song' ('Oh roses for the flush of youth').

216. *blossom of the peach* signifies 'I am your captive'.

275. *I lift mine eyes up to the hills* 'I will lift mine eyes unto the hills, from whence cometh my help' (Psalms 121:1).

280. *And many last be first* 'But many who are first will be last, and many who are last will be first' (Matthew 19:30). See also Matthew 20:16, Mark 9:35, 10:31 and Luke 13:30.

A Triad

Composed 18 December 1856. First published 1862. WMR writes: 'This very fine sonnet was published in the volume of 1862 ... bnt [*sic*] was omitted in subsequent issues. I presume that my sister, with over-strained scrupulosity, considered its moral tone to be somewhat open to exception' ('Notes' 480).

5.   *hyacinth* see note for l. 47 of 'Three Nuns'.

Love from the North

Composed 19 December 1856. First published 1862.

25-6. *He bore me . . . horse away* see ll. 21-2 of Keats's 'La Belle Dame Sans Merci' (1820): 'I set her on my pacing steed / And nothing else saw all day long'.

29.   *He made me fast with bell and book* the meaning of this line is enigmatic but could perhaps refer to a ritual of excommunication (as in the phrase 'bell, book and candle') or a binding spell.

In an Artist's Studio

Composed 24 December 1856. First published 1896. WMR writes: 'The reference is apparently to our brother's [DGR] studio, and to his constantly repeated heads of the lady whom he afterwards married, Miss Siddal' ('Notes' 460). Siddal died of a laudanum overdose in 1862. DGR had her exhumed in 1869 in order to retrieve manuscript poems he had buried with her.

A Better Resurrection

Composed 13 June 1857. First published 1862.

Title.   'Women received their dead raised to life again: and others
         were tortured, not accepting deliverance; that they might obtain
         a better resurrection' (Hebrews 11:35).

5.   *I lift mine eyes* 'I will lift up mine eyes unto the hills, from whence
      cometh my help' (Psalms 121:1).

8.   *O Jesus, quicken me* 'I am afflicted very much: quicken me, O
      Lord, according unto thy word' (Psalms 119:107). 'Quicken'
      means to bring to life or vitalize.

9.   *faded leaf* 'we all do fade as a leaf' (Isaiah 64:6).

17.   *broken bowl* 'Or ever the silver cord be loosed, or the golden
      bowl be broken, or the pitcher be broken at the fountain, or the
      wheel broken at the cistern' (Ecclesiastes 12:6).

20.   *cordial* see note for l. 96 of 'Three Nuns'.

'Whatsoever is right, that shall ye receive'

Composed 27 August 1857. Originally part of '"The heart knoweth
its own bitterness"' ('When all the overwork of life') – see WMR's
note on that poem. First published in *TF* 158–9. First poetry volume
1893.

Title.   'And about the eleventh hour he went out, and found others
         standing idle, and saith unto them, Why stand ye here all the day
         idle?' (Matthew 20:7).

9.   *hope deferred* see note for l. 2 of 'A Pause of Thought'. See also
      l. 49 of '"The heart knoweth its own bitterness"' ('When all the
      over-work of life'): 'Not in this world of hope deferred'.

11.   *Eye hath not seen, nor ear hath heard* 'But as it is written, Eye
      hath not seen, nor ear heard, neither have entered into the heart
      of man, the things which God hath prepared for them that love
      him' (1 Corinthians 2:9). See also note for l. 4 of 'Lord, I am
      feeble and of mean account'.

15.   *There God shall join and no man part* 'Wherefore they are
      no more twain, but one flesh. What therefore God hath joined
      together, let not man put asunder' (Matthew 19:6). See also
      Mark 10:9.

16.   *All one in Christ, so one—(please God!)—with me* see l. 56
      of '"The heart knoweth its own bitterness"' ('When all the
      over-work of life'): 'I full of Christ and Christ of me.'

'The heart knoweth its own bitterness'
['When all the over-work of life']

Composed 27 August 1857. First published 1896. WMR tells us that in 'her volume *Verses* ... she took the first and last stanzas of this vehement utterance, and, although altering the metre observably, and the diction not a little, she published them with the title, "*Whatsoever is right, that shall ye receive*" ... I think it only right to give the poem in full ...' He also notes how 'few things written by Christina contain more of her innermost self than this' ('Notes' 472).

Title. 'The heart knoweth his own bitterness; and a stranger doth not intermeddle with his joy' (Proverbs 14:10).

25. *To give, to give, not to receive* 'It is more blessed to give than to receive' (Acts 20:35).

41. *strait* narrow, constricted.

44. *A fountain sealed* 'A garden inclosed is my sister, my spouse; a spring shut up, a fountain sealed' (Song of Solomon 4:12).

49. *hope deferred* see note for l. 2 of 'A Pause of Thought'. See also l. 9 of ' "Whatsoever is right, that shall ye receive" ': 'Not in this world of hope deferred'.

51–2. *Eye hath not seen ... full 'enough'* see note for l. 4 of 'Lord, I am feeble and of mean account'.

A Birthday

Composed 18 November 1857. First published 1862. One of CR's best-known poems. Though WMR could not 'account for the outburst of exuberance evidenced in this celebrated lyric' ('Notes' 481), it seems to borrow its spirit from William Wordsworth's 'My heart leaps up when I behold' (1802). A contemporary parody about a husband dreading his mother-in-law's visit, concluding: 'Because the mother of my wife / Has come – and means to stay with me', appeared in 'some illustrated comic paper' and 'amused Christina' ('Notes' 481).

1. *My heart is like a singing bird* see l. 124 of 'Three Nuns': 'My heart is as a freeborn bird'.

2. *shoot* a new young branch of a tree or plant.

6. *halcyon* happy and peaceful.

9. *dais* throne.

10. *vair* fur used for trimming garments.

An Apple-Gathering

Composed 23 November 1857. First published in *Macmillan's Magazine* 4 (August 1861), 329. First poetry volume 1862.

1.   *pink blossoms from mine apple tree* apple blossom signifies preference.

Winter: My Secret

Composed 23 November 1857. First published 1862. WMR writes: 'This was at first named *Nonsense*; but, if there is method in some madness, there may be nous in some nonsense' ('Notes' 481).

Maude Clare

Composed probably between 8 December 1857 and 14 April 1858. First published 1862.

2.   *mien* demeanour.
24. *lilies* see note for l. 60 of 'Three Nuns'; *beck* brook.
25. *faded leaves* see note for l. 25 of 'Song' ('Oh roses for the flush of youth'). See also note for ll. 4–5 of 'Consider'.

At Home

Composed 28 June 1858. First published 1862. WMR informs us that DGR 'considered this to be about the best of all Christina's poems' ('Notes' 482).

14. *eyrie* a nest or habitation found at high altitude, as on a cliff.
28. *loth* reluctant.

Up-Hill

Composed 29 June 1858. First published in *Macmillan's Magazine* 3 (February 1861), 325. First poetry volume 1862. WMR writes: 'This was . . . the first poem by Christina which excited marked attention' ('Notes' 481).

The Convent Threshold

Composed 9 July 1858. First published 1862.

6.   *sea of glass* 'And I saw as it were a sea of glass mingled with fire: and them that had gotten the victory over the beast, and over his image, and over his mark, and over the number of his name, stand on the sea of glass, having the harps of God' (Revelation 15:2); 'And before the throne there was a glass like unto crystal: and in the midst of the throne, and round about the throne, were four beasts full of eyes before and behind' (Revelation 4:6).

7.   *lily* see note for l. 60 of 'Three Nuns'.

12.   *selfsame* the very same.

14.   *wash the spot* Lady Macbeth's murderous guilt manifests itself in an illusion of permanently blood-stained hands: 'Out, damned spot! out, I say!' (William Shakespeare, *Macbeth* V.i.38); *snare* trap.

26.   *Racked, roasted, crushed, wrenched limb from limb* various forms of martyrdom of the saints.

27.   *offscouring of the world* 'Thou has made us as the offscouring and refuse in the midst of the people' (Lamentations 3:45); 'Being defamed, we intreat: we are made as the filth of the world, and are the offscouring of all things unto this day' (1 Corinthians 4:13).

59.   *laves* washes (from the French *laver*).

73.   *Have pity upon me, ye my friends* 'Have pity upon me, have pity upon me, O ye my friends, for the hand of God hath touched me' (Job 19:21).

87.   *clomb* climbed.

88.   *pinions* wings.

91.   *cars* chariots.

101.   *aureole* halo.

118.   *tester* canopy.

'What good shall my life do me?' ['Have dead men long to wait']

Probably composed between 6 August and 15 October 1858. Originally part of the unpublished ' "Only believe" '. First published in *TF* 238–9. First poetry volume 1893.

Title.   'And Rebekah said to Isaac, I am weary of my life because of the daughters of Heth: if Jacob take a wife of the daughters of

Heth, such as these which are of the daughters of the land, what good shall my life do me?' (Genesis 27:46).

5.   *Dust to dust* 'In the sweat of thy face shalt thou eat bread, till thou return unto the ground; for out of it wast thou taken: for dust thou art, and unto dust shalt thou return' (Genesis 3:19).

22. *Those who sowed shall reap* see note for l. 6 of 'Vigil of St Bartholomew'.

25. *clomb* see note for l. 87 of 'The Convent Threshold'.

29. *In watered pastures fair* 'He maketh me to lie down in green pastures: he leadeth me beside the still waters' (Psalms 23:2).

33. *Love casts out fear* 'There is no fear in love; but perfect love casteth out fear: because fear hath torment. He that feareth is not made perfect in love' (1 John 4:18).

Winter Rain

Composed 31 January 1859. First published 1862.

20. *lea-crops* crop growing on pastureland that will eventually be replaced by another crop.

22. *leas* grasslands, meadows.

23. *grass* see note for l. 16 of 'Sweet Death'.

25. *moss* see note for l. 21 of ' "Consider the Lilies of the Field" ' ('Flowers preach to us if we will hear').

28. *pied* see note for l. 4 of 'Shut Out'; *daisies* see note for l. 6 of 'On Keats'.

31. *lily* see note for l. 60 of 'Three Nuns'.

L.E.L.

Composed 15 February 1859. First published in *Victoria Magazine* I (May 1863), 40–41. First published poetry volume 1866. WMR writes: 'Christina's poem *Spring* [original title] relates to herself, and not at all to the poetess L.E.L. (Letitia Elizabeth Landon). I suppose that, when the publishing-stage came on, Christina preferred to retire behind a cloud and so renamed the poem *L.E.L.*' CR's manuscript note references Elizabeth Barrett Browning, and WMR speculates that the poem alludes to the line 'One thirsty for a little love' in Barrett Browning's 'L.E.L.'s Last Question' (1844) ('Notes' 482).

Epigraph. See note above.

14. *lilies* see note for l. 60 of 'Three Nuns'.

26. *lavender* emblem of distrust, also assiduity.
27. *rosemary* symbol of remembrance; *myrrh* signifies gladness.
31. *ruth* pity or compassion.
36. *scathe* harm, injury.

Goblin Market

Composed 22 April 1859. First Published 1862. This poem is perhaps the most popular with modern readers. Its dark, fairy-tale atmosphere recalls Lewis Carroll's *Alice's Adventures in Wonderland*, a story it helped to inspire. Although WMR tells us that CR claimed the poem 'did not mean anything profound', he admits that its 'incidents are . . . at any rate suggestive'. These 'suggestive' incidents have spawned a colourful illustrating history (see Lorraine Janzen Kooistra's *Christina Rossetti and Illustration*, Ohio University Press, 2002) from DGR's original drawing to *Playboy*'s interpretation in 1973. WMR notes that 'at times . . . people do not see the central point of the story, such as the authoress intended it' ('Notes' 459). The poem's themes of temptation, resistance and sacrifice encourage parallels with Christianity, while its endorsement of sisterhood is strengthened by its original dedication to MFR.

3–4. *"Come buy"* 'Ho, everyone that thirsteth, come ye to the waters and he that hath no money, come ye, buy, and eat; yea, come buy wine and milk without money and without price' (Isaiah 55:1).
10. *Swart* see note for l. 144 of 'The Lowest Room'.
22. *bullaces* damsons.
23. *greengages* greenish fruit resembling a plum.
27. *barberries* deep red berries, from the spiny barberry shrub.
29. *Citrons* lemon-like fruits with thick peel.
76. *ratel* badger-like animal, also known as a 'honey badger'.
83. *lily* see note for l. 60 of 'Three Nuns'.
120. *furze* a yellow-flowered shrub with spiny leaves, gorse. It signifies enduring affection.
126. *precious golden lock* in folklore, fairies prize golden hair, kidnapping or seducing golden-haired girls for fairy brides (see Katharine Briggs, *A Dictionary of Fairies*, Viking, 1976).
129. *honey from the rock* 'He made him ride on the high places of the earth, that he might eat the increase of the fields; and he made him to suck honey out of the rock, and oil out of the flinty rock' (Deuteronomy 32:13).

160. *daisies* see note for l. 6 of 'On Keats'.

179. *Pellucid* translucent.

185. *Like two pigeons* 'And if she be not able to bring a lamb, then she shall bring ... two young pigeons; the one for the burnt offering, the other for a sin offering; and the priest shall make an atonement for her, and she shall be clean' (Leviticus 12:7).

220. *flags* types of iris, symbolizing eloquence.

258. *succous* containing juice or sap.

260. *Her tree of life* see note for l. 140 of 'Three Nuns'.

290. *drouth* drought.

300. *cankerous* ulcerous.

318. *rime* frost.

331–47. *Came towards her hobbling ... Gliding like fishes* see ll. 110–18 of Robert Browning's 'Pied Piper of Hamelin' (1842):

> And out of the houses the rats came tumbling.
> Great rats, small rats, lean rats, brawny rats,
> Brown rats, black rats, grey rats, tawny rats,
> Grave old plodders, gay young friskers,
> Fathers, mothers, uncles, cousins,
> Cocking tails and pricking whiskers,
> Families by tens and dozens,
> Brothers, sisters, husbands, wives –
> Followed the Piper for their lives.

395. *Cross-grained* contrary, intractable, perverse.

410. *Like a rock of blue-veined stone* 'He is like a man which built an house, and digged deep, and laid the foundation upon a rock, and when the flood arose, the stream beat vehemently upon that house, and could not shake it; for it was founded upon a rock' (Luke 6:48).

415–16. *orange-tree / White with blossoms* orange blossoms signify chastity.

451. *dingle* hollow or dell.

471. *Eat me, drink me* 'And when he had given thanks, he brake it, and said, Take, eat: this is my body, which is broken for you: this do in remembrance of me' (1 Corinthians 11:24). See also Christ's words to his disciples during the sacrament of the Eucharist (Matthew 26:26–9, Mark 14:22–5 and Luke 22:7–20). See also Chapter 1 of *Alice's Adventures in Wonderland* (1865) where Alice follows the instructions 'Eat me' and 'Drink Me'.

479. *fruit forbidden* Adam and Eve are expelled by God from the Garden of Eden when they eat fruit that has been forbidden to them. 'But of the fruit of the tree which is in the midst of the garden, God hath said, Ye shall not eat of it, neither shall ye touch it, lest ye die' (Genesis 3:3).
491. *aguish*, feverish.
494. *wormwood* a bitter ingredient of vermouth and absinthe, used as a tonic.

'No, Thank You, John'

Composed March 1860. First published 1862. WMR writes: 'In the copy of my sister's combined *Poems* (1895), I find this rather amusing entry: "The original John was obnoxious, because he never gave scope for 'No, thank you'"' ('Notes' 483).

'Out of the deep'

Composed 17 December 1862. First published 1896.

Title. 'Out of the depths have I cried unto thee, O Lord' (Psalms 130:1).

The Queen of Hearts

Composed 3 January 1863. First published 1866.

13. *prepense* planned or intended in advance, premeditated.

Consider

Composed 7 May 1863. First published 1875.

Title. See note for the title of '"Consider the Lilies of the Field"' ('Flowers preach to us if we will hear').
4–5. *Like them we fade away / As doth a leaf* 'But we are all as an unclean thing, and all our righteousnesses are as filthy rags; and we all do fade as a leaf; and our iniquities, like the wind, have taken us away' (Isaiah 64:6).
7. *sparrows* 'Are not two sparrows sold for a farthing and one of them shall not fall on the ground without your Father' (Matthew 10:29). See also Matthew 10:31 and Luke 12:6–7.
15. *coil* trouble, disturbance, ado.

17. *birds that have no barn* 'Consider the ravens: for they neither
    sow nor reap; which neither have storehouse nor barn; and God
    feedeth them: how much more are ye better than the fowls?'
    (Luke 12:24).

The Lowest Place

Composed 25 July 1863. First published 1866. WMR had the second
stanza engraved on CR's tombstone.

Title. See note for the title of 'The Lowest Room'; Christ's parable
  in Luke 14:7–14. The aspiration to the 'lowest place' is a fre-
  quent theme of CR's poetry and prose. See also 'The Lowest
  Room'.

Beauty is Vain

Composed 20 January 1864. First published 1866.

1. *roses* see note for l. 1 of 'Song' ('Oh roses for the flush of youth').
2. *lilies* see note for l. 60 of 'Three Nuns'.
7. *if she were as red or white* 'My beloved is white and ruddy, the
   chiefest among ten thousand' (Song of Solomon 5:10). See also
   l. 10 of '"A Helpmeet for Him"': 'Tender and faithful, ruddy
   and white'.

What Would I Give?

Composed 28 January 1864. First published 1866.

1. *heart of flesh* 'A new heart also will I give you, and a new spirit
   will I put within you: and I will take away the stony heart out of
   your flesh, and I will give you an heart of flesh' (Ezekiel 36:26).
9. *ingrain* dyed permanently.

Who Shall Deliver Me?

Composed 1 March 1864. First published 1875.

Title. 'O wretched man that I am! who shall deliver me from the
  body of this death?' (Romans: 7:24).
6. *gad-about* moving restlessly from one social activity to another.
11. *the race* refers to biblical comparison of life and running a race;
    'Wherefore seeing we also are compassed about with so great a

cloud of witnesses, let us lay aside every weight, and the sin which doth so easily beset us, and let us run with patience the race that is set before us' (Hebrews 12:1); 'Know ye not that they which run in a race run all, but one receiveth the prize? So run, that ye may obtain' (1 Corinthians 9:24). See also l. 3 of ' "Our heaven must be within ourselves" ' and note for l. 3 of 'On Keats'.

12. *apace* swiftly.

21. *clog* a heavy weight attached to an animal's leg to impede movement.

24. *Break off the yoke and set me free* 'Stand fast therefore in the liberty wherewith Christ hath made us free, and be not entangled again with the yoke of bondage' (Galatians 5:1).

Twice

Composed June 1864. First published 1866.

16. *corn* see note for l. 10 of 'Dream-Land'.

23. *corn-flowers* also known as 'bachelor's buttons', a symbol of celibacy worn by young men in love.

24. *the singing bird* see note for l. 1 of 'A Birthday'.

38. *dross* see note for l. 36 of 'The Lowest Room'.

Jessie Cameron

Composed October 1864. First published 1866.

20. *bane* ruin.

26. *Quickening* see note for l. 8 of 'A Better Resurrection'.

33–6. *You're good for Madge, or good for Cis . . . not good for me?* see ll. 9–12 of 'No, Thank You, John': 'I dare say Meg or Mool would take / Pity upon you, if you'd ask: / And pray don't remain single for my sake. Who can't perform that task.'

59. *unked* grim, uncanny, dismal. WMR explains that the Rossetti children first heard this 'country' word from 'our uncle Henry Polydore' (brother to John Polidori, Byron's physician and author of *The Vampyre*). Uncle Henry had first seen the word in the diary of 'a country-woman with whom he was lodging'. One stormy night, she had observed: ' "Oh, what an unkid [*sic*] night!" ' ('Notes' 485).

The Prince's Progress

Lines 481–540 composed October 1861, ll. 1–480 composed January 1865. Lines 481–540 first published in *Macmillan's Magazine* 7 (May 1863), 36. First poetry volume 1866.

Title.   Alludes to John Bunyan's *The Pilgrim's Progress* (1678), a Christian allegory about a pilgrim who overcomes delays and hardships during his journey from earth to heaven.

7.   *rime* see note for l. 318 of 'Goblin Market'.

25.   *lilies* see note for l. 60 of 'Three Nuns'; *rosebuds* represent youth and beauty. For roses in general, see note for l. 1 of 'Song' ('Oh roses for the flush of youth').

31.   *Red and white poppies* for red poppies, see note for l. 6 of ' "Consider the Lilies of the Field" ' ('Flowers preach to us if we will hear'); white poppies symbolize sleep.

50.   *corn* see note for l. 10 of 'Dream-Land'.

68.   *Was she a maid, or an evil dream?* see l. 79 of John Keats's 'Ode to a Nightingale' (1819): 'Was it a vision or a waking dream?' See also Keats's 'La Belle Dame Sans Merci' (1820) and CR's 'The World'.

69.   *Her eyes began to glitter and gleam* see ll. 16 and 31 of Keats's 'La Belle Dame Sans Merci': 'And her eyes were wild', 'And then I shut her wild wild eyes'.

100.   *mavis and merle* song thrush and blackbird.

101.   *hodden* woollen cloth.

103.   *daisies* see note for l. 6 of 'On Keats'.

110.   *réveillée* a signal to awaken.

123.   *moss* see note for l. 21 of ' "Consider the Lilies of the Field" ' ('Flowers preach to us if we will hear').

124.   *astunt* deceased.

161.   *weft* horizontal threads in woven fabric.

178–9.   *An old, old mortal, cramped and double . . . a seething-pot* see the Witches' spell in William Shakespeare's *Macbeth* IV.i.10–11: 'Double, double toil and trouble; / Fire burn, and cauldron bubble.'

181.   *atomy* skeleton.

185.   *brooked* tolerated.

203.   *Elixir of Life* an alchemical mixture drunk to achieve immortality.

269.   *Let him sow, one day he shall reap* 'He that observeth the wind shall not sow; and he that regardeth the clouds shall not reap' (Ecclesiastes 11:4). See also Job 4:8.

440–41. *Of wine-red roses . . . buds that unclose* burgundy roses ('wine-red') symbolize unconscious beauty, while full white roses ('snows . . . buds that unclose') signify 'I am worthy of you'.

458. *Does she wake or sleep?* see l. 80 of Keats's 'Ode to a Nightingale': 'Fled is that music: – Do I wake or sleep?'

516. *Kirtle* skirt.

Memory

Part I composed 8 November 1857; part II composed 17 February 1865. First published 1866.

7. *ruth* see note for l. 31 of 'L.E.L.'. Here, also the secondary definition of contrition or remorse.

8. 'So the last shall be first, and the first last: for many be called, but few chosen' (Matthew 20:16). See also Matthew 19:30, Mark 10:31 and Luke 13:30.

27. *bloodless lily* see note for l. 60 of 'Three Nuns'; *warm rose* see note for l. 1 of 'Song' ('Oh roses for the flush of youth').

Amor Mundi

Composed 21 February 1865. First published *Shilling Magazine* 2 (June 1865), 193. First poetry volume 1875. In *The Century* magazine, Edmund Gosse declares this poem 'one of the most solemn, imaginative, and powerful lyrics on a purely religious subject ever printed in England' (p. 217).

Title. 'Love of the World' (Latin).

1–2. *'Oh where are you going . . . along this valley track?'* see ll. 1–2 of W. H. Auden's Epilogue from *The Orators: An English Study* (1932): '"O where are you going?" said reader to rider, / "That valley is fatal when furnaces burn"'; *love-locks* curls or tresses of hair of a peculiar or striking character.

9. *seven* biblically significant number commonly associated with the Apocalypse, where seven vials containing the wrath of God (plagues) are emptied on to the earth by seven angels. See Revelation 15–17.

14. *A scaled and hooded worm.* 'The womb shall forget him; the worm shall feed sweetly on him; he shall be no more remembered; and wickedness shall be broken as a tree' (Job 24:20).

20. *This downhill path is easy, but there's no turning back* see Virgil's *Aeneid* VI.126–9: 'the way down to hell is easy . . . But to retrace

your steps, to find the way back to daylight – that is the task, the hard thing.'

'The Iniquity of the Fathers Upon the Children'

Composed March 1865. First published 1866. Flowers points out that this poem was probably influenced by CR's work with 'fallen women' at Highgate. WMR also credits Charles Dickens's *Bleak House* (1853) as an inspiration. Presumably he is thinking of the novel's heroine Esther Summerson, illegitimate child of Lady Dedlock.

Title.   'Thou shalt not bow down thyself to them, nor serve them: for I the LORD thy God am a jealous God, visiting the iniquity of the fathers upon the children unto the third and fourth generation of them that hate me' (Exodus 20:5).

1.   *rose* see note for l. 1 of 'Song' ('Oh roses for the flush of youth').
3.   *Under the rose* English translation of the Latin expression *sub rosa*, meaning 'in secret' or 'in confidence'.
40.   *flout and scout* treat contemptuously; make fun of, mock.
54.   *John Bull* after the character introduced in satirist John Arbuthnot's allegory *The History of John Bull* (1712). Represents the 'typical' English everyman: a plain-speaking, unsophisticated portly figure, often pictured with a bulldog.
95.   *grass* see note for l. 16 of 'Sweet Death'.
287.   *primroses* symbolize early youth.
442.   *grazier* one who grazes cattle.
535.   *pelf* wealth, acquired dishonestly.

A Daughter of Eve

Composed 30 September 1865. First published 1875.

4.   *rose* see note for l. 1 of 'Song' ('Oh roses for the flush of youth').
5.   *lily* see note for l. 60 of 'Three Nuns'.

A Smile and a Sigh

Composed 14 February 1866. First published in *Macmillan's Magazine* 18 (May 1868), 86. First poetry volume 1875.

Autumn Violets

First published in *Macmillan's Magazine* 19 (November 1868), 84.
First poetry volume 1875.

1. *violets* see note for l. 5 of 'Song' ('Oh roses for the flush of
    youth').
14. *Ruth* see note for l. 24 of 'Sweet Death'.

'They Desire a Better Country'

First published in *Macmillan's Magazine* 19 (March 1869), 422–3.
First poetry volume 1875.

Title. 'But now they desire a better country, that is, an heavenly:
    wherefore God is not ashamed to be called their God: for he hath
    prepared for them a city' (Hebrews 11:16).
2. *my future is a blank* see note for l. 117 of 'The Lowest Room'.
14. *Follow me here . . . follow here* Jesus's refrain to his disciples, as
    in Matthew 16:24: 'Then said Jesus unto his disciples, If any man
    will come after me, let him deny himself, and take up his cross,
    and follow me.' See also Matthew 4:19, 8:22, 9:9, 19:21 and
    Mark 2:14, 8:34.
34. *serried* pressed or crowded together, commonly used to describe
    soldiers standing in rows.
36. *love almost to cast out fear* 'There is no fear in love; but perfect
    love casteth out fear: because fear hath torment. He that feareth
    is not made perfect in love' (1 John 4:18).
38. *golden walls of home* refer to New Jerusalem, the holy city of
    God, described in Revelation 21:18 as 'pure gold, like unto
    clear glass'. For a detailed physical description of the city, see
    Revelation 21:15–22. See also note for l. 177 of 'Three Nuns'.

A Christmas Carol

First published in *Scribner's Magazine Monthly* 3 (January 1872),
278. First poetry volume 1875. A popular Christmas carol (as 'In the
Bleak Midwinter'), set to music many times, but most famously in
1906 by Gustav Holst (1874–1934). Still a choral favourite today,
with cover versions by twentieth-century pop musicians such as The
Moody Blues, Crash Test Dummies and Cyndi Lauper.

Love me, – I love you

First published 1872.

A city plum is not a plum

First published 1872.

1. *plum* Flowers identifies this in her notes as 'plumb', a rare piece of slang for someone who possesses £100,000.
3. *party rat* politician who abandons his party.
4. *sailor's cat* a braided naval whip, 'cat-o-nine-tails' or possibly a type of sailor's knot – a 'cat's paw' or 'catshank'.
5. *soldier's frog* a decorative fastening made of ornamental braiding which loops around a button.

A baby's cradle with no baby in it

First published 1872.

2. *sere* dry, withered.

Hope is like a harebell trembling from its birth

First published 1872.

1. *harebell* emblem of grief, submission.
2. *rose* see note for l. 1 of 'Song' ('Oh roses for the flush of youth').
3. *lily* see note for l. 60 of 'Three Nuns'.

A linnet in a gilded cage

First published 1872.

If all were rain and never sun

First published 1872.

4. *There'd be no rainbow still* after the Flood, God tells Noah he will never again destroy the earth by flood. The rainbow will appear as a symbol of this divine promise to mankind, and as a reminder of humanity's connection to God: 'I do set my bow in the cloud, and it shall be for a token of a covenant between me and the earth' (Genesis 9:13).

If I were a Queen

First published 1872.

What are heavy? sea-sand and sorrow

First published 1872.

Brown and furry

First published 1872.

A toadstool comes up in a night

First published 1872.

If a pig wore a wig

First published 1872.

How many seconds in a minute?

First published 1872.

What is pink? a rose is pink

First published 1872. This poem was recently released as a children's book, illustrated by Judith Hoffman Corwin (HarperFestival, 2000).

A pin has a head, but has no hair

First published 1872.

When fishes set umbrellas up

First published 1872.

The peacock has a score of eyes

First published 1872.

3.   *sound* to plunge downward or dive.

6.   *clocks* this refers to the head of the dandelion when it turns to
     fine filaments. The time of day is said to correspond with the
     number of breaths it takes to blow this 'dandelion clock' away.

The wind has such a rainy sound

First published 1872.

Who has seen the wind?

First published 1872.

When a mounting skylark sings

First published 1872.

5-8. *when a nightingale sings . . . heaven is heaven* see John Keats's
     'Ode to a Nightingale' (1819).

An emerald is as green as grass

First published 1872.

What does the bee do?

First published 1872.

I caught a little ladybird

First published 1872.

Baby lies so fast asleep

First published 1872.

7.   *snowdrop* emblem of hope and consolation.

Confluents

First published 1875.

1.   *As rivers seek the sea* 'All the rivers run into the sea; yet the sea
     is not full; unto the place from whence the rivers come, thither
     they return again' (Ecclesiastes 1:7).

9.   *rose* see note for l. 1 of 'Song' ('Oh roses for the flush of
      youth').

'Yet a little while'

'First published in *Dublin University Magazine* I, n.s. (1878), p. 104'
(*Letters* II.150), as discovered by Betty Flowers and recorded in her
edition of the *Complete Poems*. Also published *FD* 11. First poetry
volume 1893.

Title. 'A little while, and ye shall not see me: and again, a little while,
        and ye shall see me, because I go to the Father' (John 16:16). See
        ll. 13-14, sonnet 10 of 'Monna Innominata': 'A little while, and
        life reborn annuls / Loss and decay and death, and all is love.'
5.   *how long?* 'My soul is also sore vexed: but thou, O Lord, how
        long?' (Psalms 6:3).

Monna Innominata

Jan Marsh tells us that although this poem's 'exact genesis . . . is hard
to date precisely', it was probably composed from 1879 to 1880,
during which time Rossetti also attended a lecture series on Dante at
University College London (*CR* 471). First published 1881. WMR
states that this sonnet sequence is 'a personal utterance – an intensely
personal one', and that its preface is designed to 'draw off attention
from the writer in her proper person' ('Notes' 462). CR always refused
permission for the sonnets to be published as excerpts, writing in 1886
to an American publisher that 'Such compound work has a connection
(very often) which is of interest to the author and which an editor gains
nothing by discarding' (Lona Mosk Packer, *The Rossetti–Macmillan
Letters*, University of Carolina Press, 1963, p. 154). For a comprehen-
sive structural critique, see William Whitla's essay 'Questioning the
Convention: CR's Sonnet Sequence "Monna Innominata"' in David
A. Kent (ed.), *The Achievement of Christina Rossetti* (Cornell Univer-
sity Press, 1986), pp. 82-131.

  Translations in the epigraphs are by Charles Cayley (*Dante's Divine
Comedy*, Longman, Brown Green and Longmans, 1853, and *The
Sonnets and Stanzas of Petrarch*, Longmans, Green and Co., 1879), a
scholar and close personal friend of CR. Although she turned down
his marriage proposal, CR became his literary executor after his
death. She admired his translation of Dante privately, and promoted
it publicly in her article 'Dante, An English Classic' (published in

Churchman's Shilling Magazine and Family Treasury 2, 1867, pp. 200–205), and annotated Cayley's Dante volumes for a second edition (never published). Jan Marsh notes that the sequence has 'echoes . . . of Cayley's versions' (*CR* 472). CR also uses his translation in *TF*. For a fascinating study of Rossetti's relationship with Cayley, see Kamilla Denman and Sarah Smith, 'Christina Rossetti's Copy of C. B. Cayley's *Divine Comedy*', *Victorian Poetry*, vol. 32 (West Virginia Press, 1994), pp. 315–36.

Title. 'Unnamed Lady' (Italian).
Prefatory note. *Beatrice* Dante's muse; *altissimo poeta . . . cotanto amante* Dante, see *Inferno* 4.80; *Laura* Petrarch's muse; *Albigenses* members of a Provençal religious movement that preached a dualistic doctrine of material evil and spiritual good; *Great Poetess* Elizabeth Barrett Browning; *Troubadours* lyric poets of southern France, twelfth and early thirteenth centuries.

1

Epigraph. 'Since morn have said Adieu to darling friends' (*Purgatorio* 8:3); 'Love, with what force thou dost me now o'erthrow' (*Canzoniere* 85.12).
13–14. *Ah me . . . called them sweet* see lines 1–2 of 'The Key-Note': 'Where are the songs I used to know, / Where are the songs I used to sing?'

2

Epigraph. 'It was that hour, which thaws the heart and sends' (*Purgatorio* 8.1); 'I've called to mind how I beheld you first' (*Canzoniere* 20.3).

3

Epigraph. 'Ah shadows, that are but for sight inane' (*Purgatorio* 2.79); 'Now by a phantom guide it is controlled' (*Canzoniere* 277.9).
1–2. *I dream of you to wake . . . slumber on* see William Shakespeare's *Hamlet* III.i.64–6: 'To die, to sleep; / To sleep: perchance to dream: ay, there's the rub; / For in that sleep of death what dreams may come'.
12–13. *If thus to sleep . . . sweeter than to live* see note for ll. 5–6 of 'Sappho'. See also note above for ll. 1–2 of this sonnet.
14. *Tho' there be nothing new beneath the sun* 'What has been will be again, what has been done will be done again; there is nothing

new under the sun' (Ecclesiastes 1:9). See also l. 22 of 'Passing and Glassing'.

4

Epigraph. 'Great fire may after little spark succeed' (*Paradiso* 1.34);'Take flight all thoughts and things that it contains, / And therein Love alone with you remains' (*Canzoniere* 72.44–5).

8. *weights and measures* 'Diverse weights, and diverse measures, both of them are alike abomination to the Lord' (Proverbs 20:10).

5

Epigraph. 'Love, who from loving none beloved reprieves' (*Inferno* 5.103); '[Love] Required me into such sweet hopes to fall' (*Canzoniere* 56.11).

3. *leal* loyal.

11. *world without an end* 'Unto him be glory in the church by Christ Jesus throughout all ages, world without end. Amen' (Ephesians 3:21).

14. *woman is the helpmeet made for man* 'And the Lord God said, it is not good that the man should be alone; I will make him an help meet for him' (Genesis 2:18). See also ' "A Helpmeet for Him" '.

6

Epigraph. ' "Now," said he, rising, "mayest thou rightly set / A value on the love with which I flame' (*Purgatorio* 21.133–4); 'Me shall not Love release, / From such a knot, by pain or by decease' (*Canzoniere* 59.17).

4. *Lot's wife* while fleeing the destruction of Sodom, Lot's wife disobeys God's order not to look back at her home, and is turned into a pillar of salt (Genesis 19:1–26).

7

Epigraph. 'Here spring was always, and each plant' (*Purgatorio* 28.143); 'Love with me walks and talks, and with him I' (*Canzoniere* 35.14).

5. *Love builds the house on rock and not on sand* 'And every one that heareth these sayings of mine, and doeth them not, shall be likened unto a foolish man, which built his house upon sand' (Matthew 7:26). See also Matthew 7:24 and Luke 6:48.

13–14. *Tho' jealousy be cruel . . . love is strong as death* 'Set me as a seal upon thine heart, as a seal upon thine arm: for love is strong as death; jealousy is cruel as the grave: the coals thereof are coals of fire, which hath a most vehement flame' (Song of Solomon 8:6).

8

Epigraph. 'And breathe to God, "Nought recketh me, but thou"' (*Purgatorio* 8.12); 'I hope to miss not pardon – pity I mean' (*Canzoniere* 1.8).

1. "*I, if I perish, perish*"—*Esther spake* King Ahasueras is persuaded by his advisor Haman to carry out a slaughter of the Jews. One of his wives, Esther, also a Jew, risks death in approaching the king to plead for her people. She gains the king's favour, and he stops the planned genocide, allowing the Jews to avenge themselves on their enemies: 'Go, gather together all the Jews that are present in Shushan, and fast ye for me, and neither eat nor drink three days, night or day: I also and my maidens will fast likewise; and so will I go in unto the king, which is not according to the law: and if I perish, I perish' (Esther 4:6).

4. *slake* here, to quench or extinguish.

8. *Harmless as doves and subtle as a snake* 'Behold, I send you forth as sheep in the midst of wolves: be ye therefore wise as serpents, and harmless as doves' (Matthew 10:16).

9

Epigraph. 'Ah! white and honourable!' (*Purgatorio* 3.8); 'The soul, that warmest breath of virtue drew' (*Canzoniere* 283.3).

8. *turning to the wall* a position of prayer: 'Then Hezekiah turned his face toward the wall, and prayed unto the Lord' (Isaiah 38:2); 'Then he turned his face to the wall, and prayed unto the Lord, saying . . .' (2 Kings 20).

11–12. *wrestle till the break / Of day* refers to Jacob wrestling a stranger who turns out to be God – see Genesis 32:24–31 and Hosea 12:4.

10

Epigraph. 'With better light, with better stars allied' (*Paradiso* 1.40); 'Life flyeth, and will not a moment stay' (*Canzoniere* 272.1).

12. *A little while* see note for title of ' "Yet a little while" '.

13–14. *A little while . . . and all is love* see ll. 13–14 of 'Sonnets are full of love, and this my tome': 'Of love, whose blessed glow transcends the laws / Of time and change and mortal life and death.'

11

Epigraph. 'Let people talk, and thou behind me go' (*Purgatorio* 5.13); 'Counting the chances that our life befall' (*Canzoniere* 285.12).

5.   *prate* chatter idly.

13.   *make it plain* 'And the Lord answered me, and said, Write the vision, and make it plain upon tables, that he may run that readeth it' (Habbakuk 2:2).

12

Epigraph. 'Love, that discoursing art within my soul' (*Purgatorio* 2.112); 'Of loveliness appeareth day by day' (*Canzoniere* 13.2).

7.   *I too am crowned* here probably with laurel, representing poetic glory.

8.   *jocund* merry, cheerful.

13

Epigraph. 'And set we on the all-first Love our eyes' (*Paradiso* 32.142); 'But for my arms this burden was too sore' (*Canzoniere* 20.5).

3.   *lily* see note for l. 60 of 'Three Nuns'.

4.   *sparrow* see note for l. 7 of 'Consider'.

14

Epigraph. 'In His good pleasure we have each his peace' (*Paradiso* 3.85); 'Alone with these my thoughts, with altered hair' (*Canzoniere* 30.32).

4.   *roses* see note for l. 1 of 'Song' ('Oh roses for the flush of youth').

8.   *corn* see note for l. 10 of 'Dream-Land'.

Sonnets are full of love, and this my tome

First published 1881. CR chose this as the dedicatory sonnet for *A Pageant and Other Poems*. Her mother was a key figure in her life, as Mary Arseneau's *Recovering Christina Rossetti* (Palgrave, 2004) has recently explored.

8.   *loadstar* guiding star, used in navigation.

13–14.   *Of love, whose blessed . . . mortal life and death* see ll. 13–14, sonnet 10 of 'Monna Innominata': 'A little while, and life reborn annuls / Loss and decay and death, and all is love.' See also note for title of ' "Yet a little while" '.

The Key-Note

First published 1881.

1–2. *Where are the songs . . . I used to sing?* see ll. 13–14, sonnet 1
of 'Monna Innominata': 'Ah me, but where are now the songs I
sang / When life was sweet because you called them sweet?'
6.　*sere* see note for l. 2 of 'A baby's cradle with no baby in it'.
13.　*hips* rose-hips – bright, winter-blooming berries; *haws* hawthorn
berries, emblems of hope.

He and She

First published 1881.

De Profundis

First published 1881.

Title. 'Out of the Depths' (Latin). 'Out of the depths have I cried
unto thee, O Lord' (Psalms 130:1).

'Hollow-Sounding and Mysterious'

First published 1881.

Title. WMR tells us ('Notes', 488) that this phrase is from a poem
by Felicia Hemans (1793–1835), probably 'The Treasures of the
Deep' (1839): 'What hidest thou in thy treasure-caves and cells? /
Thou hollow-sounding and mysterious main! —' (ll. 1–2). Hem-
ans, a widely read and popular poet of her day, fell out of fashion
in the twentieth century, but her reputation, and her work, is
now being recovered.

At Last

First published 1881.

1.　*bane* ruin, woe.
10.　*Love all in all* 'When he has done this, then the Son himself will
be made subject to him who put everything under him, so that
God may be all in all' (1 Corinthians 15:28).

Mariana

First published 1881.

Title. See Alfred Lord Tennyson's 'Mariana' (1830) and 'Mariana in
the South' (1833), both about a woman pining for love.

6.   *violet* see note for l. 5 of 'Song' ('Oh roses for the flush of youth').

10.   *hoards up a treasure* 'Do not store up for yourselves treasures
        on earth, where moth and rust destroy, and where thieves break
        in and steal. But store up for yourselves treasures in heaven,
        where moth and rust do not destroy, and where thieves do not
        break in and steal' (Matthew 6:19–20).

Passing and Glassing

First published 1881.

5.   *withered roses* emblem of transient impression.

10.   *tiring-glass* mirror for 'attiring' oneself; from *tire* – to get ready
        or dress.

11.   *lavender* see note for l. 26 of 'L.E.L.'.

12.   *violet* see note for l. 5 of 'Song' ('Oh roses for the flush of youth').

22.   *nothing new beneath the sun* see note for l. 14, sonnet 3 of
        'Monna Innominata'.

The Thread of Life

First published 1881.

2

1.   *Thus am I mine own prison* see ll. 25–6 of Richard Lovelace's
        'To Althea from Prison' (1649): 'Stone walls do not a prison
        make / Nor iron bars a cage.' See also ll. 8–9 of William Words-
        worth's 'Nuns fret not at their convent's narrow room' (1802):
        'In truth the prison, unto which we doom / Ourselves, no prison
        is: and hence for me'.

13.   *I am not what I have nor what I do* see ll. 4–5, sonnet 1 of
        'Monna Innominata': 'So far between my pleasures are and few. /
        While when you do not come, what I do I do'.

14.   *what I was I am, I am even I* 'I am that I am' (Exodus 3:14).

3

6. *sanative* having the power to heal, curing.
7. *Death shall ply his sieve* biblical reference to the 'sifting' of souls: 'For lo, I will command, and I will sift the house of Israel among all nations, like as corn is sifted in a sieve, yet shall not the least grain fall upon the earth' (Amos 9:9); 'And the Lord said, Simon, behold, Satan hath desired to have you, that he may sift you as wheat' (Luke 23:31).
13–14. *O death ... where is thy victory?* 'O death, where is thy sting? O grave, where is thy victory?' (1 Corinthians 15:55).

Touching 'Never'

First published 1881.

5. *sere* see note for l. 2 of 'A baby's cradle with no baby in it'.
6. *daffodil* symbol of regard.
8. *roses* see note for l. 1 of 'Song' ('Oh roses for the flush of youth'); *nightingales* see John Keats's 'Ode to a Nightingale' (1819).

An Old-World Thicket

First published 1881.

Epigraph. 'A dark wood'. From Dante's *Inferno* 1.3.
1. *Awake or sleeping (for I know not which)* see note for l. 458 of 'The Prince's Progress'.
9. *ivy* see note for l. 3 of 'Song' ('Oh roses for the flush of youth').
16–20. *Such mirth ... reasonings wild or weak* see ll. 57–60 of John Keats's 'Ode to a Nightingale' (1819): 'While thou art pouring forth thy soul abroad / In such an ecstasy! / Still wouldst thou sing, and I have earn in vain – / To thy high requiem become a sod.'
54. *more blank my lot* see note for l. 117 of 'The Lowest Room'.
77. *a rebel against light* 'They are of those that rebel against the light; they know not the ways thereof, nor abide in the paths thereof' (Job 24:13).
88. *My strength was weakness* see l. 5 of '"A Helpmeet for Him"'.

Later Life: A Double Sonnet of Sonnets

First published 1881. True to its subtitle, this ambitious sequence comprises twenty-eight sonnets. WMR speculates that 'the majority of it must have been written with a definite intention that its various constituent parts should form one whole'. Yet he adds that 'when the general framework was getting into shape, two or three outlying sonnets were pressed into the service' ('Notes' 463). Diane D'Amico suggests that 'Later Life' is a response to 'Monna Innominata'. She compares the silence of the final stanza of 'Monna Innominata' with the hope of heavenly reunion at the conclusion of 'Later Life' (*Christina Rossetti: Faith, Gender, and Time*, Louisiana State University Press, 1999, pp. 154–5).

I

1–2. *Before the mountains ... God was God* 'Before the mountains were brought forth, or ever thou hadst formed the earth and the world, even from everlasting to everlasting, thou art God' (Psalm 90:2).

9. *tho' He slay us we will trust in Him* 'Though he slay me, yet will I trust in him: but I will maintain mine own ways before him' (Job 13:15).

2

5. *the race* see note for l. 11 of 'Who Shall Deliver Me?'.

3

3. *wordless tearless dumbness* see l. 1 of 'A Better Resurrection': 'I have no wit, no words, no tears'.

4

13. *the Thief in Paradise* when Jesus is crucified along with two thieves, one man derides Jesus, while the other thief defends him. Jesus then promises his defender that he will be able to enter paradise, though he is a thief (see Luke 23:39–43).

7

1–2. *To love ... that is not well* see ll. 13–14 of 'Remember': 'Better by far you should forget and smile / Than that you should remember and be sad.'

8

6. *Our life ... turn to Thee* 'Then spake Jesus again unto them,
    saying, I am the light of the world: he that followeth me shall
    not walk in darkness, but shall have the light of life' (John 8:12).

9

1. *Sirius ... Pole Star* Sirius is the brightest star in the sky. The Pole
    Star's (North Star) position in the sky is constant, making it
    useful for celestial navigation.

10

10. *"Thy dead ... nor hide thy slain"* 'Thy dead men shall live,
    together with my dead body shall they arise. Awake and sing, ye
    that dwell in dust: for thy dew is as the dew of herbs, and the
    earth shall cast out the dead' (Isaiah 26:19); 'Verily, verily, I say
    unto you, The hour is coming, and now is, when the dead shall
    hear the voice of the Son of God: and they that hear shall live'
    (John 5:25).

Footnote. ll. 82–4 from Canto 5 of Dante's *Inferno*: 'As doves, sum-
    moned by desire, come with wings poised and motionless to the
    sweet nest, borne by their will through the air' (trans. John D.
    Sinclair, *The Divine Comedy*, Oxford University Press, 1961).

11

See sonnet 10 of 'Monna Innominata'.

12

See sonnet 3 of 'Monna Innominata'.

13

4. *bruit* report.
11. *cautery* an instrument used (in surgery) to burn or sear tissue.

15

On pages 56–7 of her devotional prose-work *Letter and Spirit* (1883),
CR expands on this sonnet's theme: 'To begin with Adam and Eve;
one is so accustomed to contemplate the Fall as well-nigh simultaneous
in both, that perhaps the subsequent Christ-likeness of Adam, presum-
ably in forgiving and cherishing, certainly in retaining, the wife who
had cost him life and all things, may pass unnoticed. That Eve
responded to his love and patience we need not doubt. Nor need we

attempt to settle which (if either) committed the greater sin; Adam's faithful love . . . remains in any case.' See also John Milton's *Paradise Lost* XII:645–9, where Adam and Eve leave Paradise hand in hand.

1.   *Let woman fear . . . bear to learn* 'But I suffer not a woman to teach, nor to usurp authority over the man, but to be in silence' (1 Timothy 2:12).

16

3.   *Abstruse* hard to understand.
11. *cloyed* surfeited, too full of something rich or sweet.

17

8.   *Cathay* China.

19

6.   *ivy* see note for l. 3 of 'Song' ('Oh roses for the flush of youth').

21

WMR writes that the 'reference to foreign travel in this sonnet and its successor relates to the year 1865, when Christina, along with our mother, accompanied me to North Italy through Switzerland' ('Notes' 463).

2.   *nightingales* see John Keats's 'Ode to a Nightingale' (1819).
13. *sparrow* see note for l. 7 of 'Consider'.

22

1–2. *The mountains . . . when I saw them first* 'Wherein lies the sadness of mountain scenery? For I suppose many besides myself have felt depressed when approaching the "everlasting hills"' (*TF* 111).
3–4. *And afterwards . . . chords which burst* 'Then from a window I faced them [mountains] again. And, lo! the evening flush had turned snow to a rose, "and sorrow and sadness fled away"' (*TF* 111).
11. *forget-me-not* see *TF* 113 for a passage which recounts CR's memory of the forget-me-nots growing on Mount St Gotthard.

24

9–14. *Oh foolishest . . . in thy quest* see ll. 17–20 of 'A Pause of Thought': 'Alas thou foolish one! . . . Turnest to follow it.'

26

1.   *balk* defeat, disappointment, failure.

27

WMR observes that 'This forecast of death came singularly true; for, if one had been writing a condensed account of Christina Rossetti's last days and hours in December 1894, one might have described them in these terms. Perhaps, however, few among her Christian readers will suppose that she "may have missed the goal at last." The reference to a "saint rejoicing on her bed" may glance at Maria' ('Notes' 463).

1–2. *I have dreamed of Death . . . Not in a dream* see note for ll. 1–2, sonnet 3 of 'Monna Innominata'.

7.   *ruth* see note for l. 31 of 'L.E.L.'.

'Judge nothing before the time'

First published in *TF* 13. First poetry volume 1893. The passage in *TF* which immediately precedes this poem discusses Adam:

> Adam's initial work of production . . . was sin, death, hell, for himself and his posterity.
>
> Not that he made them in their first beginning: but he, as it were, re-made them for his own behoof. Never had the flame kindled upon him or the smell of fire passed upon him, but for his own free will, choice, and deed.

Title. 'Therefore judge nothing before the time, until the Lord come, who both will bring to light the hidden things of darkness, and will make manifest the counsels of the hearts: and then shall every man have praise of God' (1 Corinthians 4:5).

1.   *the mystery* biblically, 'the mystery' is associated with Christ and God. See, for example, Ephesians 3:9: 'And to make all men see what is the fellowship of the mystery, which from the beginning of the world hath been hid in God, who created all things by Jesus Christ.'

6.   *Measures the depth beneath, the height above* 'Canst thou by searching find out God? canst thou find out the Almighty unto perfection? It is as high as heaven; what canst thou do? deeper than hell; what canst thou know? The measure thereof is longer than the earth, and broader than the sea' (Job 11:7–9).

9.   *Silently telling her bead-history* praying (using rosary beads).

Joy is but sorrow

First published in *TF* 16. First poetry volume 1893.

1. *Joy is but sorrow* 'Verily, verily, I say unto you, That ye shall weep and lament, but the world shall rejoice: and ye shall be sorrowful, but your sorrow shall be turned into joy' (John 16:20).

7. *moon so fair and frail* see the introductory note for 'O ye who love today'.

10. *heaps up treasure* see note for l. 10 of 'Mariana'.

'Redeeming the Time'

First published in *TF* 23. First poetry volume 1893. This poem is the entry for 29 January in *TF*. The prose entry for 28 January is about using time wisely, while the entry for January 27 relates time-wasting specifically to writer's block:

> Much good work has been hindered by such an anxiety to do better as deters one from promptly doing one's best . . .
>
> Suppose our duty of the moment is to write: why do we not write?
>
> — Because we cannot summon up anything original, or striking, or picturesque, or eloquent, or brilliant.
>
> But is a subject set before us? — It is.
>
> Is it true? — It is.
>
> Do we understand it? — Up to a certain point we do.
>
> Is it worthy of meditation? — Yes, and prayerfully
>
> Is it worthy of exposition? — Yes, indeed.
>
> Why then not begin? —
>
> 'From pride and vain glory, Good Lord, deliver us.'

Title. 'Walk in wisdom toward them that are without, redeeming the time' (Colossians 4:5).

1. *hope deferred* see note for l. 2 of 'A Pause of Thought'. See also l. 9 of 'Whatsoever is right, that shall ye receive' and l. 49 of '"The heart knoweth its own bitterness"' ('When all the over-work of life').

8. *harvest* refers to the end of the world, when human souls will be 'harvested' on Judgement Day. See, for example, Matthew 13:38–9: 'The field is the world; the good seed are the children of the kingdom; but the tares are the children of the wicked one; The enemy that sowed them is the devil; the harvest is the end of the world; and the reapers are the angels.'

'Doeth well . . . doeth better'

First published in *TF* 33. First poetry volume 1893. This poem is the entry for 15 February in *TF*. The prose passage preceding it on 14 February concerns Valentine's Day, about which CR observes:

> With St. Valentine's Day stands popularly associated the interchange of 'Valentines': this custom having its origin, we are informed, in a pagan ceremony wisely exchanged for a Christian observance.
>
> And thus our social habit, even if degenerate, assumes a certain dignity: we connect it not merely with mirth and love, but with sanctity and suffering. The love exhibits a double aspect and accords, or should accord, with heaven as well as with earth.

It was CR's custom to compose a Valentine's Day poem for her mother every year. Although CR's mother was still living, when this poem was first published, her sister Maria, who never married and joined an Anglican Sisterhood, had been dead for almost ten years. WMR connects this poem with MFR: 'I consider this poem related to Maria Francesca Rossetti, who had died in 1876' ('Notes' 469).

Title. 'So then he that giveth her in marriage doeth well; but he that giveth her not in marriage doeth better' (1 Corinthians 7:38).

1. *My love whose heart is tender* 'Because thine heart was tender, and thou hast humbled thyself before the Lord, when thou heardest what I spake against this place, and against the inhabitants thereof, that they should become a desolation and a curse, and hast rent thy clothes, and wept before me; I also have heard thee, saith the Lord' (2 Kings 22:19).

2. *A moon lacks light* WMR notes that CR often called their sister playfully 'Moon' or 'Moony' ('Notes' 469). See also the introductory note for 'O ye who love today'.

A Castle-Builder's World

First published in *TF* 63. First poetry volume 1893.

Epigraph. 'But the cormorant and the bittern shall possess it; the owl also and the raven shall dwell in it: and he shall stretch out upon it the line of confusion, and the stones of emptiness' (Isaiah 34:11).

1. *Unripe harvest* see note for l. 2 of ' "Redeeming the Time" '.

Piteous my rhyme is

First published TF 75. First poetry volume 1893.

20. *all in all* see note for l. 10 of 'At Last'. See also 1 Corinthians 12:6: 'And there are diversities of operations, but it is the same God which worketh all in all.'

If love is not worth loving, then life is not worth living

First published in TF 93. First poetry volume 1893. The entry which immediately precedes this poem in TF tells of a general whose family fed a tamed robin. 'One day, coming home from shooting he aimed his last random shot at a speck in the sky.' After that, 'the tame robin never came again: and the soldier who loved it, and as he believed shot it, could not, when I listened to him, tell the story without emotion.' The entry concludes: 'Let us have mercy on each other and forgive: even a wronged robin's silence and absence were hard to bear.'

7. *vanity of vanities* see note for ll. 19–21 of 'Hope in Grief'.

Roses on a brier

First published TF 110. First poetry volume 1893.

1.   *Roses* see note for l. 1 of 'Song' ('Oh roses for the flush of youth').
12. *no more sea* 'And I saw a new heaven and a new earth: for the first heaven and the first earth were passed away; and there was no more sea' (Revelation 21:1).

'Called to be Saints'

First published in TF 114. First poetry volume 1893.

Title. 'Unto the church of God which is at Corinth, to them that are sanctified in Christ Jesus, called to be saints, with all that in every place call upon the name of Jesus Christ our Lord, both theirs and ours' (1 Corinthians 1:2). Also the title of CR's 1881 devotional prose-work.
1.   *The lowest place* see note for the title of 'The Lowest Room'.
7.   *For Right Hand or for Left Hand* 'But to sit on my right hand and on my left hand is not mine to give; but it shall be given to them for whom it is prepared' (Mark 10:40). See also Matthew 20:23.

Of each sad word which is more sorrowful

First published in *TF* 150. First poetry volume 1893.

6.   *dule* grief.

Our heaven must be within ourselves

Lines 1–4 composed 25 January 1854; dates of composition of ll. 5–12 unknown. First published in *TF* 213–14. First poetry volume 1893. The prose passage which precedes this entry in *TF* recalls the dying MFR's planning of her own funeral. MFR chides CR for wanting to wear the 'hood and hatband' mourning dress, saying, 'Why make everything as hopeless looking as possible?' The funeral guests 'all turned out in harmony with her holy hope and joy', and CR observes 'the sun . . . made a miniature rainbow in my eyelashes', and wishes that 'all who love enjoy cheerful little rainbows at the funerals of their beloved ones'.

2.   *work of faith* 'Remembering without ceasing your work of faith, and labour of love, and patience of hope in our Lord Jesus Christ, in the sight of God and our Father' (1 Thessalonians 1:3).

3.   *race of life* see note for l. 11 of 'Who Shall Deliver Me?'.

7.   *magnifical* magnificent.

9.   *While over all a dome must spread* see ll. 1–2 and 46 of S. T. Coleridge's 'Kubla Khan, or, A Vision in a Dream, a Fragment': 'In Xanadu did Kubla Khan / A stately pleasure-dome decree', 'I would build that dome in air'.

'A Helpmeet for Him'

First published in *"New and Old:" For Seed-Time and Harvest* 16 (January 1888), 22. First poetry volume 1888. On p. 57 of *TF*, CR addresses the question of women's weakness in terms which echo this poem:

> In common parlance Strong and Weak are merely relative terms: thus the "strong" of one sentence will be the "weak" of another.
>
> We behold the strong appointed to help the weak: Angels who "excel in strength," men. And equally the weak the strong: woman, "the weaker vessel," man.
>
> This, though it should not inflate any, may fairly buoy us all up. For every human creature may lay claim to strength, or else to weakness: in

either case to helpfulness. "We that are strong," writes St. Paul, proceed-
ing to state a day of the strong. *We* who are weak may study the resources
of the weak.

Title.   See note for l. 14, sonnet 5 of 'Monna Innominata'.
5.   *Her strength with weakness is overlaid* 'And he said unto me, My
     grace is sufficient for thee: for my strength is made perfect in weak-
     ness. Most gladly therefore will I rather glory in my infirmities,
     that the power of Christ may rest upon me' (2 Corinthians 12:9).
7.   *stays* supports, steadies.
10. *ruddy and white* 'My beloved is white and ruddy, the chiefest
     among ten thousand' (Song of Solomon 5:10). See also l. 7 of
     'Beauty is Vain'.

O ye who love today

First published in the preface of *FD*. First poetry volume 1893. CR's
preface to *FD* invokes 'A dear saint' who 'once pointed out to me
Patience as our lesson in the Book of Revelations'. This 'saint' is
MFR, whose family nickname, 'Moony', is alluded to in the poem's
comparison of Patience to a moon. See also the notes for 'Patience
must dwell with love, for Love and Sorrow' and also 'What is the
beginning? Love. What the course? Love still'.

6.   *apace* swiftly.

Lord, I am feeble and of mean account

First published in *FD* 12. First poetry volume 1893.

4.   *And grant me grace to hear and grace to see* 'hear' and 'see' are
     common biblical injunctions which refer to mankind's ability to
     perceive God. For example, Deuteronomy 29:4: 'Yet the Lord
     hath not given you an heart to perceive, and eyes to see, and ears
     to hear, unto this day'. In the prose passage preceding this poem
     in *FD*, CR observes:

> A reader and hearers stand in graduated degrees of knowledge or
> of ignorance . . . The reader studying at first hand is in direct contact
> with God's Word: hearers seek instruction of God through men.
> The reader requires most gifts: hearers may exercise fully as much
> grace. Most of us are hearers: having performed conscientiously
> the duty of hearers, we shall be the less prone to make mistakes if
> ever providentially promoted to be readers.

What is the beginning? Love. What the course? Love still

First published in *FD* 75. First poetry volume, 1893. In *FD*, the sentence immediately preceding this poem reads: 'It needs profound patience, patience born of love and sustained by love, to achieve final perseverance.'

As froth on the face of the deep

First published in *FD* 88. First poetry volume 1893.

1.   *face of the deep* 'And the earth was without form, and void; and darkness was upon the face of the deep. And the Spirit of God moved upon the face of the waters' (Genesis 1:2).

4.   *gourd of a day and a night* refers to an episode in the Book of Jonah when God makes a giant gourd grow in order to shelter Jonah, then infests it with a worm so that it withers and dies. When Jonah protests, God says, 'Thou hast had pity on the gourd, for which thou hast not laboured, neither madest it grow; which came up in a night, and perished in a night' (Jonah 4:10).

5.   *harvest* see note on l. 8 of 'Redeeming the Time'.

Patience must dwell with Love, for Love and Sorrow

First published in *FD* 116-17. First poetry volume 1893. In *FD*, CR makes this observation about patience in the prose passage preceding this poem:

> Patience goes with sorrow, not with joy. And by a natural instinct sorrow ranges itself with darkness, joy with light. But eyes that have been super-naturalized recognize, not literally only, but likewise in a figure, how darkness reveals more luminaries than does the day: to the day appertains a single sun; to the night innumerable, incalculable, by man's perception inexhaustible stars.

See also 'O ye who love today'. See too the introductory note for 'What is the beginning? Love. What the course? Love still'.

Hope is the counterpoise of fear

First published in *FD* 173-4. First poetry volume 1893.

1.   *counterpoise* see note for l. 16 of 'Three Stages'.

6. *bier* a stand for a coffin or a corpse before burial.
8. *sere* see note for l. 2 of 'A baby's cradle with no baby in it'.
9. *congruous* corresponding to physical structure, harmonious.
11. *chanticleer* cock. Also alludes to the episode in the Gospels where Christ prophesies that Peter will deny him three times before the cock crows. See Matthew 26:75, Mark 14:30, 14:72, Luke 22:34, 22:61 and John 13:38.
14. *ballasts* holds back with its weight (from *ballast*, load, weight or burden).

'Subject to like Passions as we are'

First published in *FD* 180–81. First poetry volume 1893.

Title. 'Elias was a man subject to like passions as we are, and he prayed earnestly that it might not rain: and it rained not on the earth by the space of three years and six months' (James 5:17).
5. *dross* see note for l. 36 of 'The Lowest Room'.

Experience bows a sweet contented face

First published in *FD* 198. First poetry volume 1893. In *FD*, the prose passage preceding this poem reads: 'Experience follows and gives thanks; faith precedes and offers praise. Experience keeps pace with time; faith outstripping time forestalls eternity.'

2. *Still setting to her seal that God is true* 'He that hath received his testimony hath set to his seal that God is true' (John 3:33).
3. *Beneath the sun, she knows, is nothing new* see note for l. 22 of 'Passing and Glassing'.
4–5. *All things that go . . . man's still recommencing race* see note for l. 1 of 'Confluents'. See also Ecclesiastes 9:11: 'I returned, and saw under the sun, that the race is not to the swift, nor the battle to the strong, neither yet bread to the wise, nor yet riches to men of understanding, nor yet favour to men of skill; but time and chance happeneth to them all.'
9. *"My God doth all things well"* 'And were beyond measure astonished, saying, He hath done all things well: he maketh both the deaf to hear, and the dumb to speak' (Mark 7:37).

'Charity never Faileth'

First published in *FD* 201. First poetry volume 1893.

Title. 'Charity never faileth: but whether there be prophecies, they
shall fail; whether there be tongues, they shall cease; whether
there be knowledge, it shall vanish away' (1 Corinthians 13:8).

7.   *myrtles* emblems of love; *olive* symbolizes peace.

8.   *Dove-eyed Love* 'Behold, thou art fair, my love; behold, thou art
fair; thou hast doves' eyes' (Song of Solomon 1:15). See also
Song of Solomon 4:1 and 5:12. *Twelve-fruited Tree* see note for
l. 140 of 'Three Nuns'.

Safe where I cannot lie yet

First published in *FD* 205. First poetry volume 1893.

3.   *fume* irritation.

10.   *in blow* a state of blossoming, blooming.

How great is little man!

First published *FD* 254. First poetry volume 1893.

'The Greatest of these is Charity'

First published in *FD* 255. First poetry volume 1893.

Title. 'And now abideth faith, hope, charity, these three; but the
greatest of these is charity' (1 Corinthians 13:13).

7.   *olive, grape, or corn* taken together, these are symbols of peace
and riches, general prosperity.

9.   *rose* see note for l. 1 of 'Song' ('Oh roses for the flush of youth').

13.   *New Jerusalem* see note for l. 177 of 'Three Nuns' and for l. 37
of ' "They Desire a Better Country" '.

14.   *palm-tree* 'The righteous shall flourish like the palm tree: he shall
grow like a cedar in Lebanon' (Psalms 92:12).

'O Lucifer, Son of the Morning!'

First published in *FD* 257–8. First poetry volume 1893.

Title. 'How art thou fallen from heaven, O Lucifer, son of the morn-
ing! how art thou cut down to the ground, which didst weaken

the nations!' (Isaiah 14:12). See also John Milton's *Paradise Lost* V.710–11: 'His count'nance, as the Morning Starr that guides / The starrie flock, allur'd them, and with lyes.'

2. *car* see note for l. 91 of 'The Convent Threshold'.
7. *nebular* consisting of or relating to a cluster of stars.

Time seems not short

First published in *FD* 278. First poetry volume 1893. In *FD*, the passage preceding this poem wonders:

> What is time? It is not subtracted from eternity, which if diminished would fall short of being eternal: neither is it substituted awhile for eternity, which thus would assume both end and beginning: neither is it simultaneous with eternity, because it is in Him Who inhabiteth eternity (not time) that we ourselves day by day live and move and have our being.

4. *amort* lifeless, spiritless.

'Judge not according to the appearance'

First published in *FD* 285. First poetry volume 1893.

Title. [Untitled 1892] 'Judge not according to the appearance, but judge righteous judgment' (John 7:24).
8. "*Fear not: it is I*" 'But he saith unto them, It is I; be not afraid' (John 6:20).

St Peter

First published in *FD* 326. First poetry volume 1893.

1. *Launch out into the deep* 'Now when he had left speaking, he said unto Simon, Launch out into the deep, and let down your nets for a draught' (Luke 5:4).

'Sit down in the lowest room'

First published in *FD* 350. First poetry volume 1893.

Title. See note on the title of 'The Lowest Room', note for l. 1 of 'The Lowest Place' and note for l. 7 of 'Do this, and He doeth it'.

'Consider the Lilies of the field'
['Solomon most glorious in array']

First published in *FD* 391. First poetry volume 1893.

Title. See note for title of ' "Consider the Lilies of the Field" ' ('Flowers preach to us if we will hear'). See also 'Consider'.

3.   *lilies* see note for l. 60 of 'Three Nuns'.

Our Mothers, lovely women pitiful

First published in *FD* 401. First poetry volume 1893.

6.   *Walk as we walked, much less by sight than faith* 'For we walk by faith, not by sight' (2 Corinthians 5:7).

7.   *scathe* see note for l. 37 of 'L.E.L.'.

8.   *dule* see note for l. 6 of 'Of each sad word which is more sorrowful'.

13. *happy eyes! whose tears are wiped away* 'He will swallow up death in victory; and the Lord God will wipe away tears from off all faces; and the rebuke of his people shall he take away from off all the earth: for the Lord hath spoken it' (Isaiah 25:8).

Babylon the Great

First published in *FD* 406. First poetry volume 1893. See also 'The World' and ' "Standing afar off for the fear of her torment" '.

Title. 'And upon her forehead was a name written, MYSTERY, BABYLON THE GREAT, THE MOTHER OF HARLOTS AND ABOM-INATIONS OF THE EARTH' (Revelation 17:5).

3.   *mesh thee in her wanton hair* see l. 9, sonnet 8 of 'Monna Innominata': 'She trapped him with one mesh of silken hair'.

7.   *No wine is in her cup, but filth is there* 'And the woman was arrayed in purple and scarlet colour, and decked with gold and precious stones and pearls, having a golden cup in her hand full of abominations and filthiness of her fornication' (Revelation 17:4).

13. *Her scarlet vest and gold and gem and pearl* see note for l. 7. See also Revelation 18.16: 'And saying, Alas, alas, that great city, that was clothed in fine linen, and purple, and scarlet, and decked with gold, and precious stones, and pearls!'

14. *set on fire* 'Therefore shall her plagues come in one day, death,

and mourning, and famine; and she shall be utterly burned with fire: for strong is the Lord God who judgeth her' (Revelation 18:8).

'Do this, and he doeth it'

First published in *FD* 410. First poetry volume 1893.

Title. 'For I am a man under authority, having soldiers under me: and I say to this man, Go, and he goeth; and to another, Come, and he cometh; and to my servant, Do this, and he doeth it' (Matthew 8:9). See also Luke 7:8.

7.   *we may sit, high or low* see note on the title of 'The Lowest Room' and note for l. 1 of 'The Lowest Place'.

10.   *And loss has left no barren trace* see l. 11, sonnet 2 of 'Monna Innominata': 'As traceless as a thaw of bygone snow'.

'Standing afar off for the fear of her torment'

First published in *FD* 418–19. First poetry volume 1893. See notes for 'Babylon the Great'.

Title. 'Standing afar off for the fear of her torment, saying, Alas, alas, that great city Babylon, that mighty city! for in one hour is thy judgment come' (Revelation 18:10).

Vigil of St Bartholomew

First published in *FD* 439. First poetry volume 1893. The prose paragraph preceding this poem in *FD* warns that scriptural study can be a distraction from the practical application of Christianity, relating its dangers to the parable of the wise virgins (see note for l. 5 below):

Symbolism affords a fascinating study: wholesome so long as it amounts to aspiration and research; unwholesome when it degenerates into a pastime. As literal shadows tend to soothe, lull, abate keenness of vision; so perhaps symbols may have a tendency to engross, satisfy, arrest incautious souls unwatchful and unprayerful lest they enter into temptation.

5.   *Virgins who keep vigil and are wise* refers to the parable of the virgins waiting for their bridegroom to arrive. The wise virgins bring extra oil for their lamps, while the foolish virgins run out of oil and have to go out to buy more. The bridegroom arrives

while they are away, and when they return, he refuses to let them in, saying, 'I know you not. Watch therefore, for ye know neither the day nor the hour wherein the Son of man cometh' (Matthew 25:12–13). See also Matthew 25:1–13.

6.   *To sow among all sowers who shall reap* 'They that sow in tears shall reap in joy' (Psalms 126:5).

8.   *And tread the uphill track to Paradise* see 'Up-Hill'.

'Who hath despised the day of small things?'

First published in *FD* 440. First poetry volume 1893. In *FD*, the sentence immediately preceding this poem reads, 'Self-willed humility is pride in masquerade'.

Title.   'For who hath despised the day of small things? For they shall rejoice, and shall see the plummet in the hand of Zerubbabel with those seven; they are the eyes of the Lord, which run to and fro through the whole earth' (Zechariah 4:10).

1.   *violets* see note for l. 5 of 'Song' ('Oh roses for the flush of youth').

2.   *daisies* see note for l. 6 of 'On Keats'.

Tune me, O Lord, into one harmony

First published in *FD* 489. First poetry volume 1893.

6.   *A little while* see note for l. 12, sonnet 10 of 'Monna Innominata'. See also note on the title of ' "Yet a little while" '.

Index of Titles

Bold numbers refer to the poems and non-bold to the notes

Amen **34**, 208
Amor Mundi **114**, 222
Apple-Gathering, An **53**, 213
As froth on the face of the deep **184**, 245
At Home **57**, 213
At Last **155**, 233
Autumn Violets **132**, 224

Baby lies so fast asleep **142**, 227
Babylon the Great **191**, 249
baby's cradle with no baby in it, A **135**, 225
Beauty is Vain **87**, 219
Better Resurrection, A **49**, 211
Birthday, A **52**, 212
Bourne, The **26**, 206
Brown and furry **137**, 226

'Called to be Saints' **181**, 242
Castle-Builder's World, A **179**, 241
Charade **3**, 197
Charity never Faileth **186**, 247
Christmas Carol, A **134**, 224
city plum is not a plum, A **135**, 225
Confluents **142**, 227
Consider **86**, 218
'Consider the Lilies of the Field' ['Flowers preach to us if we
    hear'] **24**, 204
'Consider the Lilies of the Field' ['Solomon most glorious in
    array'] **190**, 249

Convent Threshold, The 59, 214

Daughter of Eve, A 131, 223
Death's Chill Between 8, 199
De Profundis 153, 233
'Doeth well . . . doeth better' 178, 241
'Do this, and he doeth it' 191, 250
Dream-Land 15, 202

Echo 30, 207
emerald is as green as grass, An 141, 227
End, An 14, 201
Experience bows a sweet contented face 185, 246

Forget Me Not 3, 197
From the Antique 27, 206

Goblin Market 67, 216
'Greatest of these is Charity, The' 187, 247
Have you forgotten? 13, 201
He and She 153, 233
'Heart knoweth its own bitterness, The' ['When all the over-work of
    life'] 51, 212
Heart's Chill Between 6, 198
Helpmeet for Him, A 182, 243
'Hollow-Sounding and Mysterious' 154, 233
Hope in Grief 4, 197
Hope is like a harebell trembling from its birth 136, 225
Hope is the counterpoise of fear 184, 245
Hour and the Ghost, The 35, 208
How great is little man! 186, 247
How many seconds in a minute? 138, 226

I caught a little ladybird 141, 227
If all were rain and never sun 136, 225
If a pig wore a wig 137, 226
If I were a Queen 136, 226
If love is not worth loving, then life is not worth living 180, 242
In an Artist's Studio 49, 210
'Iniquity of the Fathers Upon the Children, The' 115, 223

Jessie Cameron 91, 220

Joy is but sorrow 178, 240
'Judge not according to the appearance' 189, 248
'Judge nothing before the time' 177, 239

Key-Note, The 152, 233

L.E.L. 65, 215
Later Life: A Double Sonnet of Sonnets 165, 236
Lines / given with a Penwiper 9, 199
linnet in a gilded cage, A 136, 225
Lord, I am feeble and of mean account 183, 244
Love from the North 48, 210
Love Me, – I love you 135, 225
Lowest Place, The 87, 219
Lowest Room, The 37, 208

Mariana 155, 234
Maude Clare 55, 213
May 33, 208
Memory 112, 222
Monna Innominata 143, 228
My Dream 31, 207

'No, Thank You, John' 83, 218

Of each sad word which is more sorrowful 181, 243
Old-World Thicket, An 159, 235
'O Lucifer, Son of the Morning!' 188, 247
On Albina 3, 197
On Keats 12, 200
On the Death of a Cat 5, 197
Our heaven must be within ourselves 182, 243
Our Mothers, lovely women pitiful 190, 249
'Out of the Deep' 84, 218
O ye who love today 183, 244

P.R.B., The 25, 205
Passing and Glassing 156, 234
Patience must dwell with Love, for Love and Sorrow 184, 245
Pause of Thought, A 10, 199
peacock has a score of eyes, The 139, 226
pin has a head, but has no hair, A 139, 226

Piteous my rhyme is 179, 242
Portraits 24, 204
Prince's Progress, The 94, 221

Queen of Hearts, The 85, 218

'Redeeming the Time' 178, 240
Remember 16, 202
Roses on a brier 180, 242

St Peter 189, 248
Safe where I cannot lie yet 186, 247
Sappho 6, 198
Shut Out 33, 208
'Sit down in the lowest room' 190, 248
Smile and a Sigh, A 131, 223
Some ladies dress in muslin full and white 12, 200
Song ['Oh roses for the flush of youth'] 13, 201
Song ['She sat and sang alway'] 10, 199
Song ['When I am dead, my dearest'] 11, 199
Sonnets are full of love, and this my tome 152, 232
'Standing afar off for the fear of her torment' 192, 250
'Subject to like Passions as we are' 185, 246
Sweet Death 14, 201

'They Desire a Better Country' 132, 224
Thread of Life, The 157, 234
Three Nuns 17, 202
Three Stages 27, 206
Time seems not short 188, 248
toadstool comes up in a night, A 137, 226
Touching 'Never' 158, 235
Triad, A 47, 210
Tune me, O Lord, into one harmony 193, 251
Twice 89, 220

Up-Hill 58, 213

Vigil of St Bartholomew 192, 250

What are heavy? sea-sand and sorrow 137, 226
What does the bee do? 141, 227

'What good shall my life do me?' ['Have dead men long to
    wait?'] 63, 214
What is pink? A rose is pink 138, 226
What is the beginning? Love. What the course? Love still 183, 245
'Whatsoever is right, that shall ye receive' 50, 211
What Would I Give? 88, 219
When a mounting skylark sings 140, 227
When fishes set umbrellas up 139, 226
Who has seen the wind? 140, 227
'Who hath despised the day of small things?' 193, 251
Who Shall Deliver Me? 88, 219
wind has such a rainy sound, The 140, 227
Winter: My Secret 54, 213
Winter Rain 64, 215
World, The 26, 206

'Yet a little while' 143, 228

Index of First Lines

Bold numbers refer to the poems and non-bold to the notes

A baby's cradle with no baby in it **135**, 225
A city plum is not a plum **135**, 225
A fool I was to sleep at noon **131**, 223
A garden in a garden: a green spot **12**, 200
A life of hope deferred too often is **178**, 240
A linnet in a gilded cage **136**, 225
All things that pass **156**, 234
A moon impoverished amid stars curtailed **187**, 247
An easy lazy length of limb **24**, 204
An emerald is as green as grass **141**, 227
A pin has a head, but has no hair **139**, 226
As froth on the face of the deep **184**, 245
A smile because the nights are short! **131**, 223
As rivers seek the sea **142**, 227
As violets so be I recluse and sweet **193**, 251
A toadstool comes up in a night **137**, 226
Awake or sleeping (for I know not which) **159**, 235

Baby lies so fast asleep **142**, 227
Because you never yet have loved me, dear **158**, 235
Before the mountains were brought forth, before **165**, 236
Brown and furry **137**, 226
By day she wooes me, soft, exceeding fair **26**, 206

Chide not; let me breathe a little **8**, 199
Come back to me, who wait and watch for you **143**, 228
Come to me in the silence of the night **30**, 207
Consider **86**, 218
Content to come, content to go **191**, 250

Does the road wind up-hill all the way? 58, 213
Downstairs I laugh, I sport and jest with all 65, 215

Every valley drinks 64, 215
Experience bows a sweet contented face 185, 246

Flowers preach to us if we will hear 24, 204
'Forget me not! Forget me not!' 3, 197
Foul is she and ill-favoured, set askew 191, 249

Give me the lowest place: not that I dare 87, 219
God strengthen me to bear myself 88, 219

Have dead men long to wait? 63, 214
Have mercy, Thou my God; mercy, my God 84, 218
Have you forgotten how one Summer night 13, 201
Hear now a curious dream I dreamed last night 31, 207
Heaven is not far, tho' far the sky 143, 228
Hope is like a harebell trembling from its birth 136, 225
Hope is the counterpoise of fear 184, 245
How comes it, Flora, that, whenever we 85, 218
How great is little man! 186, 247
How many seconds in a minute? 138, 226

I cannot tell you how it was 33, 208
I caught a little ladybird 141, 227
I did not chide him, tho' I knew 6, 198
If a pig wore a wig 137, 226
If all were rain and never sun 136, 225
If I were a Queen 136, 226
If love is not worth loving, then life is not worth living 180, 242
I had a love in soft south land 48, 210
I have compassion on the carpeting 9, 199
I have no wit, no words, no tears 49, 211
I looked for that which is not, nor can be [A Pause of Thought] 10,
    199
I looked for that which is not, nor can be [Three Stages] 27, 206
I never said I loved you, John 83, 218
In the bleak mid-winter 134, 224
I nursed it in my bosom while it lived 112, 222
I plucked pink blossoms from mine apple tree 53, 213
I sigh at day-dawn, and I sigh 6, 198

Is this the end? is there no end but this? 192, 250
I tell my secret? No indeed, not I 54, 213
It is over. What is over? 34, 208
I took my heart in my hand 89, 220
It's a weary life, it is; she said 27, 206
I would not if I could undo my past 132, 224

Jessie, Jessie Cameron 91, 220
Joy is but sorrow 178, 240

Keep love for youth, and violets for the spring 132, 224

'Launch out into the deep,' Christ spake of old 189, 248
Like flowers sequestered from the sun 37, 208
Lord, give me grace 190, 248
Lord, I am feeble and of mean account 183, 244
Lord, purge our eyes to see 189, 248
Lord, to Thine own grant watchful hearts and eyes 192, 250
Love me, – I love you 135, 225
Love understands the mystery, whereof 177, 239
Love, strong as Death, is dead 14, 201

Many have sung of love a root of bane 155, 233
Morning and evening 67, 216
My first may be the firstborn 3, 197
My heart is like a singing bird 52, 212
My love whose heart is tender said to me 178, 241

Not for me marring or making 155, 234

Of each sad word which is more sorrowful 181, 243
Oh fallen star! A darkened light 188, 247
Oh roses for the flush of youth 13, 201
Oh the rose of keenest thorn! 115, 223
Oh where are you going with your love-locks flowing 114, 222
Oh why is heaven built so far 153, 233
O love, love, hold me fast 35, 208
One face looks out from all his canvasses 49, 210
Our heaven must be within ourselves 182, 243
Our Mothers, lovely women pitiful 190, 249
Out of the church she followed them 55, 213
O ye who love today 183, 244

Patience must dwell with Love, for Love and Sorrow 184, 245
Piteous my rhyme is 179, 242

Remember me when I am gone away 16, 202
Roses on a brier 180, 242

Safe where I cannot lie yet 186, 247
Shadow, shadow on the wall 17, 202
She sat and sang alway 10, 199
Should one of us remember 153, 233
Solomon most glorious in array 190, 249
Some ladies dress in muslin full and white 12, 200
Sonnets are full of love, and this my tome 152, 232
Such is Love, it comforts in extremity 186, 247

Tell me not that death of grief 4, 197
The door was shut. I looked between 33, 208
The irresponsive silence of the land 157, 234
The lowest place. Ah, Lord, how steep and high 181, 242
The peacock has a score of eyes 139, 226
The P.R.B. is in its decadence 25, 205
There's blood between us, love, my love 59, 214
There's no replying 154, 233
The roses lingered in her cheeks 3, 197
The sweetest blossoms die 14, 201
The wind has such a rainy sound 140, 227
Three sang of love together: one with lips 47, 210
Till all sweet gums and juices flow 94, 221
Time seems not short 188, 248
Tune me, O Lord, into one harmony 193, 251

Underneath the growing grass 26, 206
Unripe harvest there hath none to reap it 179, 241

What are heavy? sea-sand and sorrow 137, 226
What does the bee do? 141, 227
What is pink? a rose is pink 138, 226
What is the beginning? Love. What the course? Love still 183,
    245
What would I give for a heart of flesh to warm me thro' 88, 219
When all the over-work of life ['The heart knoweth its own
    bitterness'] 51, 212

When all the overwork of life ['Whatsoever is right, that shall ye
    receive'] 50, 211
When a mounting skylark sings 140, 227
When fishes set umbrellas up 139, 226
When I am dead, my dearest 11, 199
When I was dead, my spirit turned 57, 213
Where are the songs I used to know 152, 233
Where sunless rivers weep 15, 202
While roses are so red 87, 219
Who has seen the wind? 140, 227
Who shall tell the lady's grief 5, 197
Whoso hath anguish is not dead in sin 185, 246
Woman was made for man's delight 182, 243